Rob Hirst was born in Camden, New South Wales. As a founding member of the internationally successful Midnight Oil, over the last twenty-five years he has co-written the words and melodies for many of the group's best-known songs, including 'Beds Are Burning', 'The Dead Heart', 'Short Memory', 'The Power and the Passion', 'Forgotten Years', 'King of the Mountain' and many others. His singing, song-writing, drumming and guitar can also be heard on three Ghostwriters albums, plus the latest CD, HANOI, by Australian blues legends the Backsliders. Rob has written and spoken on behalf of music education, produced up-and-coming musicians, co-produced an album of songs for the 2000 Sydney Olympic Games, and compiled OIL DRUMS, a collection of Midnight Oil songs scored for percussionists. When not on tour, he lives at home in Sydney with his family.

Willie's Bar and Grill

Rob Hirst

momentum

First published by Picador Australia in 2003
This edition published in 2012 by Momentum
Pan Macmillan Australia Pty Ltd
1 Market Street, Sydney 2000

A CIP record for this book is available at the National Library of Australia

Willie's Bar and Grill

EPUB format: 9781743340554
MOBI format: 9781743340660
POD format: 9781760081614

Cover design by Matt O'Keefe
Proofread by Hayley Crandell

Macmillan Digital Australia: www.macmillandigital.com.au

To report a typographical error, please email errors@momentumbooks.com.au

Visit www.momentumbooks.com.au to read more about all our books and to buy
books online. You will also find features, author interviews and news of any author
events.

For my mother, Robin,
who always writes me the best letters

Author's note

The following is based on Australian band Midnight Oil's tour of the USA and Canada in October–November 2001, with additional material from three bsequent tours of North America in 2002 and an Australian tour in the same year.

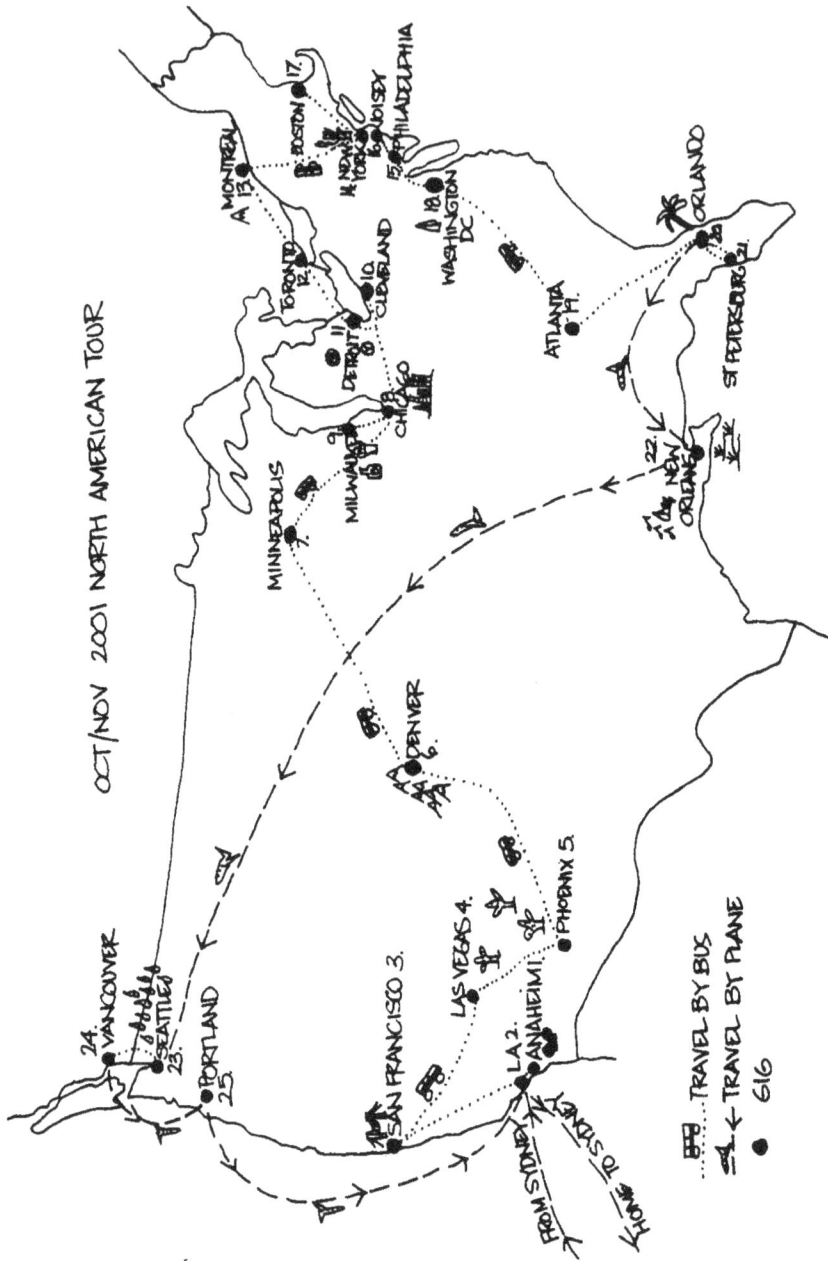

OCT/NOV 2001 NORTH AMERICAN TOUR

A. MONTREAL 13.
BOSTON 17.
B. NEW YORK 16.
BOISEY
5. PHILADELPHIA
18.
WASHINGTON DC
TORONTO 12.
10. CLEVELAND
DETROIT 11.
CHICAGO 9.
ATLANTA 14.
ORLANDO
ST PETERSBURG 21.
MILWAUKEE 8.
MINNEAPOLIS
NEW ORLEANS 22.
DENVER 6.
PHOENIX 5.
LAS VEGAS 4.
SAN FRANCISCO 3.
LA 2. ANAHEIM 1.
VANCOUVER 24.
SEATTLE 23.
PORTLAND 25.

FROM SYDNEY
HOME TO SYDNEY

🚌 TRAVEL BY BUS
✈ TRAVEL BY PLANE
● 616

We can't just sit around at home doing nothing. This is death by gardening.

Jim Moginie (Midnight Oil songwriter, guitarist and keyboard player). May 2000

DOORS OPEN: ACKNOWLEDGEMENTS

I'm on the whiskey flying
And I'll run by night
from 'Run By Night'

I'm indebted to my good friend, writer David Leser, for planting the germ of the idea for this journal – something he both regrets and regularly reminds me of. More than once I joined Dave on his regular morning walk around Cape Byron to the lighthouse, Australia's most easterly point, during which we gasped gilded memories, wheezed embellished anecdotes, huffed sordid secrets and puffed bad, convoluted jokes. There, we not only 'broke bread', as Dave would say, but devoured the entire loaf. Sometimes we even ran.

Ergo, kindly address each and every complaint or compliment, argument or affidavit, insult or injunction, rebuttal or rejoinder – anything, in fact, that might ensnare the author in hardball litigation – to Dave. It is, after all, his fault.

Many thanks to Nikki Christer at Picador for gambling her reputation on a novice; to editor Simone Ford and copy editor Jon Gibbs for judicious mercy-culling; publicist Tracey Cheetham for reintroducing me to the unparalleled joys of daytime TV; and to Lesley, Alex and Ella for humouring the jet-lagged, hall-creeping lodger with the middle-distance stare.

Thanks also to Peter and Robin Hirst for the truth that only parents dare speak; tour manager Willie MacInnes for enduring the third degree; photographer Susan Alzner for the back cover pic; Lesta for the marvellous American mud map; and renaissance man Craig Allen for his flawless memory. And, of course, thanks to Midnight Oil, management, office and crew.

Rob Hirst, Sydney, February 2003

INTRO TAPE: CAPRICORNIA

I don't need no fire and brimstone warning
I'm a long time punching bag
I won't run no race where there ain't no prize
Take a look at my face, you can see this
ain't no lies
from 'Powderworks'

On 10 September 2001, Midnight Oil were in a Sydney studio mixing 'Poets and Slaves', from our latest album, *Capricornia*, and preparing for a handful of local shows before a seven-week tour of North America. The following morning we woke up to find that nineteen terrorists had attacked the United States, killing an unknown number of innocent people.

Ten days later we set up a speaker-phone in the rehearsal room to discuss the situation with manager Gary Morris, and decided to go ahead as planned. The first run would be an exploratory one, playing to audiences that hadn't seen the band since the early '90s, meeting the folks at the new record company, and busking some acoustic songs at radio stations.

On 4 October we climbed aboard a 747 bound for Los Angeles, excited by the prospect of playing overseas again, relieved that the tour hadn't been cancelled, curious about what we'd find. Still hooked on the adrenaline of travel. Hard bitten by the music bug.

ROCKIN' IN THE FREE WORLD

Few of the sins of the father
Are visited upon the son
Hearts have been hard
Hands have been clenched into fists too long
from 'Forgotten Years'

How *American*. To be driving on a freeway, on Columbus Day, heading for Disneyland. And yet this is exactly where we find ourselves, gunning a minibus down the San Diego Freeway to Anaheim for the opening gig.

Barely a month after the September 11 attacks in New York City, Washington DC and Pennsylvania, Midnight Oil are back in the Land of the Free for our first major tour in over seven years. With us we have our road crew, stage gear, water tank and a swag of songs, ready to front up to a damaged nation with a dim, rookie president and a brand-new war.

I'm amazed and alarmed, in equal measure, at how instantly southern California's contradictory charms come skidding back. On one hand, there are the warm, dry days and hazy, cotton-palm sunsets, the rugged majesty of the San

1

Gabriel and Santa Monica mountains, and the neat shuttered haciendas draped with crimson bougainvillea. On the other, there's the macadamised mayhem of an unconscionable burden of traffic, the defiant congregation of some of the world's largest reflective surfaces, and the square-sided travesty of the disembowelled LA River.

A day or two before, curious to see LA with a fresh pair of eyes, and eternally optimistic for a decent view over the cement-rendered desert to the coast, I climb the stairs at the new Getty Center, where the waterfall in the Central Garden is just loud enough to drown out Interstate 405 below. The soaring travertine structures and the azalea maze are impressive, but I'm disappointed that smog has obliterated the south-western horizon, and so beat a retreat back to our Hollywood hotel by Metro cab.

My driver is a garrulous Russian-American. In the space of twenty minutes he's told me his life story – 'I am in America for twenty-seven years ... I cry ven I come here ven I am age of seventeen.' The cabbie is surprised to hear that I play in a band ('Vere's your big hair?') and that we have babuska dolls in Australia. He says his favourite Australian group is Air Supply (whoah!), and as for singers, 'the small bald one who used to sing with Michael Jackson' (err...). As I leave, I tell him I like his London-style Metro cab. 'You vanna buy it?' he asks eagerly.

I walk into the stygian gloom of my 'suite' and turn on CNN, just in time to catch President George W. Bush adding his folksy contribution on how to raise kids in wartime. 'I think it's essential that all moms and dads and citizens tell their children we love them,' he says. I come to the conclusion that someone's been reading him passages from Jim

Greenman's best-selling family manual *What Happened to the World? Helping Children Cope in Turbulent Times.*

Switching off the box, I scan the outlook from the Juliet balcony. Across Sunset Boulevard, the infamous Whiskey, painted devil-red, is promoting the usual pantheon of bands – one a hard-rock/hip-hop five-piece from Memphis by the name of Saliva. Directly below me stand two chorisia trees, bearing both vicious thorns and beautiful orchid-like flowers, reminding me of the similar 'drunk stick' trees I once saw in the parks of Buenos Aires. A billboard above a garage opposite is advertising *Junkyard Wars*, a TV show in which monster contraptions are built from scrap, then demolished in a series of bloodcurdling battles against death-metal foes – a kind of interactive *Mad Max 2*. Out on the street, a police car with a loud hailer barks at an illegally parked car: 'Move the Chevy before I get excited ...'

Our party of guests staying at the Bel Age Hotel, dispersed over several floors and in rooms of various size and merit, include my travelling companions of over twenty-five years, songwriter/guitarist/keyboard player Jim Moginie, guitarist Martin Rotsey, singer Peter Garrett, and, since 1987, bassist/singer Bones Hillman (né Wayne Stevens). Absent with a note is our long-time manager Gary Morris, who finds he gets more work done by remaining tethered to his desk back home in coastal New South Wales.

Jim and I have been playing music together since our mid teens; it's been a constant of our adult lives. Midnight Oil were born when a neighbour brandishing a flute, John Royle, introduced me to Jim. He and I were both in year nine, though attending different high schools (or 'weapons of mass instruction', to borrow from writer Frank Campbell). I'd get a lift to Jim's place in Sydney's north and haul my drum kit upstairs to the music room. We'd then plough fearlessly through any song we liked as well as trying our hand at writing our own tunes (well, how hard could it be?).

With first bass player Andrew 'Bear' James and Chris Hodgkinson (briefly) on rhythm guitar, and with a light show provided by the resourceful Craig Alexander, the nascent group played a few parties and harbour cruises, as well as a lunchtime concert at Jim's school, where the headmaster stormed on to the stage and told us to 'turn it down or get out' – right in the middle of our seminal interpretation of the Beatles' 'I'm a Loser'.

As drumming and singing the lead vocal simultaneously was proving an arduous task, I advertised in the *Sydney Morning Herald's* 'Musicians Wanted' section for a singer. Peter Garrett arrived in his old Peugeot 404. He easily got the gig, with his commanding presence, blond surfie hair and a quirky, falsetto reading of Jethro Tull's 'Locomotive Breath'. Also in Pete's favour were his self-operated PA system (with *white* speaker boxes) and his attractive girlfriend – who was only ever referred to by her second name.

Farm, as we'd christened the group, soon faced the classic band dilemma: no gigs because we had no experience, and no experience because we had no gigs. The solution was obvious: we'd have to promote our own shows during the summer holidays. As soon as we could legally drive, Craig Alexander and I would head south to the Victorian border or up to the mid-north coast, advertising our upcoming shows in towns such as Tathra, Bermagui and Batemans Bay, after booking the local CWA hall or school of arts for the average outlay of twelve dollars.

With our equipment crammed into a convoy of old cars with dodgy brakes, and security courtesy of our beefy schoolmate Peter Edwards, we toured as 'Top Sydney Rock Band:

FARM'. We'd make enough to pay for fuel, food, posters and the hire of the halls, and sleep at the venues or on the beach. (I remember Pete making a pre-emptive strike against the tyranny of restricted beaches one night at Port Macquarie, in which a 'No Camping' sign was excavated and launched olympically into the dunes.)

With school mate Martin Rotsey in the band playing guitar, a new name drawn from a hat (Midnight Oil – suggested by Peter Watson, a temporary keyboard player), plus a dozen original songs that Jim and I had brought to rehearsals, we were now ready to attack the country's beer-soaked pub scene with all guns ablazing.

Well, with a few left-over hungers from cracker night anyway. One of our regular gigs was at the Chatswood Charles Hotel, in a bar fitted out like a Wild West saloon. Early songs such as 'Surfing with a Spoon' and 'Eye Contact' were brought to a screaming halt by a long-serving barmaid, who'd unplug the band's amplifiers and replace them with an electric heater when her feet got cold. I threw my first genuine 'rock tantrum' at this dive, storming off to our rehearsal garage at my house down by the railway line.

Undaunted by the power-pinching barmaid and other obstacles, the band went on to play an average of 170 shows a year from 1978 until 1982, by which time we were as road-tough as the bands that had gone before us – the Easybeats, the Loved Ones, the Masters Apprentices, Chain and AC/DC. Our story from this point on reads a little like the history of modern China: a Long March followed by a Great Leap Forward, with the Old Guard eventually being replaced by a New Order. The first blurred years of pubs, clubs and RSLs – scenes like the Civic Hotel, French's, the Royal Antler Hotel, the Stage-Door Tavern and Selinas (which boasted the foulest changing-room graffiti ever committed to four walls and a ceiling), of thug-promoters, bullyboy bouncers and the Woolworths' bomber, of noise and sweat and beer and brawls, of Holden Commodores reeking of road food farts and cigarette smoke, of irascible night-bell hotel proprietors and the deadly Hume Highway – those years could easily be the subject of another book on its own.

The year 1982 was a kind of make-or-break time for Midnight Oil. We were in England for the second year in a row, having already made our first overseas recording, *Place Without a Postcard,* with legendary producer Glyn Johns (of Beatles, Stones, Who, Eagles and Joan Armatrading fame), and were working with a young producer, Nick Launay, hoping for a record that would have as much impact as the live shows. When it came out, *10, 9, 8, 7, 6, 5, 4, 3, 2, 1* opened up a wider audience for the band in Australia, and an international cult following on which we could build.

Two years later we found ourselves in Japan, recording *Red Sails in the Sunset* at Tokyo's JVC Victor Studios, followed by further bouts of relentless playing. Our breakthrough came with 1987's *Diesel and Dust,* which was largely inspired by the Blackfella/Whitefella tour of Australian outback communities alongside the Warumpi Band, with fellow travellers Charlie McMahon on didj and Glad Reed on trombone (the subject of writer Andrew McMillan's superb *Strict Rules*). That album, heralded by 'The Dead Heart' and driven by our 'hit single', 'Beds Are Burning', made the band well known around the world, particularly in North America and in Europe, though, typically, not so much in England, where we spent the most time.

Blue Sky Mining, Earth and Sun and Moon, Breathe, Redneck Wonderland and *The Real Thing* all followed, as well as a live album, a compilation album and stand-alone songs for special causes. We continued touring, although less so in Europe and America, with our original line-up unchanged except for bass players: Peter Gifford replaced

Andrew 'Bear' James in 1980, and was himself replaced by Bones Hillman in 1987. 'Giffo' eventually substituted the hammering of our rhythm section for the humming of a factory full of sewing machines, turning out huge quantities of the world's smallest bikinis in subtropical Byron Bay (with 'Urgent G-String Delivery' written on the side of his mini-van).

Meanwhile, Peter Garrett became Australia's most distinctive rock 'n' roll voice, the nation's best-known environmental spokesman, a Greenpeace International board member and president of the Australian Conservation Foundation (ACF), as well as the father of three of the thirteen 'Baby Oils' (the children conceived in the highly charged intervals between tours). Gary Morris, the surfer, golfer and dreamer/scammer who saw the band at one of the early sweat-box shows – at the notorious Antler, our homebase pub on Sydney's northern beaches – stood by the band through the best and the rest, as its manager, mauler and agent provocateur.

And Jim Moginie honed his skills to become the band's musical director, key songwriter, multi-instrumentalist and studio guru, without whom very little in the way of Midnight Oil music would ever have been heard.

Los Angeles certainly looks, sounds and smells familiar, with its wattle, bottlebrush and gum trees lining the freeways, but now that the barbarians are at the gates, the wheels are really falling off Tinsel Town. Post–September 11, the happy pills aren't working, the table-thumping televangelists are being taken seriously, the fearful are fleeing to Lake Tahoe, and the driving wounded are looking shell-shocked and exposed, as if a golden horde of Mongols had just galloped through their Bircher-muesli breakfasts.

The US flag is everywhere, sold in its thousands by those guys at intersections who clean your windscreen whether you like it or not. It hangs from private verandahs and office windows, and it's stuck to the bonnets and boots of countless Chevies, Hondas and Beemers. Some have been justly hoisted in sympathy and solidarity for the victims of 'the Incident' – 'TIME TO PRAY' urges one hotel's flashing billboard, next to a massive flagpole from which the Stars and Stripes ripple splendidly. Elsewhere a blunter message is conveyed: 'IT'S BUTT-KICKING TIME' reads the slogan on a baseball cap clearly visible through the rear windscreen of a rusty Dodge. Another enterprising jingoist is selling t-shirts warning 'DONT FUCK WITH US. WE FUCK BACK.' (just the sort of succinct, coded statement the Oval Office would doubtless love to release).

Since our arrival four days ago, a succession of grave, heavily made-up senators and retired military figures with improbable names have been filing through the nation's TV studios, offering up patriotic verse to newsmen such as Larry King, Lou Dobbs and Wolf Blitzer (a nom de guerre, surely). Fox News hired its own 'lieutenant colonel' – whose total military experience turned out to be forty-four days in a New Jersey boot camp. CNN's 'twenty-four/seven' news-only channel regularly snares between 600 000 and 800 000 viewers, but since September 11 the network is finding treasure in tragedy, rating up to 3 million during peak periods. All the news networks offer blanket coverage of the unfolding 'Operation Infinite Justice', or 'Enduring Freedom', or 'Operation Let's Go Get 'Em' – whatever they're calling it.

If ratings are any indication, though, most Americans are about as interested in their devolving international conflict as they've traditionally been in the ballot box, remaining resolutely glued to sitcoms like *Friends* (which regularly pulls in over 30 million viewers). Perhaps they've just taken Lou Dobbs's advice after some of CNN's audience complained of 'threat fatigue' after so many war-related stories; 'God created the remote control,' said Dobbs, with such hubris he could only have been referring to Himself.

Top brass such as Pentagon spokesman Rear Admiral John Stufflebeam and Deputy Secretary of Defense Paul Wolfowitz regularly appear on all the channels, warning that there's a 100-per-cent chance of further terrorist aggression (this is a country that's *extremely* fond of statistics). As a result, Disneyland, an enduring symbol of the Great Satan if ever there was one, has become a high-security zone.

Today it's virtually deserted, the much-loved old theme park looking less like a fun place for kids and more like Fort Mickey. As soon as our minibus breaches the military cordon, a uniformed posse of goons go to work on it, crawling underneath with flashlights, prodding inside the engine bay with bomb detectors, and dusting (presumably) for any trace of weapons-grade plutonium. Band members stand around contemplating the scene, wondering aloud why any terrorist hell-bent on getting even with Mickey and Donald (or 'Fascist Mouse!' and 'Bourgeois Duck!', as lighting tech Nick Elvin calls them) would arrive at their target disguised as an Australian rock band.

We're soon dismissed, with instructions to 'exit the facility' and some bogus directions to the Downtown Disney Shopping and Entertainment Mall, which houses the venue for tonight's gig. For the next half-hour we cruise the backlots of Anaheim, lost among the clean-livin', God-fearin', pre-*Simpsons/South Park/Osbournes* television families of our childhood. At one point I'm sure I see Fred McMurray from *My Three Sons* arriving home from work in his Woody wagon, hugging his perfect '60s boys (a perilous proposition these days). Eventually we find ourselves back at the original boom gates, only to promptly leave again with fresh directions.

This time we reach the venue within minutes.

The venue is the House of Blues (or 'house of booze', as tour manager Willie MacInnes calls it), one of a chain of theatres that have sprung up all over the USA. Founded by visionary Isaac Tigrett, who was also behind the Hard Rock Cafe franchise, and launched with celebrity investment from the likes of Dan Aykroyd, Aerosmith, Isaac Hayes and *The Late Show with David Letterman*'s Paul Shaffer, the HOB's charter is to 'teach history through art and music'. The original restaurant concept is now an empire that includes hotels, amphitheatres, a booking agency, a digital media company and a charitable foundation, all thematically bound together by Southern blues tradition and cuisine.

The HOB venues come in a variety of shapes and sizes. The one on Hollywood's Sunset Strip (where our second gig will take place) looks, from the outside, like the kind of rusty tin shed full of redbacks that you see abandoned on the outskirts of any Australian country town – and so fits LA perfectly. Interestingly, the corrugated iron comes from an old cotton gin near 'The Crossroads', outside Clarksdale, Mississippi, where bluesman Robert Johnson is said to have made his Faustian pact with the devil. The Chicago House of Blues is even more striking, as we discover later in the tour. I can't decide whether it looks more like a huge Moreton Bay bug (perhaps inspired by the Big Prawn at Ballina, New South Wales) or the inner sole of a giant jogging shoe. Whichever one it is, being a band that's played almost everywhere over the years – a women's prison, an outback schoolyard, a French bullring, a German U-boat factory and a flat-bed truck – we don't even blink at the idea of performing inside a crustacean or a shoe.

Inside the big bivalve, it's an eclectic potpourri of styles. The walls of this folk-art voodoo lounge are filled with a combination of patchwork curtains and native paintings by Southern artists in recycled timber frames, along with replicas of 'communication' quilts used by slaves in days gone by. Other notable features include furniture studded with old bottle tops, glass mosaic and fringes, plaster masks of great bluesmen and women – from Mississippi Fred McDowell to Johnny Winter – statues of deities from the Occident, the Orient and Africa, and pithy epigrams such as 'In Blues We Trust' and 'Unity in Diversity'. It all perfectly describes the fabled underworld of bluesy rock 'n' roll, and the fashionably eccentric characters and tortured souls that inhabit it. An old sign from a Barristers' Gallery hanging over our dressing-room door sets the tone: 'Adultresses, Whores, No Lien Dopes/Pushers.'

The HOB's devilishly clever creators also remembered to put some of the budget aside for more prosaic considerations, such as good sound and lighting systems, hydraulic stages for easy load-ins and -outs, TV monitors of the performances throughout the venues, and good sightlines from every level. As a result, bands, crews and audiences usually seem to have a good time at these venues – which seem to work just as well when hosting an Alice Cooper concert as they do a 'Gospel Brunch'.

The Anaheim HOB may also have an interesting facade, but since we enter through the loading dock, I can't be sure. Unpacking their equipment are our 'special guests' for the tour, Will Hoge, a four-piece guitar band from 'the New South', whose music is steeped in the tradition of Bruce Springsteen, Van Morrison and Neil Young. Will, Tres, Brian, Kirk and road manager Ryan become good mates over the next six weeks, managing to play strong shows *and* have fun, despite the long drives. (To make ends meet, the band drives their own van, towing their gear in a U-Haul covered trailer.) They've got an album, *Carousel*, and have been out promoting it, supporting John Mellencamp and Rod Stewart, and generally being treated poorly by the headline acts' road crews. I only hope they came away from our trip together with the sense of something gained, as the lot of an opening act – performing to near-empty rooms, warming up an often apathetic crowd, squeezing on to the lip of the stage, lugging their own equipment – can be a soul-destroying exercise in frustration.

We do our soundcheck, that ritual of checking levels, tones and effects for the monitors (what we hear on stage) and 'the front-of-house' (what the audience hears). Monitor tech Ben Shapiro performs his distinctive brand of vocal gymnastics as he adjusts the equalisers, speaking an arcane language that only other soundmen understand:

'*Ah yeah, one sssue, ay ay* [tongue click, tongue click], *ay ay, one sssue, yeah sue* [tongue click]. Put three-quarter one five back to where it was … *ssue* … now pull it out two dB … *yeah, ssue* … Try a bit of 100 cycles back in … *sssue* …'

Drum tech Clem Ryan sets up the kit exactly the same way every night – which is comforting to know whenever we've missed the soundcheck and walk out cold on to an unfamiliar stage. Clem's a drummer himself, a formidable golf opponent and a bush mechanic of percussion, fashioning replacement parts for drum kits that have been beaten into submission. He maintains and tunes my main kit and the stand-up 'cocktail' kit (a recent addition for acoustic songs, the mini drum set is dubbed 'Little Bob' by Bones). At the gigs, Clem soundchecks them when the band can't make it, adjusts my microphone and monitor levels, and puts up with sweat, volume and much gnashing of teeth on a nightly basis – as well as my occasional 'spontaneous combustion'.

These meltdowns can be triggered by a number of things. Perhaps it's a lack of oxygen, as was the case at a big-bill, multi-race concert we played at Ellis Park in Johannesburg, where the mile-high altitude wreaked havoc with the lungs of the Uitlanders. Or maybe illness is the culprit – like during the 1992 tour when tsunamis of tiredness from a prolonged bout of glandular fever made it a challenge to even pick up a pair of drumsticks. Sometimes it's just that you've had a dog of a show, when nothing has gone smoothly, or – in the words of Bob Dylan – 'Everything is broken' …

When the best-laid plans go horribly, horribly wrong, the crew are the masters of keeping it light. Lighting tech Nick Elvin and former soundman James 'Oysters' Kilpatrick would occasionally drop everything and perform their infamous Theatre of Annoyance, a face-slapping, ear-pinching Shakespearean mini-opera meets the Three Stooges. Nick's never been caught short for an apt rock 'n' roll quote in any situation, emerging backstage after particularly hot shows with Bon Jovi's 'I've seen a million faces and I've rocked them all!', or mimicking heavy-metal singer clichés (my favourite is 'Scoop up the butterfly, draw it to the heaving breast, then re-lease …').

On German tours, bets would be taken to see if anyone could last a single day without 'mentioning the war' – even a clicking of the heels would mean instant disqualification. Of course, Germany's defeat in both of the twentieth century's calamitous world wars has long been an Anglo/Aussie ob-session (and Basil Fawlty didn't help). So former production manager Michael Lippold's riposte to the unrepentant laun-dry *frau* who lost our stage clothes during our '92 European tour should have come as no surprise: 'Two–nil,' he said.

Bones, likewise, never fails to see the amusing side of any gaffe or disaster, defusing many a potentially explosive situation by turning it into a joke, awarding a nickname or breaking into song. But even Bones, on stage tonight in Disneyland wearing a t-shirt with 'The Bass Player' printed on the front, can't understand why the front few rows of the audience have dissolved into fits of mirth, until after the gig it was pointed out that his bass strap and a fold in his shirt had obscured some of the letters – leaving 'The ass layer' written boldly across his chest.

KING OF THE ROAD

There's a road train going nowhere
The roads are cut, the lines are down
I'll be staying at the Roma Bar, till the
monsoon passes on
from 'Truganini'

Perhaps we just get off on the wrong foot with our bus driver, Slim, a craggy-faced highway veteran from Nashville, Tennessee.

'What kinda group are ya?' he enquires, early on in the tour.

'We're female impersonators from Australia,' Bones replies, with the result that Slim pretty much keeps to himself, volunteering little, until almost two weeks later, when he wanders into one of the band's soundchecks and realises he's been had.

'Funny guy, that Bones,' he drawls. So begins a verbal jousting contest between the two men that lasts until the end of the trip.

Slim grew up in Tulsa, Oklahoma, attending Will ('I never met a man I didn't like') Rogers High, the same school that, just a few years later, produced some promising young musicians in J.J. Cale, Bread's David Gates, and Claude Russell Bridges, who would later reinvent himself as pianist/arranger Leon Russell. According to Slim, 'J.J. Cale didn't lark tourin' and didn't smoke dope or do cocaine' – regardless of Cale's hit song that may have indicated otherwise.

After he left school, Slim joined the Marine Corps, and was based in San Francisco. 'All young men should spend a year or two in the Marines,' he informs me gravely, as if revealing a universal truth, 'so they can learn how to make their beds and fold their underpants.' From that moment on, I resolve to leave an immaculate bunk and little piles of origami underwear, for fear of being put on latrine duty or bus-wash detail.

Slim's been driving tour buses on or off since the mid '70s. He says he's just about ready to write the story of his life on the road and the truth about the famous characters he's met. Previously, he's baulked at the idea, imagining that a publisher might only be interested in a 'sensationalised version' of the monotonous reality of ferrying entertainers around the USA. He had his own band once, a gospel group that played a circuit around several states. This was back in the days before buses had beds – they'd just remove several rows of seats and sleep on the floor.

Today's Prevost motorcoaches may lack the grace and style of the famous Airstream Clippers, but they more than make up for it in grunt, space and gadgets. Our bus, like the crew's, has twelve bunks, each with its own mini-TV, reading light, air vents, doona and privacy curtain; two lounges with writing desks; two sound systems; video, DVD and satellite TV (so that tour manager Willie can check on the baseball scores); a small kitchen with sink, fridge and microwave; plus an icebox, a wardrobe and a toilet. Underneath there's a whopping 475-horsepower Series 60 Detroit Diesel, tamed by a six-speed Allison gearbox. On the outside it's all chrome, glass and steel, the hideous airbrushed sunsets of previous buses thankfully passed over this time in favour of tasteful teal green and silver, with a signature motif. The combined effect is that of a huge, supercharged brick wrapped in tin foil, retro-fitted with tyres and windows, then signed like a runaway blank cheque.

The only frustration on this trip is the absence of a bus destination scroll, which used to enable us to change our band name at will. On the 1988 tour we could choose a new identity as the mood took us, becoming anyone from Dolly Parton to Burt Reynolds. Ms Parton became a band favourite after a convertible, occupied by two attractive young women, pulled up next to the moving bus, summoned 'Dolly' to the window and repeatedly lifted their tops. 'Burt Reynolds' turned out to be a big hit with older women, many of whom queued for hours to meet the sexy beast when we displayed his name during our day off in Niagara Falls. I ferried countless autograph requests to the back of the bus, where Burt was 'resting'; they were then signed by Pete with the kind of manly flourish one would expect from the stogie-chompin' star of *Deliverance* and *Smokey and the Bandit*.

If we feel like talking to the driver or listening to the truckers' chatter on the CB radio, or simply enjoy staring absentmindedly down the endless roadways of North America, one of us can ride shotgun next to Slim in the padded throne-like seat usually reserved for the tour manager. Bones spends the most time up the front, photographing America-the-beautiful as well as America-the-Burger-King, on Super 8, 16 mill. and video tape, and smoking Drum rollies out of the sliding window. Conversations with Slim are broken at best; his hearing loss and our Aussie/Kiwi accents prove to be a frustrating combination.

Over the years of touring in the States, we've discovered that there are at least four distinct 'Americas', depending on your route and means of travel, and each of them leaves a very different impression. The monotonous fast-food, truck-stop Americana you pass on today's interstates is altogether blander than the front-porch, small-town America that hugs the old highways of the pre-freeway age. And this again is different from the coal-dust, old-industry USA seen from a Pullman railway car, or the mile-high, relief-map America you look down on from the window of a 737.

Nonetheless, even on the big, wide roads you come across some interesting folk, from titanic truckdrivers wedged into the cabins of their gleaming Freightliners or Kenworth rigs, to tiny, sleepy schoolchildren with their faces pressed hard against the tinted windows of yellow and black buses. We see removal vans with 'Cowgirl Wanted: Must Look Good in Tight Jeans and Boots' written on the back; and large, bearded men riding Harley Davidsons with 'Does Not Play Well With Others' on their black, cut-off t-shirts. One trucker has thoughtfully printed 'I'm Naked from the Waist Down' on his cabin window. Perhaps unsurprisingly, we rarely see hitchhikers.

Occasionally there's wildlife – those resilient critters that haven't yet been hunted to extinction, a bronze monument or fluffy toy substituted in their place. A red-tailed hawk wheels over the bus, a turkey-vulture circles for a road-killed armadillo or raccoon. Elsewhere, a black bear heads for a roadside garbage dump, or a prairie dog pops out of its hole and stands as motionless as a rock (or maybe it *is* a rock). Recently we spotted chipmunks on a mountainside of dense aspen, and a rattlesnake and copperhead in a forest of hickory, ash and oak, alive with the sounds of hummingbirds and woodpeckers. You've got to be quick though. Before you can scramble to a window, the sound of the bus will frighten a deer or an elk back to shelter beyond the tree line, away from the perils of hurtling traffic.

More frequently there are farm animals, fenced into huge cattleyards, piggeries or stables. And there's even the occasional small herd of buffalo, reintroduced to provide an alternative red meat, which few Americans seem to like (or have the heart to eat). At about 400 000 head, these 'bison', as the ranchers call them, still number a fraction of the vast herds that once free-ranged over the great American plains.

As for Slim, he's seen it all. He's a highly qualified road man, and as such, he's always in demand. Bands and crew often request specific people that they know and trust, so old hands like Slim work an average of 300 days a year, doubtless preferring the perpetual motion to sedentary suburbia. As you lie in your bunk, you quickly become accustomed to the manner in which individual drivers nurse 46 000 pounds of metal, fuel, water, luggage and human cargo down the country's interstates.

Bunk selection can be critical. You can choose from a dozen inviting options – ranging from Mild Claustrophobia to Profound Discomfort – although every bunk feels as if you're entombed in a constantly vibrating chest of drawers, while above and below some ogre rummages for lost socks. The bunks at the bottom can be hot and too close to road hum, while the top bunks can develop a nasty sway, leaving the occupant sub-consciously gripping the bed-rails all night. The rear bunks are prone to diesel noise, gear-changing clunks and the regular thud of door-slamming insomniacs. Which leaves the forward middle bunks as the preferred option, although it's all quite academic really. If you can't switch off and let go, then wherever you try to sleep – even in a specially extended bunk or stretched out in the aisle – you're in danger of becoming an irascible, red-eyed bus-zombie *with issues*. If you're still awake in the morning, gazing groggily down the freeway as heat chimera form and dissolve, while the sunrise cuts mercilessly through the bug-splattered front windscreen, it's best to admit defeat. Make some coffee and embrace the new day, the new state, the next exciting episode in this boys'- own adventure.

For all this, the tour bus is still the travelling band's best friend in America, where a ten-hour drive in almost any dir- ection will find you in another city of at least 250 000 people. The alternative, post 9/11, is to spend up to three hours in the nation's security-obsessed airports, waiting for a lousy one- hour flight – not an economic (or ergonomic) proposition. Plus, to be honest, flying in this country can be white-knuckle hell right now. On a recent United Airlines flight the purs- er put the fear of Almighty God into everyone by asking on the intercom for 'anyone who speaks Iraqi or Assyrian'. Then, one passenger, who was waiting for the toilets, began tapping nervously on the lockers above my head. 'Let *me* do the drum- ming,' I told him.

The bus, on the other hand, is our cocoon, our retreat, our entertainment complex, our moving target should we inadver- tently utter something un-American about the War Against Terror, or smuggle any protest songs across state lines. On the occasions when they gleefully wag school to join us on tour, the band's kids always have particular fun on the bus, sleep- ing with enviable effortlessness and adjusting immediately to the eat-crap-food, stay-up-late, do-zilch-homework life on the road.

Our motorhome is where you can read, listen to music, tap away on your iBook or catch up on a movie, there being only a few, non-negotiable, strict rules:

1. **no fornication** – with girlfriends, concubines, strangers or with each other.
2. **no crapping in the toilet** – you've got to wait for the next truck stop.
3. **no yelling in the sleeping quarters** – the culprits know who they are!
4. **no distracting the driver** – unless it involves offers of hot stimulants.

Not that Slim just drives; he's also the navigator, and as such has developed the alarming habit of resting a laptop on the huge steering wheel as the shiny steel juggernaut hurtles onwards. He uses the computer to update on the traffic systems of upcoming cities, although he knows them all back to front, as well as the fastest route to hotels and gigs. He also checks his share prices ('mainly retail'), having bought Cisco at the bottom of its recent plunge. For the safety of everyone on board, I sincerely hope Cisco holds.

The bus stops now and again for refuelling and for food. Eating in roadhouses in the USA can be a trap for young players. Seasoned road hounds that we are, we've learned from bitter experience to avoid anything with a title like 'Moons Over My Hammy' – a sandwich filled with scrambled eggs, two cheeses and a huge slab of piglet – or 'Adam and Eve on a Raft' – scrambled eggs on an angry sea of soggy fries, smothered with a biblical sunset of ketchup. For breakfast I usually confine myself to the relative safety of cereal with a side order of 'fresh fruit', washed down by hot tea (as distinct from iced tea) and milk (rather than long-life cream), with a 'soup 'n' sandwich' for lunch, and a variety of dinners. (Hint: the Catfish Dinner is probably not as lethal as it sounds, and infinitely preferable to the Open-Faced Turkey.)

Once you realise that Paul Bocuse is unknown in the truck stops of America, you can avoid culinary disappointment. You just *know* you'll never get a good cup of (unbagged) tea, the coffee will be insipid, the meals will be bland, the eggs too yellow, the butter too white, the bread too sweet, the servings *huge*, and the overall effect debilitating. On the other hand, the service will be unfailingly efficient and the waitresses (usually Bonnie, Bethany or Brandy) will be friendly and chatty. On top of that, the water's always icy-cold, the bill's reasonable, the air's smoke-free, the piped music's innocuous – 'Ah'm only goin' halfway down,' sings a lonesome radio cowgirl – the other customers are quiet, and the merchandise is suitably tacky or quirky, or both. I mean, how could you resist a bottle opener that exclaims in a throaty male voice, 'Oh yeah! Time for a beer!' every time you squeeze the handle?

For traditional home-style cooking, you need to get off the interstates and into one of the myriad towns that occupy America's heartland. Places with names like: Normal, Illinois; Mystic, Iowa; or even the far-fetched Truth or Consequences, New Mexico. It's there you'll find such gems as the Heaven on Earth restaurant (exit 86 off Interstate 5 in Oregon), where the roast dinners, cinnamon rolls, apple-butter and 'marionberry' desserts are epicurean pieces de resistance. Then there's the Yankee Smokehouse at West Ossipee, New Hampshire, whose speciality is barbecued pork ribs. 'We will sell no swine before its time' is the proprietor's solemn vow. It's even got its own calendar, with months named Hogust, Sowtember, Octailber and Novemboar.

You meet a different type of person in these out-of-the-way chow-downs – friendlier, more direct. Like the guy and his dog who pulled up outside the Smokehouse in a Dodge utility, with a large sticker on the tool box: I WOKE UP

THIS MORNING STICKY, BROKE AND CONFUSED. (I assumed it was the opening line from a local blues song.) Even the signs on the rest-room doors, 'Cowboys' and 'Cowgirls' – or the exotic 'Gutt' and 'Jenta' at the Norske Nook in Osseo, Wisconsin – are tolerable compared with the insufferable 'Dudes' and 'Chicks' we encountered in a Chicago rehearsal room. Then there's the ridiculous, though admirably inventive and strikingly visual, 'Outboards' and 'Inboards' of a certain Bar Harbor diner.

Of course, we can always make ourselves a half-decent meal on the bus, where strong coffee is the rule along with bagels, muffins and fruit purloined from the previous night's band rider. Willie MacInnes, who's been our tour manager around the globe for almost fifteen years, is the expert when it comes to road food. Years ago he got us hooked on Legal Sea Food's clam chowder – from his home town of Boston – and has been known to Fed Ex gallons of the stuff, in giant bladders, to wherever we are in the country.

Apart from food and fuel stops, the only other hold-ups are at level crossings, to let unhurried Santa Fe or Union Pacific railroad trains wind past, or to empty the toilet on the highway verge. Other delays include changing one of the bus's eight giant tyres, or shopping in Wal*Mart, where you can buy everything from a pump-action shotgun to a hearing test. ('Take the gun and get the test for free, sir.') Occasionally we encounter obstacles on the road, like accidents, gridlocks, roadblocks or ice – or even a moose refusing to move from the middle of the road, as we experienced one evening in the Canadian Rockies, during our 1988 tour with Yothu Yindi.

Hurricanes can also create a lot of havoc. In 1990 we passed through Limon, Colorado, the day after a nasty twister had tracked right through the middle of the small town. The place looked like it had been shelled, though selectively. 'The

7-Eleven's fine,' said Chris, our bus driver at the time, 'but the lawyer sure got it.'

The Canadian border is another hurdle, particularly as we often negotiate it late at night, when the customs people are tired and have lost whatever's left of their sense of humour. Usually we're herded off the bus, passports and driver's licences in hand, and called up one by one so that faces can be put to names, and job descriptions given. Sometimes an official will lead a sniffer dog through the bus ('Got any drugs on board? I hope not'), or one of the touring party will be taken away for 'special treatment'. One unlucky recipient was Willie's friend Robyn, who was once interrogated by a female customs agent at the Detroit Bridge checkpoint for more than an hour, regarding some unmarked headache pills, then escorted back to the bus, 'shaken, not wanting to talk about it'. Other times we'll just have to wait for ages in a brightly lit office decorated by a few flags, the mug shots of missing persons, and the photos of the current prime minister or president – depending on whether we're travelling north or south – while they check our records for anything 'felonious'.

Slim takes all this as par for the course. Like most drivers who are in it (literally) for the long haul, he seems to have an unlimited well of patience, even when a three-hour drive becomes an eight-hour ordeal due to 'the way you turkeys stop'. However, going AWOL, or requesting unscheduled sightseeing excursions, could just about get a man court-martialled. (Years ago we bullied our bus driver into making a dash to the Grand Canyon, arriving after dusk, just in time to peer out over a vast purple void where the canyon *may well have been* ...)

Rather than wasting time and money on unnecessary side trips, Slim concentrates on the safety of his driving and the presentation of the coach. He manages to manoeuvre the fourteen-metre-long rig into the tightest of parking spaces with the precision of a master mariner. He somehow gets enough sleep – while the band is at soundchecks, interviews, radio shows or playing the gigs – to drive all night, *every* night if necessary, to the next city. Meanwhile, the bus's interior is always scrubbed and vacuumed to within an inch of its life, unmade beds are made, underpants are folded, notes are taken ('No mint chocolate for bunk #3'), while the exterior chrome and wheel nuts glisten like spit 'n' polished Marine Corps boots.

On an earlier tour, our bus driver at the time, lacking Slim's experience and even temperament, used to wait until we'd all retired for the evening, at which moment he'd ingest a few chemicals and start driving like the deranged truckie in Spielberg's *Duel*. It became a choice between lying deathly pale in your bunk with your buttocks in a walnut-cracking clench, surrendering to the hegemony of luck, fate and the grip of the Goodyear tyres, or taking turns in the front seat with other sleepless itinerants, ready to leap onto the steering wheel before our crazy mullet-haired test pilot ran us off a bridge, Teddy Kennedy–style.

On the current tour, there's little chance of Willie or Pete honing their own bus-driving skills, as they have in the past, because Slim jealously guards this divine right and the responsibility of his chosen career. Contributions by laymen regarding the health of the engine are also unwelcome, as I discover later on our overnight run from Denver to Minneapolis. When an acrid stench repeatedly fills the cabin, I make the mistake of suggesting, 'It smells like burning brakes.' Slim's tone changes dramatically, as if he'd just popped a mood-altering pill, and I'm dismissed out of hand as the mechanical philistine I surely am: 'What would a

drummer know about a *burse?*' he mocks. Affronted, I explain that I come from a long line of *burse* drivers ...

In retrospect, this was clearly the turning point in the
relationship with our now increasingly cantankerous driver,
who begins to exceed his share of 'senior moments'. Turning
his hearing aid to the 'off' position, he succeeds in stone-
walling Craig Allen, our tour accountant, who's in the final
stages of desperation for a toilet stop. 'What do I have to
do to get this guy to stop the bus?' pleads Craig, looking as
if 'BUSJACKING BY TERRORIST ACCOUNTANT' could
well be tomorrow's headline.

By the last couple of weeks of the tour, Craig's not the only
one 'pacing up and down the aisle like a stallion on steroids',
as Bones puts it. When boredom has threatened in the past,
we've resorted to everything from bus surfing competitions to
games of Celebrity Forehead, even awarding an art prize once
for the best caricature of Willie (won by Martin). Much of
the esoteric computer-speak between Jim, Martin and Bones
is lost on a lagging luddite like myself, who still thinks that
a USB port is something you sail a ship into. Similarly, my
eyes glaze over during conversations about the relative merits
of rare vintage guitars with binding, mother-of-pearl inlaid
necks or Bakerlite knobs.

This time, as highway signs for Dr Pepper, Days Inn,
Wendy's, Conoco fuel and Indian Casinos ('with loose slots!')
fall past with mind-numbing repetition, we rely on the music
itself to stave off ennui, and spend time moving older songs in
and out of the set list. 'Renaissance Man', 'Common Ground',
'Concrete', 'Blot', 'E-Beat', 'The Real Thing' and even 'No
Reaction' (from 1979's *Head Injuries* album) all make re-
appearances. 'US Forces' gets the occasional airing, mainly
over the Canadian border, where it's warmly received; and
'Dreamworld' settles in as the set's finale, leaving the post-9/
11 audience with a cheerful, going-home mantra from

Midnight Oil: 'Your dreamworld is just about to END, END, END, END ...'

And perhaps it is, if the daily diet of blood and guts we receive via the bus's satellite TV news programs is any indication. As the Incident is left semi-submerged in the wake, the national horror over the terrorist attacks is increasingly diverted by the carnage in Israel and Palestine, the sabre-rattling between India and Pakistan over Kashmir, and the dark mutterings in Washington regarding Iraq and North Korea. Not that the wounded American soul is getting any rest, though, with bio-terrorist alerts and weekly bomb threats to banks, malls, ports, airports, apartments, petrol tankers, mailboxes and New York City landmarks. Most of these turn out to be hoaxes or, some say, cynically fabricated to save life-insurance-company butts.

As the tour moves into its final days, Slim's barbs become totally out of order. The bus driver now takes obvious pleasure in provoking the 'hippies with volume', as Pete called us at a recent gig in Sydney, while we cruise south over the old Mason–Dixon line.

'We should do to the Arabs what we did to the Indians,' he blusters. 'Kill 'em all and steal their oil!'

'You're really ignorant, Slim!' shouts Pete, from his preferred spot in the back lounge, although, unfortunately, not loud enough for the driver to hear.

Florida's balmy climate sees Slim warming to his theme, referring as he does to some hapless young guy on a moped as 'a fag on a bicycle', and enquiring if 'the fucking tea-maker has died'. When we finally part company at Orlando Airport, neither band nor crew are on speaking terms with their drivers, with the crew plotting murder most foul in an exclusive smoking huddle outside the departures hall. Apparently their driver insisted on hosing down his bus while the lads were catching up on some much-needed kip. I figure then that the messages on the t-shirts of soundman Tim Millican – 'Your village called. Their idiot is missing.' – and monitor-tech Ben Shapiro – 'If I throw a stick, will you leave?' – must be more than mere coincidence.

As for Slim, he announces what an easy run it's been for him. 'You boys are clean, real dean,' he says approvingly. 'That was one of the most pleasur'ble trips arve had.'

'Guess what?' replies Pete, looking him straight in the eye. 'That was one of my least.'

LA WOMAN

There are canyons full of movie stars
Churches made of metal
There are mountains made of muscle
from 'Bedlam Bridge'

For three disrhythmic days my breakfast *haj* has been to the same coffee-stained plastic table that rocks annoyingly outside a Hollywood deli. My observations here, over green melon and granola, have convinced me of two irrefutable 'facts':

1 That the only people not in a car are (a) walking to or from their cars; (b) in our band; (c) smog-jogging desperados; or (d) skipping parole/medication.

This last category is included for the customer dressed in orange army fatigues at the next table who, in between sorties onto Sunset Strip to direct traffic and hurl abuse at categories (a), (b) and (c), engages himself in an angry dialectic about America's imminent Armageddon.

2 That advice on correcting the slightest physical imperfection can be found with a quick flip through the *LA Weekly,* where the advertisements for 'personal enhancement' are evidently

an irresistible siren song to the present imperfect. According to these ads, even horrifying afflictions with unspeakable names can have a happy ending – although once you've begun, it might be hard to know where to stop.

If you've got scoliosis, psoriasis, keratoconus, rosacea, unwanted male breast tissue ('manboobs'), a hairy back or 'unsightly hammertoes', now there's an answer. If you want tumescent liposuction, collagen implants, skin rejuvenation, microdermabrasion, facelift, hair transplant, breast augmentation ('through the navel!'), labia reduction, penis enlargement, rhinoplasty, tummy tuck, fuller buttocks or an endoscopic brow lift, then all of these are possible in the city of years-defying, age-denying angels.

If you're in pain, you could try rubbing Super Blue Stuff, with emu oil, into your hands and body. If your sixpack more closely resembles a wine bladder, you could experiment with a fitness belt ('The equivalent of 600 sit-ups in 10 minutes!') without leaving the comfort of your armchair or passing up a single beer nut. If you've got sweaty armpits, you can have Botox injected into your underarms – thereby risking the scientific probability of sweat breaking out doubly somewhere else. More commonly, you can ditch that harridan frown with a few Botox jabs in your forehead, which has the added benefit that, for the following few months at least, even the worst news can be met only with an expression of mild surprise. Now, if I could just get rid of this hump ...

Indeed, who could blame *anyone* for getting *everything* done, as long as young, beautiful and sexy remain the prime-time attributes for Hollywood's television career women, even those who host the so-called serious news channels. CNN's recent ad for Paula Zahn's new show featured a male voice asking: 'Where can you find a morning news anchor who's provocative, super-smart – oh yeah, and just a little sexy [cue sound of opening zip]?'

As for male news presenters, they're kindly requested to keep their zips firmly fastened. Maureen Dowd reported from Sydney that even (US) *60 Minutes* noticed the contradiction and joined the chorus of complaints about the CNN ad: 'Why doesn't someone say Wolf Blitzer is sexy?' *60 Minutes*'s Don Hewitt enquired. 'He must be sexy to *somebody*.'

Film stars come under even greater pressure, though not every actor feels that lifting their faces will automatically lift their work prospects. 'If you start doing that,' says Robert Redford, 'you start chipping away at little pieces of your soul.' (So how does he look so good?) And if the jobs do dry up along with your skin, you can always enrol in actor Richard Dreyfuss's motivational class, entitled 'How to be an Unemployed Actor in LA and Enjoy it'.

Clearly there's some urgency to get out of LA before the temptation to have some work done, or to buy the latest 500-horsepower V10 Dodge Ram muscle car, becomes over-powering. Who knows? Perhaps we'd eventually succumb to the Left Coast fashionistas ourselves, adopting the ripped and ragged *nostalgie de la boue* look – featuring worn-out-at-the-knees jeans from all that endless floor-scrubbing – currently favoured by the young, white and wealthy. These creatures usually hunt in packs, but can be easily stun-gunned, tagged and released any day of the week in Hollywood's boutique hotels. There, they habitually drag their bags in and out of beautifully appointed shoe-box rooms with wafer-thin walls and no hot water, 'created' for a six-figure sum by an interior designer almost certainly named Carl.

Our own hotel fits the bill exactly. It keeps a courtesy car parked out the front, an avocado-green Chrysler PT Cruiser, which exactly matches the colour of the receptionists' shirts.

Another establishment further down 'the Strip' hangs its sign self-consciously upside down, and features a lounge where beanbags bob on a sea of blue Astroturf. Human flotsam wearing navel jewellery and 'discreet' tattoos lie around sipping pheromone cocktails, feigning boredom and waiting to be rescued 'by my agent' – like the smug survivors of a Caribbean cruise disaster.

Two blocks down, on Santa Monica Boulevard, the men are even more buffed and coiffed, if only for a quick weekend excursion to the U Wash Doggie. Meanwhile, at the freeway exit a black man in a sharp suit plays his clarinet for change, to a line of air-conditioned cars with their doors centrally locked and their windows wound up tight.

As is often the case, the latest fashions look best on the terminally thin, and thus should be avoided by anyone larger than Gwyneth Paltrow. Tour accountant/'CIA agent' Craig Allen, armed with black wraparound sunglasses, cell phone, third-dan black belt in karate, and strict instructions from management to 'look afda da boyz', follows Bones into a bar, where they notice a full-figured lass with jeans cut so low she's got what's known at home as plumber's arse ('belt-cleavage' in the USA). She proceeds to absentmindedly scratch the aforementioned arse right in front of our heroes, an egregious habit that eventually drives them both back onto the street. At least it inadvertently saved them in the nick of time from a notorious darts hustler.

I give the stars 'n' bars a miss and go browsing in LA's music equipment stores, where I'm bamboozled by choice and fiscally humiliated by the exchange rate. I come across Keith Moon's *Tommy* drum kit, which the Who's legendary performer used in Ken Russell's film adaptation of Townshend's sprawling rock opera. Not for sale. Other vintage drums, guitars and keyboards are also out of reach by those in possession of the ailing Pacific peso, although Jim is later seen wheeling an old Wurlitzer piano in through the hotel lobby.

I'm drawn further into the seedy underbelly of LA guitarland by the sound of an Eddie Van Halen clone stretching strings and murdering arpeggios in the 'soundproof' booth. It sounds about as appealing as Aussie gangsta rap or French rock. The facial contortions, long black hair, jackboot on the wedge and screaming weapon in hand convince me that this man is carrying out a personal jihad against the shop assistant. I attempt to rescue the poor chap, but I'm knocked backwards by the aural assault of a Marshall amp cranked up to 'eleven'. As I look up from the carpet I notice that the walls of the booth are plastered with photos of English groups from an, err ... *artier* era: Pink Floyd, the Who and the Beatles (whose recently departed George Harrison is putting on a brave face, while his guitar gently weeps).

Back in my hotel room I decide to play a little guitar myself, of the quiet, acoustic variety. Leaving the door ajar for ventilation, I begin strumming gently on the balcony. I'm making some headway with a couple of new songs when in drops 'Wayne', a producer and songwriter from Nashville, who's 'missin' ma own geetar' and hankering to play one of his compositions. I dutifully hand over the instrument. Wayne tells me he's hoping that Neil Diamond will perform the song – a Jimmy Webb-esque ode to September 11 – 'in an upcoming film starring Alec Baldwin'. The moment he's finished singing the final heart-wrenching chorus, he rushes out of the room, like Kramer in *Seinfeld,* suggesting a co-write on his return to LA next Friday. I'm left alone on the balcony, wondering if Wayne was an apparition, or whether – in the city where careers are made faster than you can say 'Mulholland Drive' – I've just had my Big Break!

As it turns out, Wayne's Homeric 9/11 epic is just one of many to be written and recorded over the following twelve months, most of which are overtly patriotic, replete with heroic tales from the inferno (like 'My City of Ruins', from Bruce Springsteen's reverential *The Rising*), or at least carefully worded so as not to ruffle the fragile feathers of the Washington hawks. All except, that is, for Steve Earle's 'John Walker's Blues', from his *Jerusalem* album, in which the so-called 'American Taliban', John Walker Lindh, with chains around his feet, still 'has got to fight for what he believes'.

Tonight's gig at the House of Blues on Hollywood's Sunset Strip is a bottler, with much imbibing, chanting and idiosyncratic dancing followed by severe lower back pain, for both band and audience, proving that even in jaded, self-conscious Los Angeles, the audience will 'give it up' as long as you bust your gut – and in our case, vent your spleen. So far, in fact, everything about the tour has been *just so*.

'Time to get sartorially decked out in our agit-rock uniforms again,' says Pete before the show, alluding to the latest bespoke stage clothes that arrive belatedly from Australia in a suspicious brown paper package. They're matching gun-metal grey/khaki drill with variations-on-a-theme screen prints. Like most of the stage clobber we've had made through the years, this lot will inevitably be discarded over the following weeks – too dull, hot or contrived – or the dye will bleed in the first laundry load so that the entire band will turn puce. Thus, for better or worse, we'll wind up looking exactly like we always have – 'Daggy, but nice', as glamorous trombonist Glad Reed once neatly summed us up.

Meanwhile, Craig churns out fresh juices, dispenses herbal tonics, bags the wet stage clothes and attaches the in-ear monitors. He also doles out Monday per diems, writes left-handed cheques and advises on topics as diverse as taxation, dog breeds, archery, automobile specifications and the correct method of performing stomach crunches. Martin plays practical jokes on Bones, who in turn stirs Craig, who then takes it out on the venue owners or staff. Both the guitarists, Martin and Jim, buy new amps, guitars and effects pedals, in the land where a '60s Gretsch, a Fender Pro, a Big Muff, a Hot Cake or a Woolly Mammoth is just a log-on away. Access to the Net is a constant frustration, though, perhaps because guitar tech Dave Mayer has the only AOL account:

Pete: 'Did you get on last night?'

Jim: 'Yeah, I got on straightaway, no worries.'

Pete: 'I couldn't get on at all' (cry of exasperation).

Jim often arrives early at the gigs, where he spends hours programming sequences, samples and click-tracks, as does Martin, 'to see if I can get the buzz in my amp any louder'. Martin and Jim, ever searching for the perfect guitar sound, seem to swap their equipment on a near-daily basis ('I just want something that makes me happy,' Martin laughs).

Pete does countless 'phoners', calling up music reviewers in upcoming cities and delivering sound bites and good copy, growing *taller* with every week. (By the time we reach Wisconsin, midway through the tour, journo David A. Kulczyk writes: 'You can't really argue with a seven-foot-tall bald man, can you?')

Other reviews are even further from the mark, with one writer referring to our album before last as *Rhythmic Wonderland* – it was *Redneck*, of course – and stating confidently that 'Midnight Oil is a sidebar career for the group' (perhaps she had some inside information). A *Rolling Stone* scribe back home calls us 'a proud, but worried, bunch of Australian blokes' (what, us worry?); while Mark Brown from Denver's *Rocky Mountain News* writes: 'Think of them as very loud folk singers ...' An astrologically inclined Gold Coast woman later asks me if the title of the new album 'is based on any Capricorns in the group'. Another journo refers to one of our later festival appearances, straddled between 'Puppetry of the Penis' and a pair of World Championship Wrestlers, as 'typically nutritious'!

The three nominated interviewees – Pete, Bones and myself – each approach the media in our own quirky manner, fielding every predictable question, from the most asked, 'What's more important to Midnight Oil, the music or the message?', and the second most, 'How much longer can you guys keep going?', to the age-old, 'What are you going to do when it's all over?' Bones has taken to answering the last of these with: 'Form a boy band and call it Blue Steel.' Actually, most of the entertainment writers are genuine music fans, and still care about old-fashioned concepts such as taste, content and credibility – even if their editors don't. 'We're in the business of selling very thinly sliced trees to real humans,' said the instantly likeable Keith Blanchard, editor of men's mag *Maxim*, to *USA Today* journalist Peter Johnson.

After the show, a couple of party girls manage to breeze past the security mammoth and stumble, drinks in hand, into our dressing room – only to recoil in horror from the pan-sensory assault of wet socks and Y-fronts strewn across the floor. Shortly afterwards, our own stickered and laminated friends show up backstage.

First in is our long-time booker, Mitch Rose from Creative Artists Agency (CAA), who, with his wife Leone, has more than once had us over to his place for home-cooked meals during our LA stopovers. Our former tour accountant, Geoff Halstead, and his wife Cassie also drop by. Over our years together the naturally mild-mannered Geoff fought a series of heated pecuniary battles on our behalf, from the pits of Saarbruken to the pubs of Sao Paulo, where he once performed a splendid impersonation of De Niro in *Raging Bull* when 500 dollars US of the band's cash mysteriously vanished from a hotel safe. Next up are my friends Bill and Laura Wolfe, who've been sending me updated versions of the perfect Midnight Oil set list for more than a decade. Last to arrive are our friends Shen and Ema Schulz, daughter of *The Gong Show* creator and *Sonny and Cher Comedy Hour* writer/producer Chris Beard, and niece of thespian Robina Beard, aka 'Madge "You're soaking in it" Palmolive'.

The following morning there's a choice between taking the minibus over the Mexican border for sightseeing and shopping (a Lorena Bobbitt machete *senora?*), or spending an afternoon with friends in Malibu. I opt for the latter, and an hour later find myself outside a tiny wooden cottage in a hidden valley flanked by gums, pepper trees, jacarandas and a few remaining redwoods. The place is beautiful, and uncommonly still and silent.

Naomi, a gifted blues singer, and Vic, a wood-carver of nationwide repute, together with their son Gabriel, are the self-described 'poor cousins of the canyon', surrounded by the compounds of colourful entertainment identities such as Don Henley, Pierce Brosnan and 'a German Johnny Carson'. Barbra Streisand used to live further up the single-lane road, until she donated the five-home estate to the Santa Monica Mountains Conservancy, which now uses the property as a centre for ecological studies. Singer, songwriter and drummer Don Henley (of the Eagles), also well known for his environmental passion – particularly his successful Walden Pond preservation project in Massachusetts – spends at least part of the year on the property across the creek. Meanwhile, on any given day, nannies can be seen perambulating the valley's fortunate heirs and heiresses up and down the gated community.

It all appeared to be extremely blissful and bucolic, until I heard about the Old Testament punishments regularly visited upon this coastal Arcadia. What with bushfires, earthquakes, floods, mudslides and the dreaded Santa Ana winds, this area is a natural disaster waiting to happen. To raise the anxiety level even higher, a plethora of dangerous critters right out of a *National Geographic* feature roam with apparent impunity around this neck of the woods, including bears, mountain lions, rattlesnakes, coyotes, wild boars, horned owls and yellow jackets (not flying fish, but particularly spiteful wasps).

As if to somewhat even up the score, my lunch today is 'boar on the barbie', killed by mein host himself with a bow and arrow in the mountains beyond. These creatures may have copped the blunt end of God's ugly stick (years ago, several of them successfully stared us down in a thorn veldt in South Africa) but I highly recommend them on a plate – mmm, goluptious! And all this only an hour from greater Los Angeles, where wild animals live in the zoo (and in the room above my hotel suite), and where everyone knows that bacon, beef and biltong come from the freezer at Ralphs.

Vic told me that the land we're lunching on was originally owned and occupied by the Chumash Nation, once the largest cultural group of the western American tribes, until successive invasions by Spanish, Mexican and American settlers 're-duced' the local indigenous population. It's a tragic pattern repeated right across North America. Any development application here must include the results of an archaeological dig, to determine the existence of Native American sacred sites on the property. A seismic trench is also required, to discourage potential home-owners from rolling out the welcome mat directly above a fault line.

This was a lesson not lost on tour manager Willie and his ex-flatmate, production manager Steve 'Chopper' Borges, who, following the 1992 riots, moved out of LA's Studio City neighbourhood to a new home in Granada Hills. In January 1994 the Northridge Earthquake opened up a gaping hole in their house, and prompted a spectacular fire at the gas main at the end of their street. Willie and Chopper, armed to the teeth like Yosemite Sam and Davy Crockett defending the Alamo, took turns in holding the fort as gangs of looters swarmed past the property, following the line of destruction. The home, an 'L-shaped ranch house which became a U', as Willie puts it, was later repaired at their own considerable cost – 'Act of God' insurance being prohibitively expensive – before being resold at a loss to the not-unhappy former owners.

All of these perils seem only to add to Malibu's uniqueness, and, consequently, real-estate prices. Don Felder, Henley's former band-mate, has apparently parted with his walled estate for about 6 million dollars. Down on the beach, Cher is allegedly asking 25 mill for her faux-Egyptian colossus (although you may be able to pick it up for a lot less, as anything overtly Middle Eastern is currently right out of fashion). Other locals you might bump into with a supermarket trolley include Bruce Willis, Cindy Crawford and two antithetic Anglos, John 'Rotten' Lydon and Julie Andrews.

I'm curious whether the former Sex Pistols frontman and *The Sound of Music*'s Maria would share anything in common. Perhaps they could hook up for a duet, an age of terror anthem called, for instance, 'Anarchy in the Abbey', with John snarling the verses and Julie adding 'Yodel ay, yodel ay, yodel ay, ah-ha' in the choruses.

WILLY AND THE POOR BOYS

When I'm locked in my room
I just want to scream
Now I know what they mean
Only the strong
from 'Only the Strong'

'Willie's funny ... I like Willie.'

So said my younger daughter Ella about our long-time, international tour manager, Willie MacInnes. On European tours, Willie both charms and terrorises the locals by adopting an exaggerated Franco-Prussian accent, which he suffixes onto his natural mild Bostonian brogue. In America, he's equally as charming, except when doing battle with the lumpenproletariat. Apathetic rental-car clerks, asinine airline staff, rude security guards, opportunistic porters, recalcitrant venue owners and hotel cashiers have all felt Willie's wrath when he's provoked. He's even been known to interrogate unblinking traffic cops as to their citizenship status (more about that later). Every confrontation is approached with the same technique – speak softly and carry a big phone – while any joke or quip is followed closely by a monumental coughing/

snorting/choking belly laugh, punctuated by shots of Ventolin and/or Crown Royal whisky.

Willie's amazing. He's the last to sleep and the first to start work in the morning, getting up early to make travel and accommodation bookings, followed by a round of gentle wake-up calls. He makes sure we're on time for rehearsals, gigs, soundchecks and recording sessions, and bundles us into countless hire cars and taxis bound for airports and railway stations. When we need a mini-van for day trips, Willie handles the driving – with only a passing interest in the road rules ('Nothing handles like a hire car!') – and occasionally does the honours with the tour bus if the driver needs a break. He'll even help carry the luggage into hotels and the acoustic-show instruments into radio stations.

There's just no stopping the man. Hosting after-show suppers in his room, arranging food deliveries on the bus or great restaurants for our days off, organising sightseeing excursions, passport collections, couriers, doctors and guest lists – Willie does the lot ('These guests are a boil on my ass!'). At the beginning of the tours he regularly shouts us dinner and drinks, and when the weeks turn to months he's been known to send flowers to the girls back home, or cards to needy friends. And he graciously answers a constant barrage of never-ending questions from the likes of Bones and myself, most of which have already been covered in the tour itinerary he's provided.

As well as a superb tour manager, Willie's an actor *manque*, with an unrivalled air-maracas routine – most recently performed in a Spanish restaurant in Old San Diego; a party-all-the-time entertainer, with a phonebook the size of a road case; and a passionate sports fan, with an intimate knowledge of his beloved Boston Red Sox baseball team. He's also a great raconteur, with a lifetime of graphic stories from his years on the road. Over three decades, Willie has worked as tour manager or production manager with the Doobie Brothers, the Tubes, Steve Miller, Journey, the Beach Boys, the Brothers Johnson, Pablo Cruise, Warren Zevon, the B-52's, Boy George, INXS, the Violent Femmes, Laura Branigan and Duran Duran – the only band he's ever quit, after an unfortunate fracas in Japan.

Willie's marriage proposal to his fiancée Deborah, whom he met ten years ago at one of our concerts in San Francisco, was typically orchestrated for maximum theatrical impact. They were in Paris, in a second-floor hotel *chambre*, which had french doors opening out onto a balcony over a laneway. Opposite the hotel, renovations to a Versace store were in progress. While Deborah took a shower, Willie whipped downstairs, bought an engagement ring, and hurriedly returned to the room. With Deborah still mi-*douche,* Willie flung open the doors of the bathroom and shower screen, and wolf-whistled to the French workers on the building site to gain their attention; he then fell to his knees and slipped the ring onto the naked, dripping Deborah's soapy finger – provoking, as he'd intended, much yahooing and Gallic catcalling from across the impasse.

The other love of Willie's life, and one we share, is the Great American Scenic Drive. Once, with driver Dominic at the wheel and Willie riding shotgun, we surfed a giant tour bus all the way down Highway 1, the spectacular, single-lane, coastal road from San Francisco to LA. When we finally pulled over for food and photos, I couldn't help but marvel at the huge serpentine traffic jam we'd created in our wake, many of the passing motorists kindly honouring us with an identical digital salute.

Over the years we've made many detours to see North America's natural wonders – Arizona's Painted Desert and Petrified Forest, the Grand Canyon (almost, as mentioned earlier), Niagara Falls, the Florida Keys, the Canadian Rockies, the Humboldt Redwoods, the Adirondacks in mid-fall, and Robert Redford's Sundance Valley ranch, nestled under the spectacular Mount Timpanogos in Utah. All of which more than compensates for the hours spent on the New Jersey Turnpike – or, for that matter, the days, weeks and months spent in hotel rooms.

Speaking of hotels, this is one area where even Willie's skills cannot guarantee deep, uninterrupted sleep.

You may have chosen the most promising digs in town. You may have requested a non-smoking room on the highest possible floor, well away from the traffic noise, the elevator 'ping', the ice-machine hum and the guest laundry. Like Bones, you may even have insisted upon a room with a window facing Mecca (a long-standing joke quickly retracted after 9/11). As with bunk selection on the tour bus, regardless of the best preparation (by Willie or anyone), you can still find yourself in Hell's Teeth.

Before long, the heater will start up, then expire with a wheeze and a shudder (and again, and again ...). The two sailors in the room next door, fuelled by cheap rum and an overdose of World Championship Wrestling, will re-enact the hunting of the *Bismarck* until she finally sinks in a sea of fire and oil, wreckage and moans at precisely 3.32 am local time. The hookers arrive 10 minutes later, followed by such loud, protracted, *gymnastic* sex – 'Yes! Yes! Yes! YES! YES! Ooh! Ooh! OH! YEEEESSSS!' – that you feel like knocking on their door and asking if they need some help, just so that pink dollars and fluids can be exchanged faster and the whole tawdry business can be over and done with. Worse still is the concupiscent businessman in the room above, who, with one hand on the video's remote control and the other on the *morganplanke*, begins bouncing onanismically up and down on the bed around five o'clock in perfect jismic rhythm to the last half-hour of *Brenda's Big Day*. Then the radio alarm clock, programmed at maximum volume the previous night by a hard at hearin' curtain-ring salesman from Walla Walla, Washington, will burst into life at 6.15 am – right in the middle of the guitar solo in 'Carry On, My Wayward Son'.

Alas, o best beloved, the storm is not yet spent. At seven in the morning, the Hmelnitski family from Baltimore, all sporting matching satin jackets, holds an extended day-planner summit right outside your door. The hotel maids then deliver the coup de grace at 9 am. Treating the 'Do Not Disturb' sign written in four languages hanging from your doorknob as a personal challenge, they set about bashing their vacuum cleaners against the door repeatedly, ramming the adjacent room's bed hard against the wafer-thin dividing wall, lisping Hithpanic instructions down the hallway or, when all else fails, calling you up on a bedside phone so loud that its effect is, I imagine, akin to the opening salvo of electro-convulsive therapy. It all became too much once for Jim's former guitar tech Spanky. The sleep-deprived 'Groover from Vancouver' flipped open his Leatherman knife and carved 'LEAVE ME ALONE' into a New York City hotel-room door.

Meanwhile the gardeners have arrived, armed with machines that sound like heavy artillery at the Somme. A chainsaw is used to trim off old palm fronds, even though a bushsaw would do the job perfectly. A leaf-blower is blasted along footpaths when the soothing swish of a broom, or the zen of a rake, would certainly be healthier for the rest of humankind. Then a motor-mulcher is reversed into place – BEEP BEEP BEEP BEEP – followed by tortured screams as rainforests of greenery are reduced to woodchips. All the while you lie fuming inside your four walls, developing tumours previously unheard of, abusing the poor girl at reception one more time, or plotting the fastest way to feed both of the yardsmen through the mulcher.

Chronic room-changers and ear-plug wearers fare little better. If the police sirens, taxi horns and air-brakes on one side of the hotel don't get you, the garbage trucks and the early-morning tradesmen in the back lane surely will. One Chicago hotel we stayed at recently even had a sign in the car-park, 'Please Sound Horn' – directly below Martin's room – presumably so that reception (and half the hotel) knew of new guests' arrival.

And be not fooled. There's absolutely no correlation between the number of gents in stove-pipe hats and penguin suits standing around at the front door, m'lud, and the quality and duration of one's repose. The Philippe Starck–designed Paramount Hotel in New York City, for example, may be considerably enhanced by the asymmetrical furniture and the Italian Masters above the bedheads, but the conical stainless-steel toilets in the neighbouring rooms flush with such gusto that it sounds like you're being sucked into the East River. And I can only assume that Philippe's budget must have expired before he got around to double-glazing the windows or fitting high-wattage light bulbs. (Will someone please drop some more quarters into the power box? This place is dimmer than a nuclear winter!)

In fact, I spent a much better night in Washington DC's Hotel Bastardos, where the receptionist was protected by a bulletproof screen, the chenille bedspread was dotted with cigarette burns, and the view was over a boneyard (o blessed silence, thy name is death). Even 'the white-trash wing' – Jim's description – of a $39-a-night penitentiary-hotel in Bangor, Maine, with a giant axe-wielding John Bunyan statue right outside the window, is tolerable during our recent three-day sentence there. (They grant us day-leave to see the 'quillpigs' (hedgehogs) at nearby Bar Harbor.)

And at least people treat you normally in a crap hotel. Even the humblest traveller could eventually be seduced by the fawning ninnies who inhabit the lobbies of four- and five-star accommodation, forgetting that everyone you meet has already been slipped a buck to make damn sure that you do indeed have a nice day. A little bowing and scraping is bearable sometimes of course but, as *Redneck Wonderland* producer Magoo would regularly remind us, 'It's not the '80s now, you know.'

The only problem with el cheapo hotels is that many possess neither room service nor mini-bar, and some don't even carry a lousy chocolate bar dispenser in the hallway. Martin recently woke up starving in the middle of the night and, in a hunger frenzy, emptied the contents of his suitcase over the floor, searching for a solitary peanut. In true *Survivor* fashion, he broke the shell in two and devoured one half-nut, putting the other precious half aside in case he needed it to last until breakfast. As he remarked later, 'The number of stars on your album review and on your hotel seem to closely correspond.'

Tim and Clem, soundman and drum technician, respectively, recently divulged the secret to making great Italian coffee in hotel rooms that lack a hotplate. Step 1: grab hotel iron, switch to full heat, turn upside down on the ironing board, and steady it on both sides with a pair of leather boots. Step 2: rest coffee pot on top until beverage is brewed to taste and intoxicating smell permeates the atmosphere. Step 3: pour coffee. Step 4: for froth, hit the steam jets. Voila! Now you can enjoy an industrial-strength cappuccino while ironing your work shorts (optional). 'Clean living under difficult circumstances', as the English Mods used to say.

Occasionally the planets align and you attain somniferous nirvana in majestic surroundings, as at Colorado's Boulderado Hotel, with its sweeping balustrades and stained-glass ceiling, or Cincinnati's gracious Vernon Manor, home to the Dustin Hoffman character in *Rain Man*. At worst, it can be noisy enough to rattle your teeth out onto the pillow, such as at the legendary Skyways Motel right next to LAX Airport. The Skyways's roof sign once made a handy final line-up point for the pilots of the heavy jets that thunder into LA every fifty seconds.

Sometimes dangerous creatures, uninvited guests from the insect world, end up inside your hotel room. Craig Allen was once rudely awoken at the Sportsmen's Lodge in LA by an unidentified spider, which had already bitten the full-paying guest on the fist and the arm, and was readying for another assault (to be fair, the gardeners' noise was probably responsible for the spider's antagonistic disposition). Our tour accountant's hand swelled up to the size of a Christmas ham, but he remained philosophical about the incident. 'If it'd been an Australian spider, I'd be dead by now,' Craig reasoned. As for the spider, the angry arachnid subsequently met a grisly end on the hotel-room wall. Jim, meanwhile, had a restless night on the last Australian tour battling the dreaded bed bugs of Bathurst, which burrowed into his skin at a car-motel close to our Leagues Club gig. ('Park Nose In', read the signs. And they did.)

Critters aside, over the years, the members of our band and crew have taken considerable physical punishment, mostly self-inflicted. Apart from the predictable hearing loss, we've cracked ribs by pole-axing off darkened stages, wrecked backs by steadying falling road cases, broken toes on recalcitrant foot pedals, sliced open fingers and thumbs on cymbals and hi-hats, grappled with bouts of arthritis and survived potentially lethal encounters with malevolent chicken pies and volcanic fajitas. In the great pantheon of misfortunes, though, these are all mere bagatelles. The touring party is disgrace-fully well preserved – 'in the formaldehyde of rock 'n' roll', as Martin says – and has missed surprisingly few shows in our twenty-five years of playing.

Sometimes it's others that are injured. One such casualty was a cop who got knocked out cold when he hit his head on a post, as Pete scrambled back on stage following a roam around the audience at Santa Clara's Great America theme park. Only some fast-talking international diplomacy by manager Gary Morris convinced the police chief (who closely resembled actor Dennis Weaver) not to press charges.

On a few occasions, others have wished us harm. Take the angry crowd of loggers and their wives who rocked and ham-mered our car on our way to a dawn concert in 1993 at the Black Stump, a clear-felled site at pristine Clayoquot Sound on Vancouver Island. Our safety, along with the security of the local Native Canadians, the Douglas firs, the endangered deer-mouse and the delicate fungi and lichen, seemed of little concern to the blockading bushfolk, who spat on the ground at the mere mention of our name. They made us feel about as welcome as gout, holding up signs such as 'You're Barking Up the Wrong Tree' and screaming out friendly greetings like, 'Get the hell out of our community!' One of the cops who helped us slowly through the mob had some friendly advice: 'Next time, fly in, *please.*'

Other actions have been mostly incident-free, although Pete slipped off the top of a PA stack during the midtown Manhattan lunch-hour protest show following the 1989 *Exxon Valdez* oil disaster – only to recover triumphantly and climb straight back up. A sit-in with Greenpeace at Sao Paulo's busiest intersection, where we donned face masks to highlight the massive Brazilian city's solid air crisis, left us only with burning eyes, toxic skin and, in my case, a week of erupting yellow phlegm (out, vile jelly!).

More dangerous still may have been our performance at the Sydney 2000 Olympics Closing Ceremony. Performing 'Beds Are Burning' with Glad Reed and Kathy Wemyss on brass, and dressed in the clandestine 'Sorry' suits, the appearance lasted less than four minutes – quite long enough for me, considering the pulse-arresting fit of the jeans that had been made especially for the performance. And long enough for everyone present also, if recent allegations are proven to be true – that a senior commander of al-Qaeda, deported from Australia in 2001, was involved in a plot to launch a terrorist attack on the Games.

Sometimes it's the weather making life hell, like the wind-driven, horizontal rain that almost drowned the band, crew and audience at an open-air show at Toronto's football stadium. Then there was the Earth Day concert in Boston in 1992 when, as the on-stage temperature plummeted below freezing point and our fingers flatly refused to play the instruments, we took to the stage padded up like Michelin men. (Unlike the heroic members of Fishbone who, defying shrinkage, stripped down to their underwear.)

During one previous tour, I really got whipped by the elements. I made the critical error of assuming that an ozone layer existed above Columbus, Ohio, only to discover that a five-minute sunbake had burned a hole in the cornea of my right eye. The result was that the slightest glare became unbearable, rendering me almost sightless in that eye for the rest of the tour. I was instructed to wear an eye patch, Moshe Dayan–style, which some of our audience evidently took as a bizarre affectation.

The crew, of course, in an act of pure *schadenfreude*, resolved to have some fun, setting the visually challenged drummer's kit up backwards – with the bass-drum pedal on the left, hi-hat on the right – enjoying it immensely as I flailed away hopelessly like a punch-drunk shadow boxer.

Not surprisingly, no-one ever came forward to claim responsibility for the prank, although I'm confident that our drum tech and osteopath at the time, the gentle Doc Nelson, had nothing to do with it. That leaves the two 'Michaels' on the crew, Messrs Lippold and Kerr, who were caught on video lurking and smirking by the side of the stage ...

Any low points are soon forgotten, however, when Willie arranges a mini-vacation to one of the thousands of small lakes that dot the North American countryside. Lakes and rivers serve many of the same functions in the USA as beaches do in Australia – for fooling around in boats, wetting a line, or just lying face down and groaning – and are often a better swimming option than the oceans. Access to these waterways can also be scenic, as it usually involves driving through Starbucks-less towns of white timber houses with welcoming front porches, on which plastic swans and Adirondack chairs are aesthetically arranged, while out the back large, clammy folk sitting astride ride-on mowers carve crop circles into their lawns.

On a later tour I went for a swim in Lake Michigan, at Chicago, where there are a couple of small beaches downtown. The only obstacle was a line of 'Orange-Shirts' – overzealous lifeguards sitting on rowing boats in water no deeper than a metre, corralling the bathers close to the shore. I'd just read an account of Jim Dreyer's solo marathon swim across the middle section of Lake Michigan in 1998, a masochistic ordeal lasting some forty-one hours that inspired me to head for the horizon. I galloped through the shallow water and made a break for the wide-open inland sea, but was stopped short by an adolescent lake nazi.

'You can't swim beyond the boat,' he instructed.

I gazed out over a body of water seemingly devoid of waves, rips, currents or sharks, then refocused on the kid.

'Well, move the boat, then,' I replied, assuming that he'd realise from my accent that he's talking to a water-loving, buoyant Aussie, not a pizza-logged Illinoisian.

'Sorry,' he said, terminating the discussion.

I was forced to wallow along the shore like a bunyip in a bathtub, wondering whether the extra security had something to do with the sighting of a terrorist's periscope in the Great Lakes. As it turned out, it was safer in the water than on the beach, where a little shoving and sand-kicking between rival 'yoofs' from the 'hood – some wearing large Ali G–style fake silver medallions, black head scarves and Phat Farm tracky-daks around their ankles – was threatening to degenerate into a gangland Desert Storm.

Even less successful was an afternoon on 'the beach' at Madison, Wisconsin, where the total absence of swimmers in murky Lake Mendota had reduced the bored-out-of-her-brain lifeguard to a crumpled heap on the towel, perhaps quietly sobbing over her end of term college results. Rather than risk the probability of a double course of antibiotics, I abandoned the ridiculous notion of a dip and instead read the paper on the grass, while my daughter Ella fed bread rolls to the ducks.

The truth is, clean, white sand beaches are rare, and the sea is often too cold, treacherous or polluted to be really in-viting (with the exception of Hawaii's opalescent ocean). The Jupiter Beach Hotel in Florida, for example, ever prepared for the real possibility of a menacing oil slick or hospital-waste discharge, once thoughtfully provided a packet of 'beach tar remover' to use after our dip.

Pete's recent attempt at an ocean swim in Oregon was rendered less appealing by the presence of a dead seal lying under a stinking pile of driftwood and seaweed. Another op-portunity at Cardiff State Beach, north of San Diego, was foiled by 'urban slobber' in the water, and heavy earthmoving machinery on the beach. We got talking to one of the local surfers, who warned us about the nearby toxic cocktail, with the colour and texture of old borscht, which floats downriver every day from the city of Escondido. 'I never swim on an outgoing tide,' he said.

SAN FRANCISCO

Over liquid tarmac wastelands of cactus and heat
Down cobblestone alleyways of
washing day sheets
Up ghost prairie mountains of sunsets and space
Down the road a familiar face
Across the wilderness, out further than the bush
I will follow you
from 'King of the Mountain'

High up on the hill above San Francisco's Japantown shops stand clapboard and shingle row houses unscathed by earthquake and fire, their distinctive wide eaves, bay windows, timber columns and street numbers in the thousands a welcome sight for any jaundiced road warrior. Interspersed are sombre apartment blocks with steel fire-stairs suspended vertiginously in midair, and clusters of boutique shops for the well-heeled: gift shops, coffee houses, hairdressers, jewellers, oyster bars, pet-grooming salons, florists and milliners.

I push up through streets lined with familiar trees: red-flowering gums, native daphne, pohutakawas, figs, even a few scrappy Cootamundra wattles, a long way from home

but battling on bravely. By the time I reach Pacific Heights
the views are breathtaking, stretching from the Golden Gate
Bridge and distant Sausalito to Alcatraz Island's grim cliffs,
jail and water tank, quarantined from the foggy, white city in
the middle of a deep, cold bay.

It's a relief to be back in a smaller city built on a human
scale, where dwellings sit lightly, if tightly, on the land. In San
Fran you can walk, take a bus or cab, catch a ferry, or ride a
rattlin' ringin' streetcar, its brakeman still calling out the stops
and leaning hard on the burnished levers. Walking is a real
pleasure here, as long as you've got Cathy Freeman's legs and
Phar Lap's heart, or at least a handy supply of puffers. Cars
get short shrift, parking precariously on the steepest of grades
– in San Francisco, 'runaways' refers to vehicles with dodgy
handbrakes, not just missing teenagers.

The wharfs and foreshore districts are looking better than
ever. Along the Embarcadero where boarding-house 'crimps'
once shanghaied their crews, a new SF Port Development is
under construction, while the Bay Trail, a 650-kilometre hike,
jog, skate or bike ride, will ultimately join more than 130
open spaces and cross seven of the Bay Area bridges. The plan
is to restore non-car mobility to the town not possible since
the gold-rush days.

As long as the bridges survive, that is. The governor of
California, Gray Davis, recently made an appearance on the
major networks with the startling revelation that four of
the state's bridges, including San Francisco's Bay Bridge and
Golden Gate Bridge, could be subject to terrorist attack in the
near future: 'The best preparation is to let terrorists know that
we know what you're up to, we're ready for you,' he said.

Davis emerged about a week later, bridges intact, evidently
as blameless for going public with uncorroborated FBI terrorist warnings as he claims to be about California's crippling
energy crisis. Two police cars remain permanently stationed

on the northern shore of the Golden Gate Bridge, however, just in case.

I wander down Geary Boulevard past our hotel, with its rice-paper-screened rooms, Japanese garden and the deepest baths east of Okinawa, to the legendary Fillmore Auditorium, the venue for the third date of the tour, where the crew is readying for our soundcheck. Dodging the ticket touts – one of whom offers me a double pass to our own show – I climb the outside stairs and enter the building.

Inside the old ballroom, soundcheck under way, Clem wallops the drums one at a time. Starting with the old Boosey and Hawkes marching drum that I've been using as a tom-tom, he moves through the kit: bass drum, snare, floor tom, tympani, upside-down snare, cymbals, ice-bell, tambourines and water tank. He finishes with the vocal mic, which swings reliably backwards and forwards on 'the Clem Ryan Magic Singing Drummer' boom-arm (patent pending).

We run through 'Golden Age' and 'Overpass' from the new album, then check the acoustic-guitar and cocktail-kit levels with 'Time to Heal' and 'Blue Sky Mine'. I ask Ben to turn Bones's vocal up in my monitors, so I can track his famously consistent harmonies, then increase the entire band mix level, so that up there on the riser at the rear of the stage, it doesn't feel like I'm playing in an entirely different room. When soundmen Tim and Ben are happy, we leave the stage so that Will Hoge can do their soundcheck. We head for dinner in the upstairs lounge, handing over a meal ticket for the chance to line up, army-style, at the bain-marie.

The sight of the bain-marie takes me back to the boiling vats of bubble-and-squeak we were served at our school cadet camp, a compulsory two-week, midwinter torture in years nine and ten at Singleton in New South Wales, an ordeal which could only be made marginally more tolerable by joining the band. Our cadet band, therefore, attracted some of the least gifted 'musicians' ever assembled in one place, and eventually degenerated into an adolescent version of *Dad's Army* manned by dropouts and delinquents, reprobates and recidivists, plus a few sly-grog opportunists and conscientious objectors, their long hair tucked tragically up under their slouch hats. They even allowed a few drummers in.

As far as I can ascertain, the only lasting benefits from these camps were mastering a buzz-roll on a Legato snare drum while goose-stepping up and down a parade ground, and the newfound ability to fold a pair of underpants. Plus the premature breaking of my voice, following a two-hour punishment drill in which I was compelled to bark orders at a post.

I banish these thoughts, shake my head, and refocus on the Fillmore walls, which are entirely covered by hundreds of posters advertising impossibly exciting, multi-bill concerts of yesteryear. Cream and the Paul Butterfield Blues Band; the Jimi Hendrix Experience and Jefferson Airplane; Creedence Clearwater Revival, Steppenwolf and It's a Beautiful Day – the list goes on and on.

We've had some top nights at the Fillmore, treading the same boards as some of the greatest bands of our generation, as if those halcyon times of music and magic had permeated our own hearts and minds and muscles. Tonight's show is no exception.

The gig gets under way like a sprinter out of a starter's block. Bones sings chorus vocals then skips back to the drum riser for cues, quips and knowing winks. Jim hops up and down on the spot as he tortures note-bursts from his Gretsch, while Martin grins as he windmills his Tele in 'Been Away Too Long'. Pete's dancing, conducting, radiating, *engaging* the crowd. It's not until five songs into the set that there's a long enough break to cast a discerning eye over the house.

The audience is a sea of mainly white faces, stacked tightly together like Vietnamese water puppets, more male than female, late-teens to fifty-somethings, and includes hundreds of 'Peter Garretts' – those wearing our black 'Terminator 2' t-shirts, with Pete's face printed on the front, and the band reflected in his mirror sunglasses. There are also a few familiar 'Powderworkers' (our much-devoted, cyber-chatting fans) down at the lip of the stage, from which shrill cries of 'Jimmy Sharman's Boxers!' and 'Stand in Line!' can periodically be heard. Pete tells the post-9/11 audience, 'The way forward is to play with more heart, more passion' – and promises that the chocolate wheel, which contains the names of our repertoire of songs, and was spun on previous tours by members of the audience to determine which tune we'd play next, will return 'by popular demand' in the not-too-distant future.

We encore with 'Tone Poem', a new song from *Capricornia*. It's a trippy guitar theme and rhythm guitar/ride cymbal swing reminiscent of the Bay Area's Summer of Love, that unique experiment in peace, protest, pop, pot and bad blue-windowpane acid which climaxed at the first and only Monterey International Pop Festival in June 1967. With the motto 'Music, Love and Flowers', the festival featured San Fran's own Big Brother and the Holding Company, Canned Heat, Country Joe and the Fish, the Grateful Dead and the final performance by LA's the Mamas and the Papas.

On an earlier tour we were introduced to the legendary Bill Graham, the colourful booker, benefactor and pit-bull promoter of the Fillmore (and later the Carousel Ballroom and the Winterland). Over the years he successfully staged hundreds of peaceful gigs, including the feted New Year's Day breakfasts. Graham once said he was 'in the business of turning people on', and until his death in a helicopter crash in

1991 he did just that, time and again, while controlling the majority of venues from the Pacific Ocean to as far east as Denver. The foundation that bears his name continues the tradition of auctioning posters designed by the venues, and signed by the bands, for a variety of charities.

Alas, those days of good vibes and good will, beards and braids were not to last – although the fashion, at least, is lately making a determined reappearance. Two years after the hippies' blockade of the intersection of Haight and Ashbury streets to celebrate 'the Death of Hip' (followed closely by the sweet-sounding Second Annual Grope for Peace), the hippie dream came to an abrupt end on 6 December 1969 at nearby Altamont Speedway, where a man was murdered at a free Rolling Stones concert. As history tells us, Sir Charlie (they knighted the wrong Stone) and the lads, denied the use of Golden Gate Park for their US tour's final concert, made the regrettable decision to hire members of the Frisco Hell's Angels as security at the alternative, unsuitable venue. The price? Just 500 dollars' worth of full-strength beer.

Obviously, once the Angels had offered their services, it would have been ill-advised to renege on the deal. Midnight Oil were once informed by the Hell's Angels that we would be appearing at a 'family-friendly' festival on their Broadford property in the Victorian countryside. On the designated evening we dutifully drove to the gig, guided by beer-carton signs carved into arrows gruffly reading 'Concert', arriving after dusk at a scene which brought to mind Colonel Kurtz's barbaric upriver village in *Apocalypse Now* (lots of smoky fires, spotlights, unnatural acts, bodies hanging from trees, etcetera).

My all-important job during the gig – which was played so fast that our eighty-minute set lasted just on forty-five – was to keep an eye out for our host and master of ceremonies, Ball Bearing's signal (one raised finger), which would indicate when we were to stop. When the time came, we gratefully obeyed. Then, at the anxious insistence of our tour manager at the time, Constance Adolf, we walked straight off the stage, into the hire car, and fish-tailed out of there in one of our fastest exits since the Long Jetty Hotel riot of '78. As we disappeared over the hill we could still hear Ball (Mr Bearing to us) devouring the microphone.

'D'ya reckon we got good value outa Midnight Oil?' he growled.

'Yeeeaaah!!' moaned the hopelessly drug-fucked crowd, wearing leathers, jeans, boots and chains. Some had given up using the Porta-Loos after one had been rolled down the hill, whilst occupied, earlier in the day, and thus had resorted to pissing through the barbed-wire security barrier or projectile vomiting in the direction of the stage.

'Orright then,' said Mr Bearing, 'we'll bring the strippers back on.'

The following day we bid farewell to the manicured streetscapes above Japantown and cruise out of the city through a very different neighbourhood, the Tenderloin. Here, homelessness and poverty, loan sharks and drug dealers seem to have engulfed more of the town every time we visit, although it's comforting to see that Original Joe's restaurant, near the Warfield Theater, is holding out in spite of the onslaught.

We pass Pac Bell Park, with its statue of the great Willie Mays, the new home for the San Francisco Giants baseball team since they quit the notoriously windy and foggy Candlestick Park by the edge of the bay. 'The Stick', as it was affectionately known, was also the venue for the Beatles' last-ever scheduled concert, on 29 August 1966. I wish I could have been there, even if, like the group, I could barely have heard a note, their inadequate PA system competing with a stadium-ful of screaming pubescent girls.

I was in the middle of my own Beatles epiphany. Around about this time, my mother, in all innocence, bought me John Lennon's books *In His Own Write* and *A Spaniard in the Works*, along with some ascorbic acid and home-delivered Sharpe Bros lemonade to help me recover from the flu. By the time I could recite 'The Fat Growth on Eric Hearble' and 'Scene Three Act One', I was painfully aware that somewhere *out there* existed another world, filled with cruel farce and fantasy and pharmaceuticals, one totally foreign to our own prosaic, yet loving, family harmony and calamine-stained medicine cabinet.

Soon we're motoring through desert country irrigated by the California Aquaduct, which is fed by creeks originating in the high Sierras and by Lake Tahoe. There are citrus groves, stone-fruit orchards, almonds, alfalfa and cotton fields, growing right up next to the highway. A few skeletons of wind-power generators line the tops of bare ridges, the legacy of a technology sidelined here in the stampede for energy via fossil-fuel, hydro or nuclear power.

We stop for a Mexican feast in Bakersfield, with multiple margaritas all round, then climb over the Tehachapi Range at sunset. As the last colours of the day fade, we cross the Mojave Desert, with Edwards Air Force Base on our right, and pass close to the aeroplane graveyard which we used as the location for our 'My Country' film clip (from *Earth and Sun and Moon*). Director Claudia Castle, along with her director-of-photography sister Jane, made several other clips for us in the late '80s and early '90s: 'Forgotten Years' in Verdun, eastern France; 'Blue Sky Mine' in Kalgoorlie, WA; and 'Bedlam Bridge' in New York City.

For 'My Country', Claudia had a camera tracking on a circular dolly, while the band sweated it out, performing take after take in the sweltering heat of desert country dotted with joshua trees. Sheltering under a plane wing while film was re-loaded, Jim picked out the piano theme on an ancient upright that just happened to be lying there in the sand. To date no film clips have been made for *Capricornia*, just a short EPK (Electronic Press Kit) shot by Bones and edited by our long-time friend Youth.

Jim switches on the bus's TV for the evening news, where it's all hail to Bush the Popular, on every network. The president is clearly making political hay while his approval rating shines, introducing an aggressive anti-drug policy that appears to link casual drug use with terrorism, challenging Congress to pass a US$48 billion hike (yikes!) in military spending, and signing Military Commission Order No. 1 – tribunals which abandon the 'beyond a reasonable doubt', unanimous verdict and right of appeal protections of US law. A new pre-emptive strike policy against countries in the black-listed Axis of Evil ('Git 'em 'fore they git us!') has also been mooted. Not all of America's allies seem to be as convinced of the need for this as the bellicose Bush, however, particularly as the toll of friendly-fire victims, including 'about forty' Afghans at a wedding in Kakarak, increases daily.

Any heathen or heretic, traitor or tragic who opposes these initiatives is taken out and (almost) shot. The right of dissent is on the run everywhere except Santa Clara, California, where a 'Barbara Lee Day' has been declared, in honour of the congresswoman who alone voted against awarding George W. the vast new war powers. Meanwhile, Treasury Secretary Paul H. O'Neill is doing the rounds in four African nations along-side U2 vocalist Bono, who calls for increased aid and trade between the USA and Africa as a way to relieve poverty –

while the Republicans proceed to do the exact opposite, protecting and subsidising American farmers. The *in*Grain*ed* Belt is also exerting influence in a briefly resuscitated debate, the ol' prayer-in-school, church vs state chestnut of the 1940s, with some states proposing a daily moment of silence to 'reflect, meditate or pray'. Other states, in one of America's 'episodic fits of puritanism', to quote P.J. O'Rourke, want to make the Pledge of Allegiance compulsory, or hang the slogan 'In God We Trust' around school grounds.

In the workplace, another kind of 9/11 opportunism is taking place. It seems that employers around the country are using the security crisis as an excuse to run background checks on their employees, investigating their records, credit histories and compensation claims. As a countermeasure, civil-liberties watchdogs and unions are fighting an uphill battle to maintain workers' privacy and to prevent unfair sackings and harassment. Little wonder that working people are becoming more understanding of each other's problems; Bones notices that men no longer just shake hands when they greet each other, they embrace with a kind of awkward, sympathetic bear hug – particularly after a beer or nine.

The bus approaches Las Vegas at about 10 pm, guided by searchlights sweeping the heavens and the blazing light bulbs of the city's 2 million inhabitants. The lightshow reminds me of the *favella* on the mountainside above Rio de Janeiro, a city-within-a-city controlled and protected by the drug czars, where do-it-yourself electricians have tapped into the grid, and spun a spectacular web of twinkling fairy lights.

As we get closer to 'Lost Wages', however, it becomes obvious that this sparkling sanctuary of super-abundance in the near distance, though tasteless, is no slum. The billboards, in fact, promise a veritable feast of upcoming attractions, from the Amazing Johnathon to Rita Rudner to Sting (arriving soon slumped in the rear seat of a Jag?) and, as we triumphantly enter the city gates, 'VASECTOMY REVERSAL – or your money back. Dial 1–173 Reverse.'

We check into a resort hotel and receive our keys and rooming list. Within minutes the band and crew, all dressed in regulation black, have dragged our suitcases single-file down a long, winding pathway past shrieking, night-swimming children to our 'family holiday suites' – and chain-locked the doors.

Half an hour later, Bones, Craig Allen, monitor tech Tim 'Rat' Davis and I head off to check out a couple of real Las Vegas casinos, which turn out to be even trashier than we'd anticipated. There isn't a slick-haired, sharp-dressed, *'fock'*-saying good fella anywhere to be seen, nor Sharon Stone for that matter, just thousands of ordinary folk in t-shirts and jeans playing the pokies, standing around the blackjack tables and roulette wheels or ogling the shadow dancers, monstering the cigarette girls and swilling beer. The overwhelming impression is of *The Jerry Springer Show*'s audience let loose on a James Bond set.

Realising after an hour that it's unlikely that we'll be identified as members of an SMS (serious money syndicate) and summoned to the high-rollers' room, we head for the exit. All except for Tim, who's still chatting up one of the drinks waitresses (a 'nine-inch idea' as Willie might say). After buying some chocolate money chips as gifts, Bones, Craig and myself join the 2 am crush on the Strip.

A phalanx of hawkers is thrusting cereal packet–sized cards into the hands of passers-by, including one advertising 'Barely Legal Blondes'. (I come to the conclusion that in Vegas, there must be a statutory minimum level of 'blondeness', under which you're exposed as a hoax, then publicly humiliated on a catwalk with other 'failed blondes'.) Another glossy hand-out features a photo of a sexy young woman, with the promise 'Have this girl in your room in 20 minutes' written across. 'Twenty minutes!' I shout out, deeply impressed. 'Now that's *fast*! Balgowlah Pizza guys, take note!'

Our show at the Las Vegas House of Blues the following night is less than a sell-out, with 700 or so tourists and locals, and a couple of college kids majoring in excessive and compulsive avarice (hons), showing up. Nonetheless, it's obvious that Americans are refusing to let 'the enemy' win, and are out partying again at night, dervish-dancing and throwing down comfort grog and consolation food like there's no tomorrow. In addition, the shared chemistry of the band after so many shows together really comes through – the ahead-of-the-beat *charge* of Martin's guitar and my nervous bass drum, some wild-card guitar from Jim, plus a form-fit, unilateral polemic from Pete. All in all, it's a tough and satisfying gig, with a great sound both on stage and off.

When the audience is on the small side, I often think of a courageous performance by New Zealand band Mother Goose, at a free lunchtime concert at Sydney University, where for a few years in the mid '70s I squandered the public purse 'learning to love the law', as my erudite lecturer Professor Morrison would have it. (Midnight Oil eventually saved me from the law, which was, *res ipsa loquitur*, a mutually agreeable outcome.) Anyway, I learned a valuable showbiz lesson that day: if no-one turns up, play harder!

It was Mother Goose's first trip to Australia, before the band gained some notoriety with the trans-Tasman classic 'Baked Beans' and their outrageous costumes. The theatre was deserted therefore except for myself and one other bloke eating sandwiches, plus a dozen year-four students and their teacher, who evidently thought that they'd come to a kids' pantomime. Confronted instead by six fully grown men in drag, the horrified teacher dismissed the class and out they all filed, after which the other guy soon disappeared also. And so, alone, I stayed for the entire routine, a campy music-hall/mock rock show that predated Sydney's first Gay and Lesbian Mardi Gras by a few months, watching a hairy-legged ballerina and a hoary Kiwi bumblebee put their heart and soul into the act, resolving at that moment to forever be as professional if our own then-nascent band ever got up and running. And to *never, ever,* wear a tutu.

For a town built by the mob, or perhaps because of it, there's surprisingly little (unorganised) crime in the new fun-for-the-whole-family Las Vegas. Although, since the casino hotels went high-rise, the problem of 'jumpers' – people who 'fall' to their death from tall buildings – is on the increase. Bearing this in mind, I scan the tops of the Stratosphere Tower, the Eiffel Tower, the Pyramid, the MGM Grand building and the Statue of Liberty, searching for any sign of a struggle.

My gaze comes to rest on a sign advertising Mr Entertainment himself, Wayne Newton, *still* appearing at the Stardust Resort and Casino after forty-five great years. (Wayne must have signed one of those 'in perpetuity' contracts with Vegas when he was ten.) Actually, Mr Newton is looking good, darn good, and apparently working as hard as ever. According to *Showbiz Weekly,* in his current show Wayne 'lands' on stage via an unseen UFO, 'setting the mood' (fearful? sceptical? comical? ropeable?), before singing, joking and playing a dozen instruments. I truly want to see it, but the man's off to Europe now to entertain the US troops, in the manner of the great Bob Hope.

The other Vegas must-see is the Liberace Museum, complete with the Grinning One's piano, jewellery, costumes, cars and antiques, though no mention of 'brother George'. There's also a Madame Tussaud's Wax Museum, featuring a much healthier Michael Jackson than the one I've just seen in his latest film clip. Another option is *The Secret Garden of Siegfried and Roy*, not a homoerotic German revue, but rather a magic show where white lions, tigers and snow leopards mix with black panthers (with one raised glove?) in an 'exotic jungle setting'. You can even visit 'Paris' without having to suffer the tiny rooms and bad plumbing, or endure the supercilious pouts of French waiters as they refuse to be bullied into speaking American English. (I realise now why many Americans say 'Paris, *France*' – to differentiate it from the friendlier, more accessible 'Paris, Vegas', or even the cinematic Paris, Texas.)

The place that I really want to investigate, but which will have to wait until the next tour, is the indoor gun range, which advertises 'world-class firearms training'. According to the ad, hand guns are available, from pocket pistols to 44 Magnums, while 'submachine guns include Thompsons, Uzis … and more!' One of the facility's happy customers, kindergarten teacher Michelle Martin, writes: 'I had an extraordinary time at the submachine-gun course … This course is a must – especially for women!'

I share a cab back to the hotel, making a mental note to ask the local crew if any of them have toddlers enrolled at Frau Martin's kindergarten. During the night I'm periodically woken by a thunderous *boom* outside my window, which in my comatose state I take to be distant cannon fire from Taliban tanks, en route to the sacking and burning of Las Vegas – desert fortress of the godless infidel!

I needn't be too concerned. The War Against Terror's front line is currently half a world away from Vegas, in the desert mountains around Kandahar, Afghanistan. Still, it seems destined to move westwards to the Tigris and Euphrates valleys if the hard men of Mesopotamia refuse to allow un-restricted UN inspections of their alleged chemical-weapons stockpiles.

In the morning I realise that the *booms* are because our hotel sits right opposite the airport, which operates a twenty-four/seven service totally at odds with the old-fashioned notion of night sleeping. After all, this is the capital of the long, lost weekend – stay any longer and you may end up like the Nicolas Cage character in *Leaving Las Vegas*. Apparently this fate almost befell Australia's own Rick 'Jessie's Girl' Springfield, now back in shape and treading the boards in his own pyrotechnic show at the MGM Grand, *E.F.X. Alive*, which reputedly generates more heat than General Sherman's torching of Atlanta. Whether Vegas's newest overpaid induct-ee, Canadian croonette Celine Dion, finds that her own shoot-ing star rises or burns up over the Nevada skyline remains to be seen.

I can't help pondering what would have become of Elvis Presley, a regular performer here from 1969 until his death in 1977 and the sultry star of *Viva Las Vegas*, if the Colonel had succeeded in outlawing those lethal fried peanut butter and banana sandwiches, and substituted low-fat yoghurt. It's been twenty-five years now since Presley's 'death', and ten since Bones organised a private tour of Graceland for the band, guided by a Memphis belle with big hair and an accent as gooey as molasses in the summertime. On the way home from that temple of terrible taste, our slow-talkin' cabbie popped the big question: 'Do you feel like Elvis is dead or alarve?' he asked, in a goading drawl that suggested only he knew the correct answer. Before we could reply in unison 'The King is dead – long live the King!', our driver launched into a solilo-quy 'proving *con-clu-sive-ly*' that Elvis was not only 'alarve' but possibly immortal. His well-rehearsed spiel covered such anomalies as the delays in Lisa Marie's acceptance of the estate, uncashed insurance policies, the misspelling of Elvis's middle name Aaron as 'Aron', on the tombstone, and the periodic footsteps allegedly coming from an 'unoccupied' upstairs room at Graceland. I recall leaving the taxi wondering whether Elvis had left the building after all, or had simply been forced to join a troupe of Elvis Presley impersonators when he couldn't convince anyone of his authenticity (except for the cab driver and me).

Perhaps Mr Presley became just another anonymous entertainer *with baggage,* cruising quietly from Memphis to Vegas one evening in his twin-finned pink Cadillac and never wanting to leave, allowing the desert sand to gradually drift over him, bury him, shelter him from his past.

Maybe a similar fate befell Elvis contemporaries and Vegas regulars the Smothers Brothers, whose politically charged *Comedy Hour* on CBS in the 1960s never fully recovered from its axing following pressure from President Nixon. ('Tricky' was apparently not amused by the show's lampooning of his Vietnam 'solution'.) Pete Seeger's rendition of his Indochinese cautionary tale 'Waist Deep in the Big Muddy' may well have sealed the show's fate, while the Who's chaotic performance of 'My Generation', which climaxed with drummer Keith Moon destroying his kit with an overdose of flash powder, and Pete Townshend smashing Tommy Smothers's acoustic guitar, probably didn't help either.

The Who may never have been asked back on to the show, and Townshend's hearing was reputedly never the same, but at least the band (or what's left of it – master-bassist John Entwistle recently died in Las Vegas's House of Blues Hotel) has so far resisted the urge to play golden oldies dressed in sparkling dinner jackets at one of the casino-hotels here in Vegas, the fantasy town where 'THE TITANIC SINKS EVERY NIGHT!'

GRAFFITI MAN

In the desert in the dry
Before the breaking of the rain
The temperature in the shade
Had reached a hundred and ten again
from 'Bullroarer'

Wasn't it Steve McQueen who said that he'd rather wake
up in the middle of nowhere than in any city on earth?
Whoever it was, they were right. It's magnificent out here,
among the organ-pipe cacti and the joshua trees, surrounded
by chocolate-brown mountains and aubergine ranges, and
dwarfed by grey shale cliffs and shimmering salt pans. Big-sky
country, as Robbie Robertson said, intersected everywhere
by the puny threads of man – his roads, power lines, railway lines and jet streams. Not that everyone appreciates the
majesty of the wilderness. 'You don't need to go out there,'
said one jaded city slicker. 'Ain't nuthin' out there. Just the
great American fuck-all.'

Our tour bus cruises south down Highway 95, following
the mighty Colorado River, surfing the contours of ancient
river beds, and skirting the massive Hoover Dam (now off

limits to buses and RVs due to terrorist fears). Next stop Phoenix, Arizona. Springing the traps for us up ahead – and watched over by St Reefer, the patron saint of happy travel – is the crew bus, from which the smoke of many existentialist cigarettes is streaming from its roof vents, leaving a message of fair warning writ large in the sky: 'Abandon hope all ye who enter here.'

Around us in the heat haze lie high-security military areas and bombing ranges, rubbing uneasy shoulders with wildlife refuges and Indian reservations of the Hopi, Navajo and Apache nations. Roadside signs appear out of the dry distance. One says 'JESUS', in huge letters. Nothing else. Leaving the motorist to add his or her own punctuation, depending on his or her road-rage level. Another reads: 'World's Biggest Teepee – Turquoise – Indian Crafts – Next Right'; then a kilometre or two later, a reminder: 'Don't Forget the Teepee!' With decreasing intervals, we're told: 'TEEPEE! WORLD'S BIGGEST! LAST CHANCE! NEXT RIGHT!!' In the end, so overwhelmed are we by the frequency of the signs that we completely miss the Teepee exit. We continue on to Blythe, where we turn east, cross the Arizona border (chased by a couple of rogue tumbleweeds) and pick up Interstate 10 for a gun-barrel ride into Phoenix.

In early 1988, while Australia was throwing its backslapping Bicentennial bash, Midnight Oil and Gondwanaland slipped quietly out of town, beginning a year of playing our dilly-bag of desert songs in North America and Europe. In October of that year we joined forces with Yothu Yindi and Native American activist/poet John Trudell (aka Graffiti Man) for the Diesel and Dust to Big Mountain tour, which culminated in a benefit concert in Mesa, Arizona, to assist the legal struggle of the Hopi people, who were being forcibly relocated from their traditional homes by a mining company.

These triple-bill concerts, with land rights for the world's native peoples as the central theme, were some of the most consistently powerful nights of music and message of our touring life. They began with Trudell's mesmerising monologues over drummer/vocalist Quilt Man's rhythms and chants, stories of dispossession, betrayal and the destruction of the Indian nations – including the Santee Sioux, Trudell's own people. True stories told from the heart by this, the former chairman of the American Indian Movement, a spokesman for the Indians Of All Tribes (who occupied Alcatraz Island from 1969 to 1971) and a defender of Leonard Peltier, still languishing in prison since the 1975 shoot-out with the FBI near South Dakota's Wounded Knee. Poems of pain and loss by a husband, father and son-in-law who'd lost his family in a 'suspicious' fire in 1979 while protesting US Indian laws in San Francisco.

Then came Yothu Yindi from north-east Arnhem Land in Australia, their dancers painted in Yolngu ceremonial colours, brandishing spears at the audience, playing yidakis and clapping bilmas. Their performance was divided between Top End traditional songs and Swamp Jockey–style knock-'em-down rock 'n' roll, laying the ground for the later success of 'Treaty' and 'Djapana', a national and international career, and the annual Garma Festival of Traditional Culture.

Our own show would start with 'Bullroarer', then segue into 'Put Down That Weapon', 'Dreamworld' and 'Lucky Country'. Nick Elvin would drop down the lights at the beginning of 'Warakurna' to dusk-in-the-desert mauves, then create an orange sunrise behind our kangaroo-and-dingo 'coat of arms', and the water tank, which we'd found the year before on an outback road during the Blackfella/Whitefella tour (and is only now finally in tune). Sometimes we'd play 'Jimmy Sharman's Boxers', with Michael 'Garfield' Russell playing a marching drum in the introduction, then picking up his trumpet for the fanfare ending. By the time the big finishers came around – 'Hercules', 'Sometimes' and 'Beds Are Burning' – soundman James 'Oysters' Kilpatrick would be punishing the PA, and Jock Bain would be wringing the last desperate decibel out of the monitors. Meantime, Graffiti Man and Yothu Yindi would already be on their way to the next city, the next hotel, the next gig, ploughing their way through a six-week, thirty-date tour spanning four time zones and some 16 000 kilometres.

Thirteen years later, our Phoenix show on the current tour is in a 'theatre in the round', thankfully not rotating, and feels more like a cramped TV studio than a live concert. Ahead is a sixteen-hour overnight bus trip to Denver, a long night of fractured semi-sleep, a night of wrestling crocodiles in our bunks, alternately overheating and shivering.

The reward in the morning is a great view of the Rocky Mountains, with some early-season snow on the highest peaks, and a grassland sea replacing the desert wilderness. By the time we stop for breakfast in the tiny Colorado town of Las Vegas (another one), the temperature has dropped six or seven degrees Celsius and the air is thinner, creating an enviable sense of lightness and well-being. We cruise through the old mining town of Pueblo and hit Denver at rush hour, eventually pulling up at the Monaco Hotel.

I go for a leg-stretch down 16th Street Mall, past an elderly clarinettist in an Uncle Tom hat playing American standards, past street beggars, ageing punks, Rastas, lumberjacks, skiers, business people, defence personnel and other diverse denizens of Denver. Plenty of big people, friendly people, in brown or green suits rather than black – unhurried Coloradans. With an hour to spare, I drop in at the Denver Art Museum to see

the Alice Neel exhibition, which is full of graphic, tragic portraits of the artist's family, friends and lovers in and around
New York City in the 1930s.

In the morning we're shuffled off to nearby Boulder for a
live radio performance and chat, where we play 'Luritja Way'
from the still unreleased *Capricornia,* plus the persistent 'Beds
Are Burning'. Like most of these acoustic radio shows, the
line between triumph and debacle is a fine one, and largely
depends on the quality of the recording environment and the
talents of the station's audio engineers, who in Boulder are
efficiency personified. Even if these radio gigs end with great
sorrow and weeping, though, we rarely complain. They all
seem positively joyful when compared with one of the suggested alternatives, the much-feared 'in-store performance', an
exercise in certain professional suicide that usually involves
playing in a brightly lit, antiseptic shopping mall during lunch
hour while a local retailer named Crazy Larry tries desper-
ately to flog your current CD. Mercifully, the cursed in-store is
where this loud and proud band of gypsies has always drawn
the line.

Between the songs, radio DJ Ginger, still reeling from a
recent drop-in by Russell Crowe and his 'Grunters', asks us
what it's like to be on an Australian stamp.

'It's good,' says Bones, 'we can lick ourselves now.'

As it is, radio airplay is proving to be scarcer than a rock
drummer at a doof party. Although there is some willingness
to program the new *Capricornia* songs, we appear to be falling between the cracks of American radio formats – Rock,
Alternate, Hot AC (adult contemporary), CHR (contemporary hit radio) or R 'n' B – or forever destined to inhabit
the 1980s Classic Rock file. At a multi-format, digital radio
network in Washington DC on a later tour, we're warmly welcomed with 'Hi! I'm Celeste from the '80s Channel', while
Tom Petty's 'Free Falling' plays ominously in the background.

Later we're introduced for a live broadcast in Maine as follows: 'If, like me, you're a fan of '80s music, then you'll probably remember Midnight Oil …' Actually, the DJ's a well-meaning young girl, even if, as my friend Mark Diamond might say, her driveway doesn't go all the way to the garage.

At home in Sydney a few months down the track, our US record company rep Mason Munoz (or 'm2', as he signs off in his emails) informs us that seventy-nine stations have responded to our recent American presence by playing the fifteen-year-old 'Beds Are Burning' (again). 'Beds' is also the subject of a cover-version request from a European record company, who've suggested a German rewrite of the lyrics with the recent flood disaster in mind. The results, in part, translate as follows:

Day after day nothing but rain
From Mediterranean Sea to Ural
The continent is lapsing into wetness
The Great Flood does not need a passport
How can you be glad when the world is striking back?
How can you dream well while your bed is floating?

Another obstacle for bands like ourselves, who once relied heavily on independent radio programmers, has been the deregulation of radio-station ownership by the US Congress in 1996, and the subsequent domination of the airwaves by giants such as Infinity Broadcasting and Clear Channel Communications, which owns 1200 stations and more than 100 concert venues. Play lists now are tighter than coach class on United, in a safe, saccharine world where it's all about the advertisers and rarely about the music. Even a 1-per-cent change in the ratings can mean liquidation for a radio station, and decapitation for the programmers. In desperation, some DJs have gone way too far, one allegedly slaughtering a pig on his morning shift for a reason known only to himself, while another promised 30 000 dollars to any caller prepared to have the station's initials tattooed on his or her forehead. Yet another dared a couple to have sex in NYC's St Patrick's Cathedral – he and his shock-jock sidekick were later sacked.

Internet radio may save us yet, though, with about 25 million people at last count logging on to the new music alternative every day. And thank God for National Public Radio, where you can hear the likes of Evelyn C. White talk about the 'life-affirming effect' that Aretha Franklin's version of 'Respect' had on her and 'other young black women growing up in the turbulent 1960s'. Or there's the Tappet Brothers, aka Tom and Ray Magliozzi, and their infectious *Car Talk* program – a kind of automotive Roy and HG meets Cheech and Chong. Or Linsey from Dva, performing 'Knockin' on Kevin's Door'. Or whoever did that rewrite of the Police hit, 'Don't Stand So Colostomy'; and anything from *Hairway to Steven, You Me Carpark Now* or *Electric Landlady*. Plus, all the throat-singing albums, tuning-fork operas, gamelan orchestras, poetry-slam recordings and vanity CDs that you're unlikely to hear anywhere else.

Not that Midnight Oil are entirely absent from the airwaves. By the time we tour again in 2002, several stations in diverse locations – Chicago, Nashville and Salt Lake City – are playing 'Golden Age', though Pete's full-throated scream (my favourite bit) near the end of the song is apparently proving 'too scary' for the Triple A format. As a result, our album is languishing at something like number 198 with a depth charge. 'Luritja Way' is next in line to be released, but one key programmer has already warned us that 'I won't play anything I can't pronounce.' Mason, our record company man, sits in the back of the mini-van, pursuing reluctant programmers on his cell phone, appealing to their often nonexistent sense of decency: 'I ask the guys to drive 2000 miles to do the show, you've got 18 000 people on the grass, and you won't play the song? What am I supposed to say to these guys?'

Mason's facing a Sisyphean task. The music biz is not one that regularly rewards humility, patience and good manners, favouring instead the egoist, the impetuous – the asshole! Nonetheless, we're told with the best intelligence that *Capricornia,* our album with the 'golden calf' cover, has been sighted in CD stores from Lake Winnipesaukee to the Mississippi Delta, from Pismo Beach to Provincetown. But in each new city I search the music racks under 'M', often finding nothing between Metallica and Mudhoney except every Motorhead record ever made. Meanwhile a peculiar booing has lately been emanating from the pre-show crowd, replacing the familiar 'Oy-el' chant of Oz publand. Mason took a walk around one of the halls to see what was going on, and came back grinning: 'They're not booing,' he said. 'They're *mooing*!'

It must also be becoming 'more than my job's worth' for manager Gary Morris (aka 'The Wass', 'Wazza' or 'Larry Felskin', as Bones refers to him), directing operations from his coastal sanctuary in New South Wales, but rumoured to be looking at Tasmanian real estate. The daily barrage of lies, damn lies and bullshit has clearly taken its toll on the man, particularly as his contacts in North America often require his urgent attention at 3 am Australian Eastern Standard Time. Like most successful managers, Gary becomes more anonymous the better he does his job. And, as he says, 'I have to know *everyone's* flippin' job.' He's the *eminence grise* who pulls the strings and closes the deals, the funambulist who walks the tightrope between the band and the business, the self-described 'cave-dwelling shadow walker', connected to the outside world by a string of optic fibre, the 'guard dog and seeing-eye dog' who delivers the bad news with the good, the inspired dreamer of wild, tangential dreams and unlikely schemes, the desk-jockey who's most likely to sit bolt upright in bed in the middle of the night in an apoplectic fever, yelling, 'I won't stand for it!' or 'The t-shirts! The t-shirts!'

Gary's escapades over the years read like an episode of *All Aussie Adventures*. Some rock 'n' roll groups have band members who leave a trail of destruction in their wake – everything from crippled cars and disabled boats, to the wreckage of stand-up fights and the collapse of blue-sky deals. Not Midnight Oil. Our manager always got there first. Gary's our *own* Steve McQueen, preferring open spaces to paling fences, regularly disappearing into python-crawling jungles or stony deserts for weeks on end.

His legacy can be seen on a remote and inaccessible mountain near Wollombi, New South Wales, where he once had built a Swiss-style cedar home with solar power. Likewise in Queensland's Noosa Shire, where, in anticipation of a golf course, an entire valley was hand-voided of rocks, collected by Gary's long-suffering brother-in-law and Spy v Spy tour manager Shane. His greatest bequest to this nation and others, though, lies with his heartfelt organisation of countless benefit concerts, protest shows and groundbreaking tours since 1978, featuring Midnight Oil and others, for the homeless, the environment, land rights and disarmament.

We say farewell to the cheerful Boulder radio folk, rejoin the bus, and cruise off to a 2.30 pm breakfast, passing a gathering of women from the international peace network known as the 'Women in Black', who are standing in silent vigil on a busy street corner. The real prospect of peace seems more unlikely every day, though, with the *LA Times* reporting that the United States is 'creating a ring of new and expanded military bases that encircle Afghanistan and enhance its ability to strike targets in much of the Muslim world'. The response from the Arab nations is, I imagine, similar to the panic in America in 1962, when the Soviets under Kruschev began moving nuclear missiles into neighbouring Cuba. Certainly, extremists such as the al-Qaeda leader, Saudi-born Osama bin Laden, have long vowed to get rid of the US bases close to Islam's holiest cities of Mecca and Medina. 'I swear to God that America will not live in peace before all the army of infidels depart the land of the Prophet Muhammad,' he said recently in a video message. An oath that should doubtless be taken without a single grain of salt.

Within minutes we arrive at one of Willie's favourite lunch stops, the Chataugua Dining Hall, set among spacious gardens in mid-fall splendour, and dwarfed by the first rise of the Rocky Mountains. Apparently, Boulder's Chataugua is one of the four surviving 'grand meeting houses' of the 12 000-plus built across the USA at the turn of the twentieth century. The purpose of these meeting houses, according to the thoughtfully provided history brochure, was to 'establish a gathering place where people from all walks of life could enjoy food, musicians, orators and educators'. We tell the waitress not to bother with the last three, but that sustenance was a high priority.

After the meal we decide to 'work it off' by walking up to Green Mountain summit, at 2484 metres, not exactly Everest but enough to cause some serious dizziness. Signs warn us of the local perils, particularly mountain lions, bears and 'nesting raptors' (birds of prey, not free-ranging dinosaurs). I ask Will if there was likely to be any 'bear action'.

'What, five naked men in the woods?' interjects Bones, ever reliable.

'That'd be disappointing,' sighs Pete.

I consult the information board. If a mountain lion is encountered, it tells me, 'You should speak sternly to the animal, then slowly back away.' No advice is offered as to what you might actually say to a salivating, hiker-mauling bush-beast, but I have my doubts that 'Go to your room!' would have much effect. A similar approach is recommended for bears, where 'running or screaming is not advised'. I recall that Bones recently spotted a canister of 'grizzly bear repellent' in a supermarket, albeit with 'This product may not work' written in fine print across the bottom, but sherpa Hillman has wisely retired to the foot of the mountain with Willie and Deborah, leaving us to our own dubious devices.

We trek up the mountainside, keeping an eye out for four-footed man-eaters, stopping regularly to catch our breath. It soon becomes clear why the Denver Nuggets use slightly under-inflated basketballs in the cool, thin air – our lungs begin pushing hard against our ribs, craving oxygen, like self-inflating party balloons keylocked behind prison bars. Near the top a wolfish critter appears from behind a stand of conifers (cue the *Peter and the Wolf* theme). It turns out to be a sweet-natured Siberian husky named Tahji, no doubt sent by the ranger to get the Aussie rockers off the mountain before sunset. We 'summit' (a professional mountaineering term), take a few photos of the highest snowy peaks, then begin a fast descent, Tahji stepping out ahead at a discreet distance in case the dopey foreigners lose the trail.

The gigs in Colorado have always been memorable. One warm, 'erb-scented evening with UB40 in the late 1980s always comes to mind, at the magnificent Red Rocks open-air amphitheatre, which is nestled between boulders in the foothills of the Rockies. UB40's brass section – Brian, Norman and Astro – got up at the end of our set and played the outro to 'The Power and the Passion', while Robin and Ali Campbell mimed on spare brass instruments, before disappearing into their dressing room to perfect the 'Bruce' sketch from *Monty Python's Flying Circus*. 'The UBs' were great fun to tour with, even though the nexus of the two bands – cruisy English reggae meets angsty Oz rock – left the audience totally bamboozled, whipped into a righteous frenzy one moment, reaching for their roach clips the next. Backstage there was equal confusion, as UB40's Trenchtown-tainted Brummie brogue meant we barely understood a bleedin' word they said, mon, for the entire three weeks.

Tonight, the seated audience at the Paramount Theater leaps to its feet at the first blast of 'Redneck Wonderland', and stays there until the end of the show. We're not entirely surprised that the gig turns out so well, as grand old theatres such as the Paramount are usually a joy to play. They have an atmosphere about them that's hard to reproduce in the North American 'sheds' (indoor/outdoor sound-shells) or the *patinoires* and *sporthalles* of Europe, where, much to the distress of bands and audiences alike, the sound bounces back and forth unremittingly off canyons of cold concrete and other equally unmusical surfaces.

We receive a similarly warm reaction a few months later, at an afternoon show at Boulder Reservoir. While the good burghers of Boulder drink beer, smoke dope and ingest pharmaceuticals in the warm spring sunshine, resurrecting themselves briefly to award prizes for an amphibious boat-building competition (the double grand piano won the day), we judge the mood exactly and hoist a banner informing the audience about the proposed nuclear waste dump at Yucca Mountain in Nevada. If the plan goes ahead, the dump will receive more than 50 000 shipments of highly dangerous radio-active material from forty-four states over the next three or four decades, to be transported by truck, train and barge through Yucca's neighbouring states, including Colorado. Kate Pierson from the B-52's, and Amy and Emily from Indigo

Girls, later join us at a press conference, explaining the perverse and dangerous logic of the Yucca Mountain proposal and the magnified hazards of shipping nukes in 'the Age of Nasty Surprises'.

Now the tour's longest bus ride is waiting for us. The 1557-kilometre journey to Minneapolis – through Colorado, Nebraska and Iowa, and into Minnesota – begins poorly, with toxic fumes leaking into the cabin, an increasingly cranky driver, and a disturbing DVD rerun of *The Deer Hunter* to match the mood. At one point we switch on the satellite news, which inspires even greater fear (if not loathing). One CNN report confirms that the United States will feed and provide ammunition to the Taliban's foes, but that 'there's no suggestion that Islamic terrorists are related to the anthrax scare'.

In the areas of security and defence, it appears that the country is hurriedly getting its house in order. The FBI is undergoing its broadest reorganisation in its 93-year history. Director Robert Mueller is appointing new chiefs to the bureau's counter-terrorism division following revelations that a pre-9/11 memo, which indicated that al-Qaeda could be using US flight schools to train terrorists, caught the agency navelgazing. The demand for elite troops for the military's 'special operations' divisions – the National Guard Green Berets, the Navy SEALS, the Delta Force commandoes and air-force helicopter teams – is currently so great that civilians are being recruited along with career soldiers. Perhaps children will soon be allowed to join up, if the number of war toys in shops such as FAO Schwarz is any indication. Judging by a later visit to the Chicago store you can buy young Stormin' Nathan anything, from an M5 Light Tank (which is anything but light, weighing almost as much as the real thing) to GI Joe Desert

Storm marines and Vietnam door gunners. (Perhaps unsurprisingly, there were very few of these last items left in stock.)

An added sense of urgency arrives courtesy of Omaha billionaire Warren Buffett, who makes everyone's day by predicting that America will 'almost certainly' suffer a major nuclear event, a threat that New York state senator Charles Schumer is also taking seriously: 'I've seen the data,' he says, 'when you learn about it, it chills you to the bone.' It's somewhat baffling then, with all this Armageddon talk going around, that the acceptance rate of the free 'anti-radiation' pills (potassium iodide) has been so slow. The pills, which guard against thyroid cancer, have been made available to people who live within sixteen kilometres of a nuclear power plant.

We stop at a roadhouse in the early hours of the morning for fuel and a feed, joining half-a-dozen middle-age couples who are grazing on genetically modified grain or staring silently over each other's shoulders at the copper-art stagecoaches on the wall. The meal is surprisingly tasty and, of course, enormous. Far preferable, I must say, to the nouvelle cuisine we were once served in an upmarket restaurant in Zurich, at the invitation of the well-meaning, Dryzabone-clad Norman of Sony Switzerland. That lunch consisted of a beautifully presented steak the size of a kidney bean in a heart-shaped raspberry coulis, served by immaculately coiffed Aryan-looking waiters with Swiss-clock-like synchronicity. After the 'meal' Willie helpfully suggested that we fill up at McDonald's – whereupon Norman looked as if he'd asphyxiated and our Swiss album sales began a slow, but steady, decline. Rather than Macca's, I noticed what looked like a food fair in the park near our hotel, and walked briskly towards it until it belatedly dawned on me that I'd stumbled across the notorious 'Needle Park', where young junkie couples were openly injecting each other in terrifying places, or had already passed out on the fastidiously maintained narcotics' lawn.

I wake at midday after a restless bus-sleep full of Russian-roulette horrors (courtesy of *The Deer Hunter*), to a cold, wet and windy Minneapolis, home of artists such as Prince, Husker Du, the Replacement and Soul Asylum. Through a foggy window on the left the Electric Fetus CD and merchandise shop appears, near a block of flats with the sign 'If you lived here you'd be home by now' flapping hard in the gale. 'If I lived here I'd be a homicide risk,' I mutter darkly to myself.

In the morning I escape the faceless Millennium Hotel and walk briskly down the length of freezing Nicolette Mall, stopping at a street stall selling bison jerky, and gazing up at the tall, fair, Scandinavian-descent Minnesotans. I briefly ponder why it is that immigrants from Norway and Sweden, when given the chance for a new life, ended up somewhere even colder in the New World. Personally, I would have burned the oil-skins, swapped the horned helmet for a panama hat, stocked the longship with *lutefisk* and suntan cream, and set sail for Key West.

When I get back to my room, it's in the throes of being made up by a Hong Kong Chinese woman, who tells me in broken English that she's been in the States since 1971, and has a 38-year-old son 'much older than you'. I like her immediately. As she pulls up the chenille bedspread and puts two Caramello bears on the pillow, I serenade her with my guitar, playing a few new songs I'd been working on, while her supervisor fumes impatiently in the background (apparently guests are expressly *verboten* from entertaining the maids). She says that she plays a guitar like mine, but 'much bigger'. A 'Chinese cello' is as close as I can get.

Before the soundcheck at The Quest, we dash across the road to Radio KTCZ to do another acoustic show, setting up in the studio office with 'Sell Ideas' written authoritatively on a whiteboard. Our spot is hosted by a DJ called Brian, who resembles actor John Cusack and adopts a God-like voice as soon as he hits the On Air button. In between songs ('Luritja Way', 'Short Memory' and 'Beds') we talk about Vegemite, Aborigines and how few 'complaint rockers' there are these days.

As we leave the studio, Willie rushes ahead to wrangle with a traffic cop of Puerto Rican descent, who's in the process of booking our bus. Then Willie throws away some remark about the cop 'probably not even having a green card'. The cop responds by using some words I haven't heard since our South American tour. As tour accountant Craig emerges to pour oil on the cavitating waters, Will hurries inside to 'talk to his people', the band does a half-hearted soundcheck, and Clem, our drum technician, tells me about his big day of golf (or 'whack – fuck!' as Tim calls it). We then head back to the hotel for the room-service fettuccine marinara – a courageous call, so far from the ocean – and forty winks.

'When do you want your wake-up call?' asks Craig, as we disappear into the lift.

'Every five minutes until we leave,' says Bones.

The gig that night is followed by a meeting back at the hotel with our Minneapolis-based record company with the prescient title of Liquid 8. One of the head honchos cheerfully informs us that his day job is liquidating bankrupt businesses, which is how he came up with the name. As it transpires, within a year, Liquid 8 Records has itself been liquidated, self-vaporising into the thin northern air, leaving us and other acts high and dry as an Arizona mule on peyote grass.

The chat is cut short by Willie, who begins wheeling suitcases towards the bus, settling the extras on the bill and making hurry-up calls. The chatty hotel porter, who's loading our suitcases into the bus bay, greets us with 'Waz 'appenin', man?', to which Pete replies unreservedly, 'You're loading our suitcases.'

Within minutes we're moving again, into Wisconsin, bound for Chicago, passing ghostly corn silos standing tall in oceans of maize like intercontinental ballistic missiles awaiting launching against the Axis of Evil. Then come rust-red barns with names like 'Pittz', a house belonging to 'Shultz', a caryard with 'Gratz' on the sign, and a tavern called 'Blatz'.

As we cruise through Madison, the capital of Wisconsin, the Teutonic flavour of the region becomes positively sinister, with the statue on top of the Capitol Building holding what appears to be a Nazi salute, and the nearby Quisling Towers apartments really setting off the alarm bells. All of which is totally at odds with Madison's limousine-liberal, college-town reputation, with its population swollen annually by Beavis and Butthead frat-boys with heads full of Lara Croft, and pushbike-riding new age nubiles with Nordic good looks, sipping decaf soyaccinos in State Street.

TAKING CARE OF BUSINESS

But if I work all day on the blue sky mine
There'll be food on the table tonight
If I walk up and down on the blue sky mine
There'll be pay in your pocket tonight
from 'Blue Sky Mine'

'Business is great. You are business. You are great.' Or so it says at the hotel entrance.

Actually, business is not so great. We know this because there's no staff left at the hotel to stock the mini-bars, and because the company that makes the touring band's most faithful companion, the Polaroid camera, has just filed for Chapter XI bankruptcy protection.

If Polaroid goes under it'd be the end of an era. After all, how many lonely rock 'n' roll troubadours have documented their hotel adventures using these fun, cheap, instant-gratification gadgets? Evidently the company, unable to match the new digital alternatives, accrued about 1 billion dollars US in debt, only to be walloped again by the economic downturn and September 11.

Years ago I bought a Polaroid Spectra-System camera in New York, from a swarthy salesman on the evolutionary scale somewhere between fish and fowl.

'Play in a group?' he enquired. I nodded. 'Then you're gonna need da remote,' he said, with a lascivious drool.

'I just need the camera for my young daughters' birthday parties,' I protested innocently.

'Yeah right!' he chuckled, as his eyes lit up. 'But just in case, get da remote. Remember, there's a Betty-Sue in every small town in America just *beggin'* to be a film star!'

There's bad news on the economy wherever you turn, with no J-curve or dead cat bounce anywhere on the radar screen. In Greater LA, hotel occupancies are down 30 per cent for the September month, unemployment is up to 5.4 per cent (still low by Australian standards), while Universal Studios has just sacked eighty employees.

In the aircraft industry, business is not so much flying as plummeting. Boeing's much anticipated move to Chicago couldn't have come at a worse time, coinciding as it has with the dramatic fall in airline demand post 9/11, which has already resulted in the layoff of 20 000 workers. Even the venerable Rolls-Royce is shedding labour from its aircraft engine division. By the time we roll into Atlanta a month later, interest rates will plunge to about 2 per cent, the lowest in four decades, and the proportion of Americans living in poverty will rise for the first time in eight years (to 11.7 per cent).

There's some good news, though. As correctly predicted all those years ago in the opening scene of *The Graduate*, there's still a 'great future in plastics'. The Tupperware Corporation has just won the National Design Awards for 'corporate achievement', successfully moving out of the nation's living rooms – where a generation of women press-ganged their closest friends into buying things to put other things in – and into mega-malls and the Internet. Also going strong in its fiftieth year is Matchbox Toys, founded in the UK and now based in Philadelphia, whose range of fire trucks and rescue vehicles has been selling briskly since September 11; and larger-than-life-size motorcycle manufacturer Harley Davidson, whose 100th birthday is to be celebrated with a series of 'Open Road Tour' concerts, starring Bob Dylan in Baltimore and the Doors, with Ian Astbury on lead vocals, in LA.

I go for a wander around a road-stop mall to test the consumer Zeitgeist, and discover a near-deserted, brightly lit echo chamber in which forlorn shopkeeper/supermodels exchange nervous smiles with anyone who comes within trawling distance of their windows. The problem isn't that the mall moguls skipped their Commerce 1 homework; in close proximity to each other are a shoe shop, an ATM and a bar – usually a killer combination. It's simply that today, no-one's buying. The only item I see that appeals to me, a long-sleeved cotton shirt from Abercrombie and Fitch, is off limits, the young sales assistant refusing to unbutton the last one in my size from a mannequin. 'We have to keep one on display, dude,' he explains, presumably so other potential customers can ask about it, and also be denied. No wonder sales are down.

Silicon Valley (Nerdvana, Geektopia, or however it's come to be known) is the hardest hit of all. Suddenly there's an entire unemployed underclass of hightech sawdust caesars, wandering dazed and confused among the fire sales of their luxury homes, cars and yachts – and not a single 50 000-dollar dot com launch party to be seen. As Cisco lays off 8000 jobs and Hewlett-Packard chops 7000, the tech-wreck lies in pieces on a windswept coast, with no sign of fair-weather ahead. The NASDAQ index has lost a whopping 64 per cent of its value since peaking in March 2000, wiping out an inconceivable 4.1 *trillion* dollars US in market wealth.

All of this economic woe is seriously impacting on the music biz, particularly those artists who rely on sponsorship deals – to wit, almost everyone. Sponsors make the world go round in America, the land of big bucks and kickbacks. The aim is to super-size your message or product, wherever and whenever, courtesy of any sweat-shop operating, employee-sacking, strip-mining, ground-water–polluting offshore company that believes that your song, name, face, breast or butt will encourage people to *buy more stuff*! The last of the remaining British rock bands of the '60s won't even set foot on US soil these days until a seven- or eight-figure sum has been negotiated with some corporation. And it's not just musical dinosaurs who ply this swamp, real ones do as well – the 15-million-year-old T. Rex named Sue at Chicago's Field Museum is sponsored by McDonald's. Now that'd make a *serious* McWhopper.

That some acts refuse to sell their soul to the highest bidder, such as Neil Young, Bruce Springsteen, John Fogerty, Tom Waits, Rage Against the Machine (sadly, no longer together), Pearl Jam, Michael Franti, Indigo Girls and Ani di Franco – not to mention Midnight Oil – is considered quaint or 'principled' at best here in America, and dated, idiotic or criminal at worst. In our band, we used to go so far as covering up or removing the brand names from our stage gear, and over the years unflinchingly turned down every oh-so-tempting celebrity endorsement on offer (not that Raben Footwear, Stoliar Bros Army Surplus or Trims in Adelaide ever called).

You can't escape it completely though. Almost every surviving live venue, event, TV program and radio show is sponsored by someone, so if you want to play at all in the USA, you're perpetually surrounded by ads for Miller beer,

Dunkin' Donuts, or the Potawatomi Bingo Casino. One recent show in Kansas City has a scrolling sign, 'Marlboro … Come to where the flavour is', flashing right next to the stage for the entire time we play. It reminds me of the red light that producer Glyn Johns used to press, to abort a dodgy take, during the recording of *Place Without a Postcard* in England, back in 1981. (Even today, that miserable light – stop playing! – still messes with my sleep.)

Things aren't much different in Australia. At Sydney's annual *Sun-Herald* City to Surf marathon run I was surrounded by sweaty t-shirts plugging everything from Freehills lawyers to Campbelltown's Fisher's Ghost Running Club. At least the great Hilfiger hoax, in which a New York rag-trader convinced the Earth's 7 billion people to plaster his name in large letters over their torsos, seemed to have somewhat abated. (However, a new ad campaign featuring Lauren Bush, George W.'s niece, may well restore the profile.) Near the end of the race, a lofty Tanzanian swept past, creating a bow wave which knocked all of us plodding also-rans into the gutter. I looked to the heavens for deliverance and saw that some aerial idiot had written 'AGFA FILM' in the clear blue sky. Heartbreak Hill indeed!

I once attended a songwriting workshop in Sydney with the prolific American tunesmith Jimmy Webb, who played and sang excerpts of some of his greatest hits, including 'Witchita Lineman', 'By the Time I Get to Phoenix' and 'MacArthur Park'. During question time we got into a conversation about one of his compositions, 'Up, Up and Away' (recorded by the Fifth Dimension), specifically the controversy in the 1960s about its use as the BOAC airlines theme song. 'Songwriters like to eat, to feed their families,' he replied with a shrug, while Jimmy Barnes, seated behind me, rasped his approval. I took the point as well, although the recent use by the now-defunct Ansett Airlines of the Who's 'My

Generation', a seminal song from my youth, made me bristle every time I heard it.

When it comes to branding, cross-promotion and 'ambush marketing' though, sportspeople leave musicians in the dust, weeping on the blocks. Particularly in the high-profile endeavours of track and field and swimming, they're encouraged by their managers to make a killing while they're still bankable.

In many sports, of course, a sponsor can be the sole means of survival. When co-producing an album of songs for the Sydney 2000 Olympics, I flew to Perth to record the Hockeyroos, Australia's world champions of women's hockey, because the executive producers of the album were keen on including some musical participation by the athletes (*que?*). As it turned out, many of the girls had excellent voices – perhaps from all that victorious singing in the post-match bus. Nevertheless, as they pointed out, they were hockey players, not swimmers or runners, and women at that, so good-paying sponsors had been hard to find, and many had to fit the rigorous training sessions around dull as dishwater day jobs. In fact, dishwater figured prominently in more than one of their occupations.

Not all the athletes were as musically gifted. The Armani-clad Ian Thorpe wisely sidestepped 'the singing bit', the swimming star preferring to read out something he'd written, a well-observed autobiographical piece about his expectations and emotions leading up to the Olympics. Susie O'Neill likewise begged off from any musical contribution, staging instead a fifty-metre swimming race with Mental as Anything's guitarist/artist Reg Mombassa. The latter had to be rescued from Madam Butterfly's training pool in Brisbane when his oversized Mambo shorts ballooned up, then began to drag him under. 'Are you joking,' asked Susie, swimming back to the fast-submerging Reg, 'or do you really swim like that?'

The album was nonetheless completed with drumming explosions from Grant Hackett, 'vocalising' by Michael Klim and Matt Shirvington, and great singing and guitar playing by Atlanta '96 sprinter Paul Greene (who now has two albums out, as well as being the latest member of the Ghostwriters). As you might expect, considering the now legendary pre-Games glitches, when producers Rick Grossman, James Cadsky and I finally delivered the album, the Olympic suits had no sound system to play it on, other than an old boom-box with one dying speaker. We ended up listening to it, all crowded into my old Citroën DS in the carpark, like in a scene from ABC TV's classic, prophetic series, *The Games*.

Over on a different patch of the globe it seems that another magnificent folly is playing out. According to the newspapers, it's raining peanut butter and jelly in Afghanistan. Every day C-17 cargo planes loaded with small yellow packages have been departing Germany's Ramstein Air Base bound for the war-torn mountain country, where these 'humanitarian daily rations' – containing rice, barley-stew, shortbread cookies, peanut butter and jelly – are dropped from the clouds.

A fine effort, methinks. However, as this precious precipitation is labelled in English not Pashtun, the folks on the ground have no way of knowing whether the 'yellow rain' is not some new form of Koranic punishment (cluster bombs of the same colour and size are also being dropped with some horrific consequences) or a genuine 'food gift from the people of the United States of America'. Those who do comprehend are busy reselling the packages on the black market, while the jelly is apparently a big hit with the local donkeys.

I scan the backstage room at the Quest in Minneapolis, inspecting our own meagre rations. It's an eclectic grouping of items, ranging from complete junk (cola, chips and chocolates) to evangelical health-food overkill (fresh carrot, apple and celery juice blended by mix-master Craig) along with vegies, fruit, spring water and hippie tea (anyone for pennyroyal?) For the show, there are crates of Gatorade, which come in cough-syrup red, anti-freeze green or electric-kool-aid-acid-test blue – the kind of substance you'd need twelve steps to recover from – and enough 'Rock-Star' high-caffeine fuel to make you play like Suicidal Tendencies non-stop for the whole six-week tour. For afterwards there are cases of 'good local lager' and red wine, including a bottle of Greg Norman Estates Limestone Coast cabernet merlot '99. It's a fine drop (no wonder the Shark's putting has gone to the dogs). Plus there's the inevitable, medicinal, Crown Royal whisky, Willie's poison of choice.

I break off a piece of chocolate, which tastes a lot like soapy cheese, taking care not to crack open a molar, as I once did on a malicious Hershey Bar. I then begin to tap out drumming patterns on the mini-kit   diplomatically dampened by a practice pad – which we always have set up in the warm-up room. Thus begins the nightly pre-show ritual, which involves stretching the wrists, the neck, the back and the vocal cords, running through some of the older songs (or busking someone else's) on the faithful Fender Deluxe-Reverb rehearsal amp with the loose valve – anything from the Clash to Dick Dale to Radiohead – and wrangling over the set list. Once song selection and order are finalised, the results are spat out of Craig's computer. The whole process eases the transition from cold, impersonal dressing room to hot, loud, blinding stage.

Soon the band and crew are engaged in a fragmented, twelve-way conversation, involving anything from guitar change points to 'Have you seen my red belt?' 'Yeah, mate,' Craig tells me, 'it's hanging up in the wardrobe case.'

I scour the wardrobe case – more correctly, a mobile grave-yard of boots, rags and rejects. Inside I find items of musky stage gear that have been stalking us for years, used perhaps once at Shellharbour Workers Club in the distant past, and other weighty ballast that keeps the freight bills up and gives the loaders hell. Other esoteria include: rolls of gaffer tape, cast-off Diesel shoes, a first-aid kit, a broken wall-clock, a kettle, gig posters, Fierce Festival t-shirts, a Jim Ladd 'Lord Have Mercy' peace candle, two Maine numberplates, a ten-pin, a Captain Morgan's Original Spiced Rum bath towel and three 'wombat-bashers' (as former stage manager Glenn Lloyd used to refer to those long-handle metal flashlights).

Lighting tech Nick Elvin drops in to collect the set list. 'Look,' he says with a grin, 'I don't know where I am. I'm doing the best I can – it might be different tomorrow ...' In another corner of the room, soundman Tim Millican is talk-ing mixing consoles with Jim.

Jim: 'How's the board, the Soundcraft? Is it like the Yammi?'

Tim: 'It's better than the Yammi.'

Jim: 'Is it smaller than the Yammi?'

Tim: 'It's got all the VCAs, small knobs – and I've got big, flat hands from playing bass.'

With that, Jim sits down at the practice kit and starts play-ing a lopey beat, and is soon joined by Pete playing Bones's bass. Then tonight's set is re-evaluated.

'There's too many similar-paced songs in a row,' I remark, predictably. 'We need something that kicks along near the start.'

'I'll just call it,' says Pete.

'So the first break comes after "Too Much Sunshine"?' asks Bones.

'Yeah, I'll say something there, and before the acoustic set,' replies Pete, still thumbing the bass's bottom strings.

'We can segue the arpeggio at the end of "King of the Mountain" into "Only the Strong",' says Martin. 'Actually, we can segue anything into "Strong".' Martin then begins playing the overture from *Tommy*, with Bones on the other side of the room singing, 'See me, feel me, touch me – Kiwi.'

'Twenty minutes!' calls Craig, who's interrupted by a call from production manager Barry Woods on his walkie-talkie.

'We should all pull together and do it my way,' crackles Baz, speaking from out near Martin's guitar rack.

'There's no "I" in "team" – and there's no "U" either,' adds Nick, leaving with his list.

Then drum tech Clem arrives, wearing his 'I See Drunk People' badge. 'The access is from around the back of the riser. Just follow the white line,' he tells me. Clem takes his place, armed with drinks, towels and a torch, on the immediate left of the drums, behind Bones's bass cabinets.

Moments later, soundman Tim drops in again, and takes me aside. 'I'm gonna get some t-shirts made,' he confides, grinning, 'with "How Do You Spell ROCK?" written across the front, and "C-L-E-M" on the back.'

'Twelve minutes!' Craig yells out, with considerable authority.

'Really?' asks Martin. 'That was a quick eight minutes. Are you sure about that?'

'Deadly serious,' Craig replies, checking his 'good to 200 fathoms' wristwatch and approaching me holding a black gismo with what appears to be electrodes hanging out of it. 'Brace yourself,' he chuckles, as he clips the ear-monitor pack onto the back of my belt.

'By the way, Bones, that's an A at the end of the second chorus of "Last of the Diggers",' says Jim.

'Are there any lyrical problems in "Ships of Freedom"?' I ask, sounding like a cracked record.

'Not that I know of,' Pete answers, wrestling with the belt of his jeans.

With five minutes to go, Ben Shapiro's urbane voice cuts through on the in-ear monitors. 'Good evening, chaps,' he says. 'This is your in-ear check.'

'Right to go, then?' asks Barry on the intercom speaker.

'Just a minute, Baz,' Craig says into his shoulder, 'there's a whole lot of nervous weeing going on up here.' I grab some sticks, gulp down my Gatorade and head for side-of-stage, with Willie, Deborah and Craig lighting the way. As soon as the intro tape comes on, Jim fires up 'Redneck Wonderland', and then it's heads down, see you at the end of the show.

'Dreamworld' is next, followed by 'Golden Age', its steady swing and pop choruses extracting a less visceral response from the audience than 'Read About It' and 'Only the Strong', which come further down the set. During one of the breaks, Pete addresses the crowd: 'At the end of the day, we believe the best response to terrorism is to not be intimidated, to continue doing what you do. The farmer's gonna still get up in the morning and milk his cows, and the musician is still gonna come to the theatre to play his songs.'

After the gig I struggle out of sweat-soaked clothes, shower off, change, accept a beer and listen to Tim's assessment of the different rooms' acoustics. 'It was deluxe ... it was *all* good ... I had a cracker,' he enthuses. Tim was once the bassist with the Divinyls, but now he's happily mixing live sound or, as he puts it, 'at the laughing end of the multicore'.

Well, perhaps not *always* laughing. One evening on a 1987 Divinyls tour, Tim was walking to a restaurant from Hollywood's Franklin Plaza hotel, a notorious haunt of touring bands, when he became the victim of a drive-by shooting. Fortunately, the small-calibre slug was stopped short by one of his ribs, and was removed by a dismissive doctor a few minutes later at a nearby medical centre, who stung him even more painfully for the whimsical sum of 1800 dollars.

On other occasions Tim's mixing position in the middle of the audience has left him exposed to drunken punters who fancy themselves as music critics, or who insist that he pass on vital information to the band. A few years ago at Sydney's Castle Hill Tavern, Tim was accosted by one of our 'oldest fans', a barrel-chested bogan with inflammatory breath and a noble brow unruffled by the effort of thought.

'Mate, you should tell the *Oyelz* to stop playin' all that new crap an' start playin' some real *Oyelz* music,' he slobbered, spilling his plastic cup of Dog Bolter.

'Mate, could I have a blueprint of your brain?' Tim asked flatly. 'I'm building a fuckwit at home.'

STEP ON THE DEVIL'S NECK

So we came and we conquered and found
The riches of commons and kings
Who strangled and wrestled the ground
But never put back anything
from 'River Runs Red'

We're in Chicago, the 'city of big shoulders' as poet Carl Sandburg called it, and the location for the eighth stop on the tour. We motor past Polish delis, Spanish restaurants and drinking holes such as Cindy's Bar, on our way to an afternoon radio show at 93XRT. The streets on the left and right are a riot of colour, with lines of silver birches and copper beeches competing with the red, white and blue of heartland patriots. Rows of flaky-painted timber houses spill out onto the sidewalks, which, in stark contrast to many public transport–challenged cities of the USA, are full of the bustle of everyday life.

Our local driver is the heavily tattooed Bob, wearing Buddy Holly–style glasses and a sawn-off t-shirt, one of those large, garrulous Americans you meet now and again who give the impression of having an encyclopaedic local knowledge at their fingertips. We arrive at the radio station and quickly offload our 'buskers' gear' – Jim's twelve-string Martin acoustic, Martin's six-string Gibson, Bones's Modulus bass, Pete's Hohner harmonicas and my Ludwig cocktail kit – and squeeze in around the mixing desk. The sound is trashy (it's way too early in the day to sing) but we hoe through honest versions of 'Golden Age', 'Luritja Way' and, you guessed it, 'Beds Are Burning'. Our DJ, Bobby Skafish, opens up the callers' line, then asks some tricky questions himself.

'Have you ever found yourself on the wrong side of the political fence, backing the wrong horse?'

'I found myself in a Mexican transvestite bar last time we were here,' laughs Bones.

The following morning I jump into a Checker Cab bound for the National Vietnam Veterans' Art Museum, where I'm instantly transfixed by the 'Above and Beyond' ceiling sculpture made of 58226 metal dog tags – representing all of the Americans killed in their longest war. One black tag is submerged in the sea of silver, on behalf of the many more combatants who've since died from war-related injuries, whether that be from Agent Orange poisoning, illness or suicide.

Unsurprisingly, the vast majority of the vets' artwork is extremely harrowing, and clearly cathartic, with the favoured colours – reds and blacks – reminiscent of the modern German Expressionists. Alongside the paintings and sculptures are photos, letters and relics, many using recurring images of fire, agony, death and crucifixion. The works by the Vietnamese are just as painful to view. All the nations involved in the conflict are represented here through their art, including Australia, with an eight-panel acrylic painting by Kenneth Willhite entitled 'The Castrator', which depicts a 7RAR Digger's tattooed arm next to the Queen's Medal. If ever there was a powerful anti-war statement, this museum is it. I then walk back up Michigan Avenue, trying to reconcile the images I'd just seen with the perfect day outside.

As soon as I'm back in the downtown area, I head straight for a late Mexicano breakfast at the Dearborn Diner, situated opposite the Chicago Fire Department, where a memorial, entitled 'The Bravest', has been created for the firies' fallen brothers in New York. It's a moving tribute, a heartfelt shrine displaying the faces of 343 lost comrades, next to a dusty pair of fireman's boots. I study it for a while, then head off for a contemplative walk beside the Chicago River to Lake Michigan, skirting the East Wacker Drive viaduct reconstruction and looping back via Wabash Avenue.

The marinas along the lake are virtually empty, so I do some boat-spotting from the banks of the river, where the last yachts of the season are being chaperoned into safe havens downstream, away from the winter ice-vice. (After 15 November any vessel left on a mooring is in danger of being crushed, unless she has the reinforced hull of an ice-breaker.) As they open up in pairs for their patient procession, the Chicago River's road and rail bridges stretch and groan, like grumpy giants woken from the deepest slumber. The river itself is an unusual colour, a sinister bottle green, but looks and smells comparatively clean. Somewhat disappointingly, not a single garrotted gangster floats to the surface while I'm standing there.

As it turns out, the Chicago River is clean(ish) for an interesting reason. Evidently, back in the 1830s, the cry went up 'Turn the river around!', and with that marvellous American 'Can do, will do, so WHY THE HELL NOT?', that's exactly what happened. The city fathers, keen to realise the dream of connecting the Great Lakes with the Illinois and Mississippi rivers, and hence the Gulf of Mexico, resolved to dig a 155-kilometre canal. In 1871, following health concerns about the dumping of the city's raw sewage into the lake, it was decided that the canal should be deepened, allowing the waters of Lake Michigan to flow down the canal to the Des Plaines River – thereby reversing the flow of the Chicago River.

A serious outbreak of cholera, dysentery and typhoid in 1885 gave the project a new urgency. In the event, fifteen locks were built to regulate the river levels, while more rock was eventually removed from the ditch than from the Panama Canal. The Illinois and Michigan Canal, despite the many delays and considerable loss of life, was a great commercial success. The city boomed, as it still does today, on the back of trade, agriculture and industry, and the refuse problem was shifted downstream, out of harm's way. Well, to St Louis.

Never one to pass up a boating opportunity, I join Jim and Martin for the architecture cruise, on an open-top ferry especially designed to slip under the bridges. The commentary turns out to be a shameless apologia for the big end of town: the story of visionary 'starchitects' and bullish builders, of entrepreneurial zeal and engineering breakthroughs, of limitless budgets and extravagant materials, of greed, ruthless ambition and shameless competition. In short, all the necessary ingredients to transform Chicago into a high-rise American Paris.

Which, of course, it's not and nor did it ever need to be. In the space of a few square kilometres stands some of the world's best-preserved commercial architecture of the last 150 years, built on the ashes of the Great Fire of 1871, and still soaring skywards at a giddy pace. There's faux-Gothic and Beaux-Arts, Art Moderne and Art Deco, Modernism, Post-Modernism, 'Echo-Deco', plus a few side orders such as Bertrand Goldberg's delicious, hot-buttered 'Corn-Cob' style.

My own pick of these capitalist cathedrals would have to be the Carbide and Carbon Building, which, with its sooty dark green and gold-trimmed exterior, looks just as the name suggests. It's currently getting a scrub-down for its new role as (of course) a Hard Rock hotel and casino. Next would have to be the old Shriners Medinah Athletic Club Tower, now the Inter-Continental Hotel, with its Indiana-limestone exterior, friezes, statues and bizarre gold dome (or sack of wheat?) perched on top. For sheer brute scale, though, the Merchandise Mart is hard to beat, its pink, gold and blue lights illuminating the top two recessed floors and atrium in a great night-time effect.

I leave the cruise wondering whether Ludwig Mies van der Rohe, with his 'less is more' dictum, is in any way responsible for Sydney's best example of less is just less, the Blues Point Tower. And whether Frank Lloyd Wright's horizontal 'prairie style' had been intentionally forward-planned for the current age of terror, in which the tallest buildings can sometimes get in the way of air traffic. And whether anyone has ever owned up to the distinctive 'Eastern European toilet block style' of Sydney's Royal North Shore Hospital. Also, which of Chicago's architects will be involved in the remodelling of New York City's World Trade Center site? Whatever the answers, I love the 'contextualism' – the way new structures pay homage to what's already there – such as the NBC Building's modern take on the Tribune Tower's flying buttresses, and the fact that you can actually see the individual skyscrapers and their remarkable finishes, the polished granite, limestone, terracotta or Carrara marble, from numerous vantage points by the river or the lake. As our learned tour guide succinctly puts it, 'God is in the details.'

Needless to say, not everyone has shared in Chicago's bright, shining vision, or its prosperity. On my walk back to the hotel, directly across the river from the original Fort Dearborn site, a man is drumming on a plastic container, stopping to shout 'Change!' before resuming his accented, single-stroke rolls. Then a young black woman, in the space of five seconds, tells me that she's 'starting a job at

McDonald's in two weeks', but she's 'got two kids' and 'needs the bus fare to the job', so could I perhaps 'spare some change'? As I empty my pocket of quarters – the paucity of the gesture not lost on either of us – my mind rewinds a few days to an incident in Minneapolis, where an unemployed man sitting on the sidewalk politely asked a passing woman for money. 'Get a job, asshole!' she screamed. 'No-one will give me one,' the man replied bitterly.

Our booking in Chicago is for a three-night stand at (yet another) House of Blues, this one sporting the plunging roofline of the ill-fated and ephemeral clamshell period. First off is a photo session, in and around the venue, with affable photographer Paul Natkin, who introduces himself with: 'Hi! Don't worry, I'm the best!' This is probably not far from the truth, after his many years of documenting Rolling Stones tours. As soon as Paul is ready to shoot, we instinctively try to stare the camera down, in my case avoiding any perilous profiles. (I am, after all, the proud owner of a schnoz that the crew once charitably described as 'like a Concorde sticking out of its hangar'.)

Appearing at the HOB on the evening before we play is none other than Robert Hunter, Grateful Dead songwriter and high priest to the Deadhead party faithful. Hunter plays understated vocal-and-guitar versions of selections from the Dead's extensive canon, each item of which is instantly recognised and received rapturously. The audience, who appear to be aged between sixteen and sixty, are variously swaying in that distinctive trance-dance. 'I know the Deadhead rules,' says Hunter in between fretboard ruminations. 'Never repeat a song.' And there seems little need to do that, if our own search for a Grateful Dead song to cover for the *Deadicated* benefit album a few years back is any indication. (After wading through dozens of songs, we eventually lucked out on the much coveted 'Wharf Rat'.)

Hunter's meandering performance is intriguing and a timely reminder that non-radio-driven, non-dollar-fixated music once flourished in America, and still forms the basis of a vast, unique, peaceful cult. 'It's as if he's holding the shards of a forgotten culture,' says Jim. Not that the Dead are entirely alone here. 'Outsider music', made by 'eccentrics, mental patients, self-taught loners and visionary cranks', to quote the *New York Time*'s Dwight Garner, is fighting a David and Goliath battle against the over-produced, over-budgeted musak dished out relentlessly by the major record companies.

On Sunday morning we're all invited to Gospel Brunch, an HOB tradition that combines a cardiac-arresting Southern feast with the hardest-working gospel choir north of the Bible Belt. The choir, dressed in white surplices and fronted by a funky minister in a perfect suit and two-tone shoes, is joyful and charismatic, and capable of some serious vocal fireworks. The band is a driving three-piece, consisting of Hammond organ, bass and drums, and play a tight set even though this is the first time the drummer has ever played with the organist.

When the choir launches into rousing anthems such as 'V.I.C.T.O.R.Y.' and 'Step on the Devil's Neck', the whole stage starts visibly bouncing up and down. Our drums, water tank and side-fill monitors, still set up for the next two shows, wave around precariously with the ebullient 'call and response' happening at the front of the stage. As I watch the performance, I can't help thinking that the 'Midnight Oil – Sydney' stencils on our road cases, and the sign on Bones's bass rig, 'Do Not Feed the Rats and Pigeons', also written in Russian and Hebrew, look right out of place behind a Southern-style gospel choir.

In truth, I'm stunned by (and a little envious of) the rockin' good time that this choir is having. The buttoned-down, stitched-up church choir of my own youth only ever seemed to moan lamb-slaughtering psalms from dog-eared psalters, sung by the choirboys in alarming, unbroken voices. Bones, too, was a young chorister, in New Zealand, and was midway through a tour when his voice abruptly broke. For the final two weeks he mimed his part, hoping that he wouldn't be discovered singing basso profundo in a sea of sibilant sopranos.

Back in Chicago, the concert is building towards a sweaty climax, while the people seated at the tables, having wolfed down as much chicken-jambalaya, shrimp, roast potato and grits as they can, stagger to their feet and holler 'Yeah!' and 'Whoah!' All three levels of the theatre have surrendered to the spirit. Before long we're holding hands with our neighbours, shaking our hair, and running (well, shuffling anyway) on the spot, so by the time we file out into the pale sun of a Chicago Sunday afternoon we feel blessed, bloated and thoroughly entertained.

I head directly back to my hotel room, only to find that the entire foyer has been taken over by 'yappy hour', a weekly ritual in which dogs are matched up with new owners. I step aside for a couple of muscular Rhodesian Ridgebacks and attempt a flanking manoeuvre through the canine crush to the elevator. The last thing I see as the lift doors close is a chunky Rottweiler, who's towing a fake Louis XV table around the lobby.

We're still on a gospel high when we arrive for our own show that evening. Pete's already there, laid out on a slab while a steely young woman pummels the knots in his back. She asks me if I'd like a massage. I tell her that I've sworn off them ever since Bones tiptoed into a rub-down room and substituted his man-hands for those of the masseuse, dribbled stealthily on my back, then asked if I'd requested the happy ending.

Backstage, we run through 'Common Ground', from the *Breathe* album, Jim and Martin ad-libbing throughout, and Pete tapping on the warm-up drum kit and singing: 'I could never figure, the calendar's flow …' Bones then plays the bass line from 'Renaissance Man' from go to whoa, adding his answering chorus vocals as they come around, while Pete, swapping a can of Red Bull from hand to hand, executes a half-dozen slow-sweeping chi moves with alternate arms.

'Hey, Craigy,' he calls out, 'have you got the words to "Renaissance Man" handy?'

'Yeah, mate,' replies our multi-tasking tour accountant, who brings up the lyrics on his laptop, then hands out the ear monitors. In one ear now I can hear Tim Millican checking the mic lines, 'Bones vocal … okay. DI … okay …'. After finishing with a 'Thanks, it's been emotional,' Tim's voice leaves us with only the buzz of the crowd and the intro-tape music.

The show is a killer, the set rolling almost seamlessly from one song to the next. Bones jumps up on the drum riser, impales himself on a crash cymbal, and topples backwards to the microphone without missing a note. Pete spends a lot of time on the lip of the stage, winning hearts and minds, 'spray-canning as much rhetoric as we can muster'. 'Say Your Prayers', originally a benefit song for the East Timorese Independence Movement, churns along with a vengeance, Jim's overdriven Dobro sounding like an angry mozzie trapped inside his speaker box. Later that night, Mason, our record company boss, comments on the good reaction to the song. 'That's got to be on the album,' he says quietly, over after-show sushi and beer. Marshall, our avuncular truck driver and advance co-ordinator, agrees (or at least, I think so): 'Every time I hear that song I want to throw the toaster into the bathtub.'

The following morning is cold, wet and windy. On South Dearborn Street, however, Ossama's Hair Design appears to be doing good business (a sign perhaps that the prejudice directed at the USA's large Muslim community is gradually being tempered?). The crackdown on 'illegals' and 'aliens' acquiring US documentation, though, means that legitimate immigrants seeking driving licences are having a tough time, particularly in Florida, Virginia and New Jersey, where eighteen of the nineteen hijackers held valid licences. By midsummer the following year, over 600 individuals will have been detained by the US Immigration and Naturalization Service and been subject to secret hearings. Tighter border security may also result in our own twelve-month American work visas becoming a thing of the past – gone the way of drive-in movies, 'artist development' and double-sided hit singles.

On Jim and Martin's recommendation, I decide to visit the 'Van Gogh and Gauguin, The Studio of the South' exhibition at the Art Institute of Chicago (not that this rock 'n' roll tour is fast becoming a cultural junket across the USA!). The institute is focusing on the nine weeks that Vincent spent with Paul Gauguin in the Yellow House at Arles in the autumn of 1888, calling it a 'pivotal' collaboration – which it clearly never was – although Gauguin wasted no time in arranging some *collaborations horizontales* with the local girls. In fact, the tortured Dutchman and the priapic Parisian fell out almost immediately. The embittered Gauguin eventually returned to his Tahitian idyll, while Vincent committed himself to an asylum at St-Remy-de-Provence before killing himself out of frustration the following year.

However, one should never let the facts interfere with a good exhibition. The mainly female crowd at the gallery, umbilically attached to their audio-guides, seem to be universally transfixed by this uneven no-contest. (Gauguin's muse, so potent when describing naked Polynesian princesses, seems to have deserted him in Arles.) Some of the women tentatively approach the precious artworks, fixing them in a deathly stare, like a hypnotist doing battle with a cobra. I dodge around them and head straight for the merchandising shop, the sacred cash-cow for the gallery and the artists' distant relatives. I can't decide between the 'Cypresses' fridge magnets, the 'Pont-Aven' t-shirts, the 'Self-Portrait' coffee mugs, the umbrellas, the posters or the slides; so I end up buying six lousy postcards to send to the folks back home.

Our own Midnight Oil merchandising, available at the entrance to the venues, is not selling much better. 'Mike the Merch' tells me that his customers are somewhat perplexed by the 'golden calf' t-shirt, although the 'Terminator 2' t-shirt is doing 'fair' business. In fact, it's not until months later, on the Australian tour, that our iconic cow – graphically enhanced and now sporting a Colgate ring-of-confidence grin – really becomes the big selling, bovine pin-up pop star that we always knew she could be. Either way it's not a huge drama for Mike, as our swag is just a shopfront for his real earner, buying and selling Rolex watches on the Internet ...

THUNDER ROAD

Here come the Hercules
Here come the submarines
Sinking South Pacific dreams
from 'Hercules'

What fresh hell, this?

We're in Milwaukee on a cold Tuesday night, in the rain, having language problems. There's a bunch of blokes waiting for autographs as the bus pulls up, all sporting trackies, flannos, beanies and beards. On closer inspection, some of them turn out to be women. Others look vaguely familiar, but like us, a little worse for wear, as if the years since our last visit had just been one long sleepless night. 'How ya going, mate?' I ask one guy, as I jump down off the bus. 'Goin' where?' he grunts, pushing some vinyl into my hand.

Communication has been tricky ever since we arrived in America. At LAX Airport a portentous voice kept reminding us that 'You are not required to give money to solicitors.' Damn right, I thought, they've got enough already.

Previous trips were no better. When I first heard about Monica Lewinsky and her 'thong', I wondered what happened to the other one. Then I made the mistake of asking for white coffee in a southern diner. 'I think he means carf-fee wit cream,' drawled a passing waitress, thereby narrowly avoiding another Mississippi riot. Years ago a highway cop asked to see my licence at a desert roadblock, so I told him it was in the boot. 'It's in yer *boot?*' he replied, before regis-tering my accent. 'Tell ya what,' he said slowly, as he weighed up the time-consuming options, 'ah'm jus gonna let ya go through.'

The misconception is this: for many years Australians and Americans have been operating on the fanciful assumption that we have a common understanding based on a *lingua franca*, that we're Pan-Pacific *hermanos* just because American English bears a passing resemblance to our own syntax-mauling Aussie slang. Not so. Neither party has a clue what the other party is really saying. We may as well be speaking Insect. Take for example the motto on the floor plaque of our venue for this evening, the old Milwaukee Eagle Club ballroom, which reads like a clue for some sinister cryptic crossword: 'If I Can't Speak Well of an Eagle, I Won't Speak Ill of Him.'

Willie explains that the Eagle Club was once one of the more liberal of America's 'friendly societies', thankfully lack-ing the secret handshakes and shady business dealings of some of the others. In any case, we feel infinitely safer inside the place than out, where a dark and misty Jack the Ripper twi-light is descending, obscuring the hotel opposite. It was in this hotel, according to the local crew, that serial killer Jeffery Dahmer bagged his first victim. This didn't seem to worry a group of six young girls, who appear out of the murky middle distance, then trot laughing into the Rave nightclub upstairs.

Barry, our production manager, ushers us through a bead curtain into our dressing room. The room resembles a hippie-trippy pad circa 1972, complete with sloppy springless couches, scented candles, joss sticks, lava lamps (bolted down – bummer!), gilt-edged mirrors, fake potted figs with fairy lights, all on a black Astroturf floor and covered by a patchwork Indian-cotton tent reeking of incense and patchouli oil. A kind of Moroccan brothel meets Mullumbimby in Milwaukee. The only items missing from the crash pads of our youth are the Bob Marley tapes and the bucket bong.

We light the candles, adjust our auras, chant a warm-up mantra and, channelling some good energy, start the show. It sounds like Stalingrad. The drums are so horribly loud and boomy, the only reason that I know I'm playing at all is from the pressure of my feet on the pedals, and the bounce of my sticks off the heads. In my monitor ear I can just make out a tiny voice singing, which sounds like someone trapped in a vigorously agitated cornflakes packet. Later I recognise it as my own. My other ear is assaulted by snare beats, which ricochet off the unforgiving walls, then hammer back at the stage a millisecond later, like volleys of guided missiles. We're ducks in a shooting gallery. Sharman's Boxers buckling under body blows.

I try playing visually, watching Bones's fingers when he turns my way, following his bouncy left foot the rest of the time. In the end, I try playing with everyone, anyone, anything. We're all at sea, a synchronised swimming team savaged by a school of sharks.

It takes me back to the outdoor summer festivals we played in Europe. Up to 65 000 people – sun-lamped Germans and sun-struck Poms, 'neutral' Swiss and baffled Belgians, tired and emotional French, and tall, sauna-softened Swedes – would clap along to 'The Dead Heart' and 'Blue Sky Mine', getting further out of time the greater the distance they were from the PA stacks, the Len Wright tour buses and the purple line of Edwin Shirley trucks – only to fall back into time, on the *previous* beat, at the far horizon. From where we stood, it always looked impressive – a massive Mexican wave, continuously snaking from the lip of the stage to the veggie vans at the back of the field – but it also had its perils. It could hypnotise you if you watched it too closely, throwing you off balance and catastrophically out of time.

The Milwaukee echo chamber also reminds me of walking up through dark zigzag corridors to one of our concerts at an open-air amphitheatre in Berlin, listening on my overloaded video camera earphones to Sinead O'Connor, who was singing with her band on the stage above. According to the local crew, the tunnels were intentionally angled so that the Führer (who evidently enjoyed listening to his beloved Wagner at this venue) could dodge a sniper's bullet or an assassin's bomb, jump into the Merc and make a safe underground *ausfahrt*.

Fortunately tonight's audience ignores the appalling acoustics, and throws themselves into the spirit of the gig, singing along, demanding an encore. One athletic couple perform a unique 'stalking dance' over in an empty corner, circling each other, then lunging forwards with flying limbs, like the capoeira fighters we once saw on a beach in Brazil. It must be love.

The second encore catches me by surprise. Thinking that the show's over, I'm already stripped off and showered, wandering around the hippie tent in a towel, heading for the beer trough. Anxious to spare the crowd a Jim Morrison–style exposure, Pete and Jim get up by themselves and play a great version of 'In the Valley', receiving a tremendous response for their efforts. With just piano, voice and a touch of harmonium, it's by far the best-sounding song of the night.

Outside the club, a bouncer is lining up our fans along an invisible wall in the carpark, at a discreet distance from the stage door. I march straight over the DMZ and sign some vinyl, for the locals, for some Aussies, and for the heavy-duty fans who've driven all day from Michigan and Montreal. I recognise the guy who held up a sign during the show ('Bones, Don't Spit'); he explains that he was hit in the forehead by one of Bones's goobies during the previous night's show in Chicago. Inside the hall, the crew pulls down the gear, exhausted from the fifth show in a row and the monumental drives, with Tim and Ben particularly weary from having worked all day attempting to tame the bunker's cruel reflecting surfaces. Nick Elvin is trashed also, but, as always, capable of seeing an upside: 'It's good,' he says. 'I used to pay a lot of money to feel like this.'

We drive straight out of Milwaukee back to Chicago, thereby missing the old brewing town's latest attraction, the Art Museum's brise-soleil roof, which opens to resemble a great white egret in flight, hovering above the Lake Michigan shoreline. Milwaukee's one of those stoic Midwest cities, with a strong German heritage, where people still wait for the lights to change, and often seem quite fascinated by them. One of the local girls tells us that her home town is famous for beer, Harley Davidson motorcycles and teen pregnancies – and often all three at once.

The bus is quiet on the two-hour drive, with Deborah's two stuffed alligators, Boodie and Alex, fast asleep under the front windscreen. On the screen in the front lounge is a film about the life of English artist Francis Bacon, who rather liked his boys. Instead of watching it, I decide to write a few letters to family and friends, starting each one with 'Greetings from my glamorous life'. Then I drag out the big black diary, and with the roar of the Eagle Club aircraft hangar still resonating in my inner ears, I add a short 'know thyself' observation/confession/excuse/defence, correcting it as I scrawl:

<u>Herein lies the dilemma</u>
When I play in this band my back ~~hurts~~ aches,
my lungs ~~wheeze~~ gasp, my throat hurts.
When I don't my brain hurts
I've found over the years that, FOR ME, it's better
to punish the body than the brain.

When we get back to Chicago I call my friend and Ghostwriters compadre Rick Grossman in Sydney to tell him that a CD of his demo songs has gone missing in action. You know when you've been on the road too long if you can remember off by heart the thirty digits that are the 'Call Home Australia' access number, your PIN and the phone number. I deftly dial the numbers, thereby bypassing the hotel switchboard and avoiding an extras bill the size of the US military budget – and get the answer machine. Damn! I leave a message and fall asleep.

At 3.17 am, I'm woken by Rick's return call. 'Hello?' I croak, sounding like Elmer Fudd as the echo bounces back down the line.

'Hi, mate,' says Rick, 'are you all right?'

'Nothing that a real job wouldn't fix,' I reply.

'Mate, you guys have been busier than Osama bin Laden's travel agent!'

'Oh, you know us, out there every night pushing back the frontiers of music, art and culture, as Shooey might say.'

'Really?'

'No, we're really counting down the number of sleeps before we get to go home.'

'How was the gig?'

'Pretty average – very loud. The last time I felt this bad was when Steady Eddy tried to drink me under the table in Mudgee. I'm thinking of giving it all away and looking for some part-time work raking blueberries in Maine. Or maybe asking Tom Cruise if he needs a butt-double.'

'Mate, it's time you got out of this chicken-shit business.'

Actually, considering the current decline in the labour supply (even butt-doubling work is sagging), leaving the music biz now is probably not an option. The economy remains stalled, with a record number of 'fallen angels' in the past twelve months, including Kmart, Hilton Hotels and Delta Airlines, while business confidence has been shattered by the kleptocrats from Enron/Worldcom. The tech wreck continues to claim new victims, some former blue-sky shares now mere grease spots on the carpet. (I'm sure that was the aptly named Exodus Communications former CEO who just shuffled up and pulled a dog-end from the ceramic ashtray outside our hotel.)

Even the weather is in a holding pattern, the four-year drought turning the Canadian prairie cities of Calgary and Edmonton into a 1930s Okie-style desert, right out of one of Woody Guthrie's Dust Bowl ballads. By the time we reach Winnipeg on the following tour, the only visible sign of life is a posse of mall rats, scuttling around a vast subterranean shopping centre while an icy bug-storm of hungry grasshoppers and crickets rages above our heads.

Fortunately our own microcosmic music business is surviving, with as many teens and twenty-somethings turning up to the shows as in our original 1980s audience, some of whom now work for J.P. Morgan Chase or Deutsche Bank, and are no doubt currently preoccupied with anti-terrorist drills, third-mortgage repayments or their children's homework – all of which take priority over our midweek gigs. Not that our audiences are entirely young though. On a recent Australian tour we play in Albany, WA, where a grand-dad wearing a 'Sorry' t-shirt and a patch over one eye is pinned alongside his eighty-something wife/girlfriend to the security barrier, unable to move for the entire show.

By the time the northern hemisphere midsummer festivals roll around in 2002, we're playing to large crowds, in Chicago, Milwaukee and Orem, Utah, where, much to Willie's dismay, a toothy waitress refuses to put more than one drink in front of us at any given time (it must be some arcane Mormon law). In Minneapolis we join a fundraising concert to help restore the Basilica of Saint Mary (an event billed as 'A Party of Biblical Proportions'), playing to a largely unfamiliar audience while the setting sun blazes mercilessly in our eyes. Jim's unfazed by the situation, neatly sizing it up: 'We've got to hit 'em with that peculiar form of prog Oz rock we're known for,' he quips. On a return trip to Milwaukee we seize the stage after a slow blues act, with Bones joking backstage about the crowd's hot and boozy lethargy, compared with the full-speed-ahead assault of our set: 'They're out there listening to the blues. We come out playing fifty times faster, with an hour-ful of bad news! Drink up, it's all over!'

My daughter Ella gets up to some mischief of her own at a radio station–sponsored gig we play in Orange County, featuring John Waite and Cheap Trick, rewriting the set list on Craig's computer so that 'Golden Age' becomes 'Ageing Gold' – provoking a collective shudder in the dressing room.

Otherwise, we dine on sushi suppers, sign endless autographs, and lose items of laundry on a daily basis. The only items of mine not souvenired by tour's end are the 'name socks' which Midnight Oil secretary Arlene Brookes thoughtfully bought for all of us years ago, plus my ancient pair of Doc Martens, which no-one would want anyway (unlike my Adidas 'Gazelles', which disappeared within minutes).

There's many of the usual suspects at the after-show meet 'n' greets, including a number of Powderworkers, recently renamed the Chowderworkers since manna (in the shape of wine, tea and cookies) began dropping from heaven into our backstage larder. Evidently some of them have been hired by the record company as spotters, whose job it is to check that the new album is available in the stores.

Two new faces arrive in the shape of Mick and Jen from Mt Pritchard in Sydney, who won an Australian radio-station contest to see Midnight Oil in Chicago, plus enough spending money, with the hopeless exchange rate, to last them for at least forty-eight hours. They stay awake the whole time, hanging out with the band and partying hard, with drinks permanently glued to their hands and laminates swinging from their necks, eventually pouring themselves back on to a plane, after what must have been one of the strangest long weekends of their lives.

Like Mick and Jen, most people we meet are friendly and enthusiastic, and often extremely excited about finding themselves backstage. Over the years we've come to accept (to be honest, really look forward to) the often gushing quality of American compliments, and we now regularly enjoy the company of many like-minded, softly spoken Americans. In fact, several lasting friendships have resulted from these dimly lit conversations in the engine-rooms of North America's clubs, theatres, ballrooms and sheds.

Sometimes, however, the post-gig piss-ups carry a sting in the tail. One girl, with arms like Rosie the Riveter, once greeted me so vigorously that I thought that she'd crushed most of the bones in my right hand. Another woman looked shifty and suspicious, with a chiselled face like a Bob Dickerson drawing, the kind who'd steal your kidneys or boil your pet rabbit. 'I'm your biggest fan,' she claimed, before launching into a lengthy and lively discussion which came to a screeching halt following a surprising non sequitur:

'And what do you do in the band?' she enquired earnestly.

'I do the books,' I sighed, and slunk off to the waiting bus.

ROCK 'N' ROLL HIGH SCHOOL

How can we dance when our earth is turning
How do we sleep while our beds are burning
from 'Beds Are Burning'

Willie's been circulating a fax that shows George Bush, Dick
Cheney and Colin Powell as Mo, Larry and Curley from *The
Three Stooges*. Bush really looks like Mo if you draw him
a fringe – grab a black felt-tip pen and try it. Then punctu-
ate the president's speeches with 'Why I oughta!' and 'Mmm,
wise guy!' and you'll see why the country is in serious trouble.

It seems that the further the world spins away from
September 11, the greater the public's tolerance for parody
and debate – the first limping casualties of the subsequent
media blackout. But not all writers have kowtowed to the official Washington line. The usual refuseniks maintain their ob-
jectivity: Noam Chomsky, Michael Moore, Bill Maher (whose
Politically Incorrect on (American) ABC was recently axed
following 'controversial' comments by the host about the terrorists) and Chalmers Johnson, a former US naval officer and
president of the Japan Policy Research Institute in California.
As my friend and drumstick-whittler Roland Jehan said, after

118

reading Johnson's *Blowback: The Costs and Consequences of American Empire*, 'Mate, the Yanks have been in everything except a hot bath.'

The national mood is a little lighter now. *Saturday Night Live* has just featured a comedy troupe called the Dancing bin Ladens, performing their latest hit song 'Singing in Bahrain'. By early next year the shops will be stocked with Rudi 'the Rock' Giuliani and Tony 'the Ally' Blair action dolls, while the Where's Wally? puzzles will have been joined by Where's Osama? An Australian artist's website will even offer postcards of a handsome Elvis bin Laden, complete with slick black hair, beard, designer sunnies – and numerous reports of unconfirmed sightings.

America's rediscovered sense of humour is a promising sign on its road to recovery, even if the jokes mask a collective frustration: 'If we can't find him then at least we can poke fun at him!' Whether the al-Qaeda leader, now known as 'OBL' in hip circles, has his own repertoire of side-splitting gags, which he inflicts on his captive audience, may never be known. However, schoolyard taunts like 'Sticks and stones may break my bones, but Bush will never find me' have allegedly been intercepted by the CIA and translated from Arabic.

The music business has long been a stand-up comedy routine-in-progress, and most bands rely on a kind of brooding, fatalistic, gallows humour to survive. Hard rockers Anthrax, for example, are apparently resisting all coercion to change their name, joking that 'something friendlier', like A Basket Full of Puppies might nonetheless be a good career move. Tom Feran, from Cleveland's blue-collar bible the *Plain Dealer*, has his own suggestion for the band's new name: 'Considering the age of the band and its fans, "Enlarged Prostate", for example.' (Anthrax's response to Feran is unavailable – and most likely unprintable.)

Not everyone is as relaxed about the currency of fear as Anthrax. Many radio programmers have 'used their discretion' and banned a list of 'lyrically questionable' songs, including REM's 'It's the End of the World as We Know it', Jerry Lee Lewis's 'Great Balls of Fire', Steve Miller's 'Jet Airliner', and anything by Rage Against the Machine or the Afghan Whigs. Peace anthems have also been censored, including the John Lennon classic 'Imagine' and Cat Stevens's flaccid 'Peace Train'. Needless to say, any residual spins of Midnight Oil's 'US Forces' or 'My Country' (right or wrong) have disappeared faster than a big Australian insurance company.

All bands with a sense of the ridiculous love the infamous 'Hello, Cleveland' scene in the rockumentary *This is Spinal Tap*, in which the group gets lost in the bowels of a theatre on their way from the dressing room to the stage. (It's happened to us on a few hilarious occasions.) Equally well known is Cleveland's Rock and Roll Hall of Fame and Museum, a glistening US$92 million, I.M. Pei–designed glass pyramid and 'turntable' which stands proudly on the shores of Lake Erie, between the massive Browns Stadium and the Coastguard.

I look down from the seventeenth floor of the Holiday *Grim* and plot a short cut to the Hall of Fame. It's a mere hop, skip, jump, duck and stagger which would involve crossing seven railway lines, a six-row carpark, a nine-lane freeway and an airport runway.

I scan the local rag for better directions. 'It's official,' reads one article, 'Cleveland is windier than Chicago.' I glance outside my window and decide that they're probably right. It's *bleak*. This is a town only a mother could love, what coastal Americans dismiss as 'fly-over country'. The trees, which were still draped in red and gold foliage a few days ago in Boulder, are entirely bare in Cleveland, while a ferocious cold westerly is blasting across the city, tipping the muddy contents of the lake over the breakwater.

Undaunted by the elements, Pete, Jim and I are soon battling our way across the foreshore to the Hall of Fame. Pete steels himself as I take his photo in front of Claes Oldenburg's rubber-stamp sculpture, paradoxically bearing the word 'Free'. As we approach one of rock music's holiest of grails, I become increasingly curious to discover what the first fifty-odd years of rock 'n' roll has to show for itself. And why the licence plates claim that 'Cleveland rocks'.

One of the locals explains the latter question, reminding me that the city was the first with an R 'n' B radio program pitched at white teenagers as well as black, and the first to host a rock 'n' roll concert. Legendary DJ Alan Freed, sponsored by Leo Mintz's Rendezvous Records, began *The Moondog Rock and Roll House Party* in 1951, a late-night radio show on WJW-AM in Cleveland, which was later syndicated around America, and staged 'the Moondog Coronation Ball' – the first big-time rock 'n' roll concert – at the Cleveland Arena on 21 March 1952.

Since then, Pere Ubu, Chrissie Hynde of the Pretenders, the totally original Devo (from the neighbouring industrial city of Akron) and Trent Reznor of Nine Inch Nails (who moved here from Pennsylvania) are some of northern Ohio's finest to have hit the international big time. Devo's Mark Mothersbaugh, explaining the band's uniqueness, once suggested that 'all the rubber fumes in the air back in the '70s, when they were still making tyres in Akron, "vulcanized" the band'.

We pay our fifteen-dollar tithe and enter the Ahmet M. Ertegun Exhibition Hall (named after the Atlantic Records co-founder and Hall of Fame Foundation chairman), in which U2's Trabis hang, the Soviet-made cars used as stage props on the Zoo TV tour. Then, in a manner entirely contrary to Japanese tour groups to Australia, we disappear in different directions. I spend some time in the Jimi Hendrix exhibition, mesmerised by a remastered film of Jimi and the Experience, with the brilliant Mitch Mitchell on drums, at the 1970 Isle of Wight Festival in front of the final-day stoner audience (at the festival, not in the theatre).

One thing quickly becomes apparent as you wander around this museum. This is a place where, as Australia's Roy and HG might say, too much rock is never enough. There's rock music piped into the foyer, rock music in the cafe, rock music in the toilets. In fact, there's five decades of rock music on six levels, all competing with each other for space, time and volume. Art imitates the airwaves!

I'm particularly taken with some of the stage clobber, such as George Clinton's 'atomic dog' slippers, Roger Daltrey's *Tommy* lace-up chamois vest and pants (surgically removed by the rest of the Who in the '80s), and Bono's muscleman outfit, which looks so real from a distance that it must have inspired those sixpack stormtroopers in Rammstein to get their own shirts off. The star's cars are fun as well; a burn around town in ZZ Top's roadster would surely turn any geek into a local hero, legs or no legs.

There are, of course, *loads* of guitars, including the little acoustic model belonging to a ten-year-old George Harrison, and the Gibson mandolin played live by the great Levon Helm of the Band (while pianist and singer Richard Manuel filled in on drums). There's also a wooden 'sunflower' made from the sticks of famous drummers – an oxymoron if ever there was one – which must be here as a warning to all aspiring young drummers not to ignore their daddy's advice: 'Never try to make a living with your hands, kid.' Actually, one of my own sticks is here, although it's discouragingly smaller than Dave Grohl's, of Nirvana and Foo Fighters fame.

On the second floor is the Sun Studio room, which features the original recording equipment used by Memphis producer Sam Phillips to record the young Elvis Presley and Jerry Lee Lewis. The next level again is dedicated to those enduring artists who've been 'inducted' into the Hall of Fame (presumably they don't have to pay the fifteen bucks, or at least they get the seniors' discount). Recently these include AC/DC, Elvis Costello and the Attractions, the Police, the Clash, Talking Heads, Tom Petty and the Heartbreakers, and the Ramones, the latter failing to take part in the inductees' end-of-ceremony all-star jam. Talking Heads guitarist/producer Jerry Harrison offered a succinct explanation: 'The Ramones don't jam.'

I pass Martin, dressed in regulation black, sprinting down the stairs from the current featured exhibition, which takes up the top two floors. 'It's not for everyone,' he says, when asked about his impressions so far. The exhibition is 'Lennon – His Life and Work', a retrospective of the myopic Liverpudlian's handwritten lyrics and music, paintings and drawings, a documentary film, the Dakota Building bed, and some famous busts (both kinds) – all courtesy of the enterprising Yoko Ono, who seems intent on ensuring the beatification of St John of Strawberry Fields in the not-too-distant future. On the way back down, my eye catches a display of significant telegrams, those quaint relics of the 'premail' age. Included is a disturbing plea by Sid Vicious's mother (Missus Vicious?) to have her ill-fated son's body returned to her from the USA.

As for Midnight Oil, like most groups who live outside the trans-Atlantic axis of influence, we're filed on the Performer Database. This parrots out our abbreviated history plus some photos and video excerpts – all of which end abruptly in 1993. I make a mental note to add Jann S. Wenner, Lord High

Chancellor of *Rolling Stone* magazine (and Hall of Fame vice-chairman) to the guest list for our next American tour. I'll also be sending him copies of our last four studio albums, signed 'Outraged! of Sydney'. After all, we've been together long enough now to meet the criterion for induction – twenty-five years not out – although there may be a few deserving youngsters ahead of us in the tuckshop line, including AC/DC, the Sex Pistols, Black Sabbath and Iggy Pop.

On my way to the exit, I scrutinise the merchandising shop for something useful, and very nearly buy a red plastic tambourine with a chain-gang-Santa kind of sound. At the crucial moment, however, I'm gripped by an uncommon hunger, the sound of Enya's siren-like voice luring me helplessly to the cafe, where I feel compelled to order a large, shrink-wrapped fruit salad and chocolate cookie. (Moral: when it's all said and done, and Slim Shady's sung, rock is still less important than rockmelon.)

Back at the hotel there's a story on TV about Beatle Paul – Sir Paul McCartney to any misguided monarchists under thirty or over eighty – who's just hosted a huge 9/11 fundraiser concert in New York City. Like so many of our generation, I was a huge fan of McCartney in my formative years, hooked on the Beatles ever since 'Love Me Do' crackled onto the PA system at Sydney's Royal Prince Alfred Park ice-skating rink. McCartney's singing, writing and bass playing was always so strong, so *right,* that even today I can happily overlook the abyss of blandness into which most of his post-Beatles work has descended. Not that pop's wealthiest squire would give a tinker's cuss what I think.

Tonight's concert, however, is moving, heartfelt and beyond reproach, and eventually raises about 30 million dollars

US for the Robin Hood Relief Fund, set up to help the families of the victims. Meanwhile, the irritating CNN headlines scrolling underneath Macca's performance claim that Celine Dion's 'God Bless America', from an album of breast-beatin' American classics, is number 1 on the charts, first week in. Even the Postal Department has succumbed to the current Zeitgeist, rush-releasing a 'United We Stand' stamp.

Our own show, in a death-metal sweat-pit on the Cleveland Flats, opposite the local Hooters eat-and-ogle ('but don't touch!') restaurant and the river, is a tad more modest in scale, but not lacking in angsty energy. Unsurprisingly, the acoustic songs sound best in this black hole, although the cocktail kit – an ungainly instrument to play at the best of times – starts rocking alarmingly in the middle of 'Warakurna'. Clem darts out to fix the problem, but hardly has he left when the rivet cymbal begins to shed split-pins, which sheer off into the audience, followed by a large chunk of the ice-bell and splinters from the 'hot-rod' drumsticks. By the last choruses of the song, the foot soldiers in the front row are coated with more shrapnel than you'll see in the entire series of *Mash*.

After the show we make a hasty retreat to the hotel.

'Doing anything tonight?' I ask Bones, looking for distraction.

'No, mate,' he says. 'I'm just going to my room to have my way with myself.'

I walk into my own room and, hoping to cheer myself up, switch on the box – only to see a few luckless, miserable prisoners being herded around 'Camp X-Ray', the US naval base in Cuba. I search for the face of alleged al-Qaeda fighter, Australian-born David Hicks, who has been detained by the Americans. Unfortunately for him, his status as an 'unlawful combatant', rather than a POW, means that the Geneva Convention provisions – including Hicks's rightful repatriation to Australia – are evidently inapplicable. If Hicks was an American captured by the Aussies, I find myself fulminating to myself, the USS *Harry S. Truman,* with Ian Cohen MP clinging to the bow, would be blasting full-steam down Sydney Harbour as we speak. To bring one of *our* boys back home.

Seething, I turn off the fucking TV. In desperation, I grab the 'No Moleste' privacy sign swinging from the doorknob, cover up the first word, and hang it outside the door, just in case someone attractive and hard-up walks past. No-one does. I briefly toy with the notion of doing something rock-starish, such as gluing the furniture upside down on the ceiling, detonating an explosive in my room or defenestrating the TV into the hotel pool, but reject it as clichéd, out of character, costly and quite possibly litigious. Plus there's no pool, the windows don't open and I'm right out of saltpetre and Semtex.

Calming myself, I opt instead for the opium of the masses, and reach for the obligatory Gideon's Bible in the top drawer of the bedside table. Scanning the contents page, I see a chapter entitled 'Rest in Time of <u>WEARINESS</u>'. I dutifully turn to Matthew 12:19: 'He will not quarrel nor cry out, nor will anyone hear his voice in the street.' Too right, I muse, not with this howling gale and the double-glazed windows. I put the Bible down and open a surprisingly thick hardback by Bob Dole, *Great Presidential Wit,* in which Abraham Lincoln also contemplates religion, in particular, whether the fact that a rebel prisoner is a 'deeply religious man' is sufficient reason for his release from a Northern jail: 'The religion that reconciles men to the idea of eating their bread in the sweat of other men's faces is not the kind to get to heaven on,' said the stentorian Lincoln, with his usual disarming eloquence. Truly the Bob Carr of his day, I thought, laughing out aloud like a crazy man.

With every entertainment option now exhausted, I turn once more to the great leveller, television. It's business as usual post-9/11, with saturation advertising for a cornucopia of drugs, including Viagra, promoted by a star baseball-hitter with a knowing twinkle in his eye and an awesome bulge in his crotch. The people at the Fox Network, undisputed masters of the single entendre, are leading the charge back to 'normalcy', with such enlightened programs as *Celebrity Boxing*. I change channels and stumble on *When Animals Invade Your Home*, not an exposé of cable guys or repo men but rather a horror movie in which Florida housewives wage pitched battles with pythons, crazed monkeys and feral possums.

Worse is yet to come. By the time I've encountered *Naked Cops* and comedian Sean Conlon singing 'You've Got a Friend in Porn', I'm seriously wondering whether a few well-aimed dirty bombs in the offending TV producers' swimming pools mightn't be such a bad idea.

All is quickly forgiven, though, after the audiovisual assault of *The Jerry Springer Happy Hooker Hour*, an unapologetic, soul-mugging freakshow which leaves the viewer feeling as poisoned, as violated, as the knuckleheads who agree to take part. (I know, I know: God created the remote...) MTV's contribution is the scatological hit series *The Osbournes*, an anthropological study that has been examining the cumulative effect of thirty-five years of hard Goth rock on the Caucasian male. And if your family of lounge lizards can't decide between these titans of trench TV, help is at hand in the shape of a channel-surfing channel, offering three-second glimpses of the hundreds of options now available on cable and satellite. So now you don't even have to exercise your thumb.

I finally give up on the box, flip through the newspapers, and notice a story about the USA's reliance on imported oil in the *Plain Dealer.* Cleveland, birthplace of John D. Rockefeller's Standard Oil (Ohio) from 1870, is a town that knows about oil; there was so much of it in the Cuyahoga River in 1952 and 1969 that the river caught on fire. These days, the waterways are cleaner, but like many moribund north-east American cities with failing heavy industries and rising unemployment, the local economy could do with a giant Heimlich manoeuvre. Down the road in Holland, Michigan, even the humble Lifesaver is about to roll out of town, to Canada, where sugar is cheaper, after thirty-five years and a whopping 46 billion units of sucking pleasure.

As for downtown Cleveland, it puts a brave face to the ill winds of change, the solid Society National Bank, Tower City and First Merit Buildings, as well as the new Jacob's Field Stadium – home to baseball's Cleveland Indians – standing resolutely above the rust belt. But there are signs that the business of pop and rock may be the next to tremble and fall, turning the Rock and Roll Hall of Fame Museum into a rock 'n' roll mausoleum, full of the dusty artefacts of a golden age that ain't a-comin' back.

The awful truth that dare not speak its name is that rock's share of the musical pie is continuing to decline, music piracy is on the increase, and the downloading of digital mp3 files is becoming easier, faster and cheaper than buying or mail-ordering the originals. Similarly, '60s music bible *Rolling Stone* magazine is coming under increasing pressure from newer rivals, and even recording giant EMI is readying to dump 1800 jobs and 'hundreds of fading recording stars'.

Gulp! One more time, fellas: 'How do we sleep while our beds are burning?'

SUGAR MAN

Don't turn back the ships of freedom
Back to the South China Sea
Can you imagine, the first taste of freedom
For the refugee
from 'Ships of Freedom'

I know this feeling. It's called homesickness. I haven't felt such a longing for Australia since Martin set fire to some dry gum leaves on the US *Diesel and Dust* tour, thereby sending the Antipodean occupants of the dressing room hurtling back in a time-machine to the great Aussie summer.

Outside, the first light snow of the season is falling as we tumble into the foyer of our hotel in Auburn Hills, part of metropolitan Detroit. I notice that the automatic revolving glass door at the hotel entrance has trapped a pile of autumn leaves, and is insistently pushing them around. It's as if the Hilton Suites has taken hostage the last colours of fall, guarding them jealously, refusing to let them go. I take it as an ominous sign, the sinking feeling in my gut reminding me of every New Year's Eve, when the forced merriment never fails to reduce me to a state of mild panic, a sense of lost control.

After all, the approach of the northern hemisphere winter has often been an omen for Australians overseas, reminding them that it's time to collect their thoughts and belongings and fly south for the summer.

I was one of those kids who literally grew up on Sydney Harbour. (That is, after Mum and Dad, with admirable foresight, upped and left our five-acre, funnel-web–infested bush block in the badlands outside Campbelltown, New South Wales.) From my grandparents' window at harbourside Kirribilli, my childhood imagination was fired by the massive steel topsides and rusting hulls of ships bound for impossibly exotic ports, slipping silently from harbour to sea in a ghostly evening passing parade.

Sydney in the late '50s and the '60s was still a real working port, before the dirty work of shipping – everything except cruise liners, containers and pleasure craft – was shunted out of boom-town, Australia, to make way for waterfront apartments and their marinas. I was fascinated by the harbour, its crowded mix of oil and industry, its scrappy coastal colliers, merchantmen and passenger liners, and its graceful fleet of red, green and yellow Lady-class and K-class ferries, as well as the Manly ferries, workmen's launches and pilots, all framed by the giant Hornibrook cranes that were gradually assembling the Opera House.

I kept my own ships register to keep track of the constant movement, complete with the vessel's name, company, registration port, tonnage and flag, plus a hastily drawn sketch before the ship had picked up speed, passed the Sow'n'Pigs, then turned eastward to face the swells of the South Pacific.

Whenever a howling southerly was raging at the Heads, I'd jump on one of the Manly ferries with tall smokestacks and no stabilisers, the *Dee Why* or the *Curl Curl,* and install myself on the foreward deck as she approached the swell. As whitewater cascaded over the bow and stomachs were thrown high in the air, as the steam engine spat and hissed and the jazz band clung to their instruments, I glued myself to the gunwales of those majestic steel ships. Soaked to the skin. Loving every plunge and shudder and groan.

My grandparents' flat, 'noisy, cold and south-facing', was just the kind of place where a nagging wanderlust could be nurtured, and where the love of music was a foregone conclusion. My grandfather, George Hirst, played classical piano, while my father, Peter, was a jazz buff, who used to listen in to the only jazz-show broadcast in the '40s, on ABC radio. Dad would save up for heavy shellac 78s of Bix Biederbecke, King Oliver and Louis Armstrong – some of which still deliver enough music underneath the blizzard of crackles and pops.

My elder brother Stephen was a fine pianist, and still is, gaining his diploma at the Sydney Conservatorium of Music. Stephen and I were musical antagonists until our mid teens, when we declared an armistice following the totally unprovoked destruction of my treasured copy of the Rolling Stones album *Sticky Fingers*. Incandescent with anger, I manically tried to piece it back together, still finding snatches of 'Bitch' and 'Sister Morphine' in the curtains and carpet for months after. My younger brother Matthew, against the best advice, followed in my drumming footsteps, then ditched music for a real job. As for me, I was happy to watch the coloured lights of the city zigzagging across the water, to plot an escape to foreign ports, and to listen to *my* kind of music – the Beatles, the Stones, the Hollies, the Animals, the Kinks, the Who and the Dave Clark Five – on a little leather-bound transistor radio.

Years later I realised that this urgency to leave home was probably a direct result of Nan's cooking. Although she made a superb Sunday casserole, followed by a rice pudding coated in hallucinogenic quantities of nutmeg, my grandmother's idea of a week-night dinner consisted of two hard-boiled eggs, white Buttercup bread and huge blocks of Kraft processed cheese, all washed down with a glass of full-cream milk or Golden Circle pineapple juice. She insisted on carrying huge tins of this juice home from shopping excursions to 'Davy' Jones, which must at least partially explain why she lived until she was 103. I once asked her the secret to her longevity. 'I've always walked everywhere,' she replied, 'and I've never done a day's work in my life.'

Armed with the unerring wisdom of the very old, I resolved to learn how to play the drums, just like Ringo, at the earliest opportunity. On my seventh birthday, my parents gave me the Beatles first EP, on the Parlophone label, along with a pair of *real* drumsticks, which I used to systematically destroy the house and contents. I took the sticks to primary school, where with Mr Prendergast's permission I got to play a pig-skin snare drum on marches to Mosman Oval. Alongside me were my classmates from school, including future actor Tom Burlinson and a young cricket star named Allan Border, whose name now graces the oval.

At the end of my first year at high school, Dad drove me into the city, to Harry Landis in Park Street, where he bought me a Star drum kit with a nauseous volcanic finish. It was a welcome-home gift after six weeks in hospital following the removal of a nasty lump from my right leg. As soon as we got the new drums set up, I attacked them with extreme gusto, before the bone had properly healed, so my leg set at a strange angle facing out towards the bass drum pedal – where it's remained ever since.

Back in Detroit my childhood reveries are brought to an abrupt conclusion by Willie's round-'em-up whistle, which propels us towards the bus and tonight's concert. The venue turns out to be an old church, converted into a four-level nightclub. It's called Clutch Cargo's, just like that bizarre TV series of our childhood which, I recall, pioneered a revolutionary animation technique known as 'Syncro Vox' – the superimposition of real moving lips over still drawings of faces – which gave the characters a wooden, slightly grotesque quality. I suspect the program had a fate similar to Detroit's best-known lemon, Ford's Edsel, which must have also seemed like a terrific idea at the time.

I dress (down) into my standard-issue stage clothes: t-shirt, red, cotton x 1 (one); Doc Martens, cherry, one size too small x 2 (two); and work pants, navy blue, still damp and stylishly crushed from last night's show x 1 (one). The tiny subterranean dressing room is covered in the usual phallic graffiti, except for one wall, on which someone has drawn a plausible Mickey Mouse, along with the words: 'Mickey Says, Let's Keep This Wall Penis Free.' It's the shoddiest changing room we've come across since we played the Blue Moose in Mackay, Queensland, which boasted a backstage area entirely constructed from slabs of XXXX beer. ('You must have got changed quickly,' Craig later quipped, 'or the crowd would have drunk your dressing room.')

The intro tape comes on, climaxing with a series of explosions that loosen the mortar in the old church, and sound like the place has been hit by one of Defense Secretary Donald Rumsfeld's RQ1 Hellfire anti-tank missiles. The band launches into 'Redneck Wonderland', which has proven to be a strong opening song for the entire tour. Lighting guru Nick Elvin drowns the small stage in the deepest red, punctuating the guitar riff with cues that fall exactly with our picks and sticks and feet. Monitor maestro Ben Shapiro cranks the click-track and sequence to the point where it sounds like we're being bullied along by an urgent steam-powered metronome, making it physically impossible to stray out of time. Barry Woods, our 'get-three-for-one' production manager, stage manager and guitar tech, watches the proceedings from side-of-stage like a benign hawk, the smoothness of the shows a quiet testimony to his hard work and experience.

The rest of the set is charged with the kind of energy that comes from the knowledge that Detroit was, and still is, one of the great music capitals of the world. There was Motown in the '60s – the Supremes, the Temptations, the Four Tops – and 'kick out the jams' rock 'n' roll in the late '60s and the '70s in the form of the MC5, the Stooges, Mitch Ryder and the Detroit Wheels, and the Amboy Dukes (featuring one Ted Nugent, 'the Motor City Madman'). Techno, drum 'n' bass and electronica followed in the '80s – with Detroit supplying the likes of Optic Nerve, May, Atkins and Saunderson – and the hip-hop, house and rap of the '80s and '90s mob included the rantin', rhymin' machine himself, Eminem. As I write, Detroit's latest exports, drum and guitar duo the White Stripes, are playing some shows at home in Australia.

For all of these acts, the musical common denominator has been the city itself, a sprawling metropolis where the motor car is God and the music is real and often made by people without too many other life choices. People such as Madonna, who lived here with her father, stepmother and seven siblings from the age of twelve until she attended the University of Michigan. (Her childhood home was recently for sale, with an asking price of 324 000 dollars, although the current owners stopped taking bids on eBay after pranksters drove the price up to over 99 million ...)

Back at Clutch Cargo's our show is nearing completion. The mid-tempo pulse of 'The Dead Heart' jumps twenty-odd beats per minute for 'Forgotten Years', which segues into 'Hercules'. Two breathlessly rewritten encores follow, the first consisting of 'Tone Poem' and 'Read About It', and the second featuring Jim and Pete singing 'In the Valley'. We finish with 'Power and the Passion' with much harassment of the water tank, sweat and drum sticks flying – the usual *sturm und drang*. Guitar and keyboard tech Dave Mayer, much tattooed and wearing black clothes except for the white lettering on the back of his t-shirt ('Rehab is for Quitters'), nearly gets totalled as band members jump blindly off stage. Finally the Cruel Sea tape comes on, and everyone knows that the show's over, folks.

After our cooling-off period I wander out to the meet 'n' greet, and run into our old musical confidant Rodriguez, whose two albums of the late '60s and the '70s, *Cold Fact* and *Coming From Reality*, found passionate audiences in Australia, New Zealand, Zimbabwe and South Africa, although curiously not in his homeland. Rodriguez has been to most of our concerts in and around Detroit, usually positioning himself in the front row and maintaining a huge grin for the entire show. There's definitely some connection between his music and ours, if only because most of our songs are about our own country, our own people.

Since we last saw him, Rodriguez has been continuing his social work, particularly in child development programs, making a few forays into local politics, and touring in South Africa with former Midnight Oil manager Zev Eisik. Framed by one of the church's stained-glass windows, Rodriguez tells me that he's been working on new material, though it must be a challenge to produce songs as chilling as 'Sugar Man' or as compelling as 'Inner City Blues'. I love the sparse production of those recordings, the real brass and strings, but most of all I love the voice. *That* voice, right up front in the mix, as instantly recognisable as Stevie Wonder, Diana Ross, Aretha

Franklin or John Lee Hooker, all of whom managed to make a name in a town which in the last forty years has been knocked down more often than Joe Louis decked his opponents, and is only now struggling to its feet.

Torn apart by the country's worst-ever race riots, in 1967, divided by Dearborn's racist mayor Orville Hubbard, stung by the oil shocks of the early '70s and mortally wounded by the arrival of cheap Toyotas, Detroit's downtown was abandoned by those who could afford to move. They headed for the perceived safety of the fringes – a 'white flight' and a 'middle-class black flight' – which left a vacancy for poverty and crime in the old heart of town.

Not that the history of Detroit is entirely bleak. Out of rock-throwing racism, housing discrimination, unemployment and union battles came a host of positive changes. There were strong civil-rights gains, such as Detroit's Great March to Freedom, led by Dr Martin Luther King Jr, in 1963; political empowerment, including the election of one of America's first black mayors, Coleman Young, in 1974; and success in business, notably Berry Gordy Jr's Motown Records, which grew into the largest black-owned company in the USA.

Detroit's great population upheavals became obvious on an earlier visit to the Motor City when a few of us were chauffeured in the back of a pick-up around a once-grand inner-city neighbourhood of boarded-up mansions, formerly the homes of the captains of the auto industry, or at least those on first-name terms with relatives of the car czars – Edsel and Eleanor Ford, Lawrence Fisher, Walter P. Chrysler, John Dodge. They were now occupied by different folk, squatters and students ('the deserving poor'), as well as crack dealers, pushers and pimps ('the lowlife').

Our student friends showed us around their unlikely accommodation. Fresh paint, furniture and framed posters had almost restored the former opulence of the old home, with its giddy ceilings and obscenely large living room. And, as they pointed out, if you could handle the sound of nightly gunfire and a few eccentric neighbours and their clients, then the place certainly had location, location, location.

Now, on the 300th anniversary of French explorer Antoine de la Mothe Cadillac's original landing on the shores of the D'etroit ('the strait') River, the city's future looks about as secure as any other right now. Rear Admiral John Stufflebeam is on the talk shows again, acknowledging the tough, fighting spirit of the Taliban, and suggesting that they may try to poison the aerial aid packages. He confirms that air power alone won't be enough to root out the rebels – one lesson, at least, learned from the protracted 'American War', as the Vietnamese refer to it.

The visitor's guide in my hotel room is positively glowing. 'Never before has metro Detroit been so alive,' it pleads, perhaps hoping for a self-fulfilling prophecy. According to the magazine, the turnaround began in the late 1980s with the construction of the optimistically entitled Renaissance Center. The 'Ren Cen', a cluster of glass towers right downtown, is now home to General Motors World Headquarters, among others. There's a new Science Center, an upgraded Orchestra Hall, and most importantly for sports-mad Michiganians, a new stadium named Comerica Park, which fails spectacularly to match the atmosphere of the old Tiger Stadium. Other new arrivals include four 'Las Vegas-style' casinos (is this a *plus?*) and a mushroom plague of shopping malls, including the Southland Center, which offers 'a mall-wide trick-or-treating event' on Halloween called 'Mall-O-Ween', which guarantees your kids don't get attacked by some nut while they're out doing the rounds.

The way they're talking it up, a day off in Detroit is sounding less like a sentence and more like fun, particularly if you're into cars. There's the Automotive Hall of Fame, GM World and the Henry Ford Museum, the latter featuring the chair in which Abe Lincoln was assassinated, and the vial allegedly containing Thomas Edison's last breath. (How could you be sure? the sceptic-in-me asks of such a claim. And if it is true, what despicable cad would rob a man of his final gasp?)

If none of this appeals, you could leave the kids at Detroit's famous zoo (permanently perhaps) and take a look around the original Motown Studio on West Grand Boulevard. This is 'Hitsville USA', where so many classic recordings were made in Studio A, 'The Snakepit', particularly with the crack bass-and-drum combination of James Jamerson and Benny Benjamin. I still can't believe they managed to cram those big bands with brass sections and backing singers into such a small room, and the recording console, an eight-track homemade by Mike McClean, looks extremely, er ... *rustic*. Still, as Maria Muldaur once sang with unchallengeable authority, 'It ain't the meat, it's the motion.'

The reality is that despite the healthy hum of construction and the sweet sound of music, the city's troubles are far from over. Recently some Japanese and Korean auto manufacturers began offering ten-year warranties for cars that are cheaper and more reliable than anything that Detroit can produce. The city has responded by 'going back to basics'. GM's Bob Lutz claims that 'Our concepts are vehicles that people would like to drive today, not ten years from now.' With gasoline still cheaper than bottled water, the latest models are big, fast and powerful, with running costs, safety and the environment manifestly low on the list of consumer concerns. (DaimlerChrysler's new sports utility, for instance, will only give you about ten miles per gallon – that's less than four ks a litre in Australia.) The 'flight' now is one of job-seekers to Chicago, or to Kansas City, or to the South – or perhaps even to the Australian state of Victoria, where Ford has undertaken to invest 500 million dollars US in a new car plant to go into production in 2004.

Fortunately for Detroit, America's love affair with the horseless carriage and the internal combustion engine shows no sign of waning. Auto polygamy is on the increase, particularly in New Jersey, which now has 600 000 more registered vehicles than drivers. And the local bands, or at least the best of them, are as innovative, angry and in yer face as ever – Eminem, for example. Even the freeway signs that used to encourage motorists to 'Say Something Nice About Detroit!' have long disappeared.

My conversation with Rodriguez at the after-show party has been brought to an abrupt conclusion by the relentless pounding of a drum 'n' bass groove coming from the dance club downstairs. The rhythm is repetitive and highly percussive – it's got the fingerprints of one of the local GM pressing-plant workers all over it. Literally. In the early '80s the car plants of Detroit inspired 'industrial techno', a tough brand of electronic music which spawned such global interest that the recent Ford Motor Company–sponsored Detroit Electronic Music Festival attracted over a million baggy-panted punters, many making a pilgrimage from Europe to the birthplace of their favourite beats. Intrigued, I stick my head in the door of the club but I'm driven back by thick, oily smoke, and interrogated by a female bouncer with emerald-green contact lenses and a hair colour unknown in nature.

I decide instead to grab my bag and make a run for the bus – straight into the arms of a large group of autograph hunters who've been waiting, freezing, for at least an hour. Flanked by a pierced and skin-illustrated security hulk, I have my photo taken in groups, then proceed to sign everything: CDs and vinyl, including some obscure singles never released in Australia; t-shirts, one bearing an early version of

Capricornia's golden calf; Midnight Oil hand caps; tickets, splintered drum sticks, gig posters, plus a set list that's been deftly liberated from the front of the stage. The locals are cheerful and earnest, evidently as happy to see us after such a long absence as we are to see them. When Pete appears at the stage door the crowd stampedes in his direction, leaving me, mid-signature, in a little cloud of dust. I take the opportunity provided and slip away quietly onto the ever-idling bus.

We retreat for dinner, beer and emails to room 417 at the hotel, with a large laminated sign reading 'Willie's Bar & Grill' taped to the door, shattering the peace for the night-shift receptionist in the foyer, where the autumn leaves are still rotating in their glass prison. Willie and Deborah settle everyone down in front of miso soup and sushi, while *Rustler's Rhapsody*, a Western send-up, plays in the background on the bedroom TV. For a full five minutes everyone is uncommonly quiet, except for the sound of raw fish being devoured, and the occasional thunderous guffaw by Willie as he stops to catch a snippet of the movie.

Mason, our record company boss and resident sage, joins us in the Bar & Grill, having flown in earlier to smooth-talk some 'important radio people'. He informs me in hushed, reverential tones that tonight was an important show. 'This was not the biggest crowd of the tour,' he whispers, 'but it sure was the *neediest* ...'

AT THE HUNDREDTH MERIDIAN

Cos I know
This is the end of the beginning
Of the outbreak of love
from 'Outbreak of Love'

Sometimes a rock show has its own momentum. Driven along by the grunt of electric guitars pumped through massive PAs, illuminated by kilowatts of candlepower, inspired by a frenzied crowd, lifted by soaring choruses, hammered by riffs, kidney-punched by kick drums, eviscerated by the bass, and king-hit by vocal yelps, hollers and screams. Rock music at its best can and should be transcendent, an elevated state that can be attained if the musicians possess what manager Gary Morris calls 'a spiritual connectivity' (sic). It should send shivers up the spine and pub darts into your eardrums. It should make you want to play air guitar, and airhead drums, at home, and party like a dancing fool at gigs. It needs to be tough enough to interrupt your heart pattern, melodic enough to make you burst into song, fast enough to galvanise your arms, legs and hips, and loud enough to fry a terrifying number of brain cells. In the international argot of pubs and clubland, it's gotta *rock*!

The shows in Canada rock. I'm not certain whether that's due to our ex-colonial kinship, our shared sense of humour or just something they put in the Molson, but we've always had some great times here. In 1993 we crossed the country as part of Another Roadside Attraction, a multi-bill touring festival featuring Canadian acts the Tragically Hip, Daniel Lanois, and Crash Vegas, as well as the delightful, soulful Irishmen in Hothouse Flowers. For me, the highlights of that tour were the Hip's great grooves and Gordy's 'tween-song patter, the Flowers' Fiachna playing tin whistle barefoot in a turquoise silk suit, and the mind-blowing drumming of Brian Blade, sitting up high on his Gretsch jazz kit in the Lanois set, whipping those traps to within an inch of their life. We even recorded together one evening, a benefit song for Clayoquat Sound called 'Land', produced by Daniel in an all-night recording session in Calgary.

Most of all though, I remember the lack of pretence and the camaraderie of the touring party – a rare commodity in this biz. So as we breeze over the Detroit Bridge border crossing into Canada on our current tour, the memories are all good ones. It almost feels like a homecoming as we drive towards Toronto, past the Roadkill Cafe, down a highway flanked by Maple Leaf flags (now *there's* a great flag design – why can't we have one?). Willie entertains us with a story about being left at a diner here during a tour with the Cruzados, who evidently thought that Will was asleep in his bunk. He then tried to catch up to the bus in a waitress's car, before giving up and hopping on a flight to Toronto, where he met the band bus, just as it pulled into the hotel.

It's a harsh reality not lost on the Canadians that, with their proximity to the States, they've potentially got more to lose than any other country (with the possible exception of Israel) if the Americans decide to prosecute a Middle Eastern war. Particularly if the inevitable retaliation breaches 'homeland security'. Most of the folk we encounter here during our 2001/2002 shows are simultaneously shocked by the terrorist attacks and horrified at the prospect of an ill-considered, pre-emptive war on any armed to the teeth, chemical weapon–toting Muslim nation. 'We will act in the interests of the *world*,' says the American president, if the UN weapons inspectors are not given total freedom to do their job in Iraq. But the rationale for such a strike, it seems to many people in Canada, has as much to do with big oil interests and the unshakeable belief in the 'Godzone USA' concept, a notion to which a majority of Americans happily subscribe. As John Ibbitson writes later in a piece entitled 'America', for Canada's *Globe and Mail*: 'Americans are a divided society: racially divided, socially divided, divided between urban and rural, north and south. But they are as one in their belief that America is a light unto the world, uniquely free.'

Our Toronto concert is at the Warehouse, with local band Staggered Crossing replacing Will Hoge as the opening act for the night. The boomy old storage space down near Lake Ontario must have had some acoustic work done since the last time we were here, because the sound is tighter and punchier, making it much easier to play. The guitars sound particularly good, with Jim's twelve-string Rickenbacker positively chiming in 'Golden Age', and Martin's twangy Guild driving the choruses of 'Truganini' and 'King of the Mountain'. The final run of songs – 'Forgotten Years', 'Sometimes', 'Hercules' and 'Dreamworld' – leave us gasping for air, guzzling Gatorade and collapsing on the changing room floor.

Two hours later we're back on the bus for an overnight ride to picturesque, prosperous Montreal, the pride of

French-speaking Quebec. We arrive at the hotel at 8 am, so I sleep until midday and wake up 'feeling strangely fine', to borrow from Semisonic. I decide to climb the 'mont' in Montreal, to view the city and the chalet, heroically using the steps rather than the easier serpentine path. I ascend through a forest of maples, oaks and birches with leaves the colour of flaky rust, as if they'd been scorched by a recent fire-storm.

My sense of bravado is somewhat shattered, however, by a wild-eyed, bearded septuagenarian in bicycle pants, who comes running up the stairs behind me and then charges on up ahead, without the slightest visible sign of distress. The old show-off doesn't even have the decency to be breathing heavily.

Once on top, I amble along wet winding paths cushioned by the fall, happy to be lost for a while until soundcheck beckons, when I know that silence and nature will be abruptly replaced by a brain-load of decibels, and the familiar pub-stench of ash, sweat and beer. I trek down off the mountain and have a look around town, where the French preoccupation with style and cuisine immediately distinguishes this city from the big-hair, sports-bar dagginess and emotional blankness of much of the Midwest. Less than an hour, and a couple of snooty waiters, later, I've changed my mind. Already I'm missing the folksy politeness of those anonymous, grain-belt towns, out there simmering in the heat haze of the prairie, where life's neither a competition nor a catwalk. Nor a croissant for that matter. Though occasionally a croisandwich.

I meet up with my old friend Pajet, who first came to see us play 'new' songs like 'Sleep' and 'Hercules' at Le Spectrum back in 1985, when he was in his teens. Now he's the boss of an indie label, with a healthy roster of skate-punk and ska bands. Pajet's also a part-time tour manager, but his preferred means of transport remains the skateboard – a smart move in this often-gridlocked city.

He comes to the afternoon soundcheck at the Metropolis, waiting patiently while I finish an interview for a TV program dedicated to Native Canadian affairs. After the chat, we're given a large Mohawk flag, the same one which gained notoriety during the Oka stand-off of the '90s, when pitched battles were fought over a plan to build a golf course on native land. I drape it over the water tank for the duration of the show, which, according to my diary notes (scribbled next to three incriminating spots of red wine), is 'one of the best so far'.

The following day we cross the St Lawrence Seaway, back into the United States, and drive down Highway 87 through the magnificent Adirondack Mountains, red and green, and brimming with lakes. The stuff of wildlife-magazine covers. Our direction now is due south, a route that will skirt the borders of Vermont, Massachusetts and Connecticut, and pass Lake Champlain, Lake George and Fort Ticonderoga (an historic landmark from the Seven Years War and the War of American Independence). We then follow the Hudson River all the way down to New York City.

I sprawl out over the back lounge, drinking in the view, and reading 'snatches' from Mötley Crüe's hysterical 'fess-up *The Dirt,* passed on by our booking agent Mitch Rose. The band members have dedicated their book 'to our wives and children in the hope that they may forgive us for what we've done'. *Recommended* *** (consenting adults only).

We stop at Lake George, a summer holiday destination informed by great physical beauty, now so completely devoid of life that I wonder if the bio-terrorists haven't been through overnight, the survivors still hiding in the hills. Willie finds us the only restaurant in town still open, which has a fire crackling away, stuffed animal trophies on the wall and a huge moustachioed man who's apparently passed away, without anyone noticing, in a nearby armchair. He looks uncannily like Teddy Roosevelt, laid out in his State Dining Room after a long day hunting.

It soon becomes evident why 'Teddy' has expired, though. This place serves the largest steaks any of us have ever seen (and the ones we order are the medium size). Sensing that it might be considered un-American not to finish the meal, we sally forth, only to fail miserably, the belligerent beast definitely getting the better of us.

Other local animals have suffered an even worse fate. According to a brochure in the restaurant, the nearby Taxidermy Museum at Keene displays everything 'from mice to moose' – in fact, enough stuffed and mounted animals to last you a lifetime. No wonder nothing moves in the woods these days. What is it about mountains that attracts these crackpots with such unseemly obsessions?

Back on Highway 87 we catch the first glimpse of the (re-arranged) NYC skyline, with the Empire State Building again towering over everything else. The cops halt the bus at the entrance to the Lincoln Tunnel, then check underneath in the luggage bays.

'You guys in a group?' they ask. Willie nods confirmation. 'Wassa name? … Oh, Midnight Oil? So where's the tall, bald guy?' Pete's summoned from the back lounge, greets the cops, and within a minute we're on our way again.

Soon the bus pulls up outside our familiar base in Lexington Avenue, the little hotel with the big American flag. Deborah's there to meet us, having had the good sense to fly directly from Chicago to New York, where she adopts, nay, *becomes* the city, just like Diane Keaton in *Annie Hall*.

I push open the window of my room – a simple pleasure fast disappearing in American hotels – and spot two people on the street, seven floors below. One is a middle-age black man lying sideways on a subway vent; the other figure is covered by a white doona with a starfish print, his or her identity entirely obscured. Next to the couple is a wheelchair, from which a small US flag had been attached to the rear frame and flutters in the light wind. People arrive in groups of two or three, some dressed in Halloween gear, all of them taking care not to tread on the sleeping figures. By the by, a black limo glides into sight. The driver gently reverses the immaculate vehicle into the kerb, then proceeds to clean and polish it. Above, all the interior lights of the office block opposite blaze on, revealing a maze of tiny rooms stacked high with computers, boxes of books and papers, and indoor plants.

I sleep brilliantly. The sleep of the just. Miraculously, the usual cacophony of taxi horns has halved in volume and venom, presumably out of respect for the recent tragedy. More to the point, instead of my normal street-facing thunder-box, I've inherited Pete's hermetically sealed, back-lane–side enorma-suite, while he accepts the offer of a friend's apartment. The room is uncannily silent - almost as quiet as my compadres in Midnight Oil when I told them I was writing this book. (Bones later offered photos, while Jim suggested book titles, including *Sushi Was the Last Thing I Ate*, *Waiting For Pete*, and (my favourite) *Mid-Level Band Struggling With Its Own Limitations*.) The absence of background noise reminded me of another visit to New York City, when we arrived at La Guardia Airport just prior to a marauding coastal hurricane. Many of Manhattan's office windows had been taped up, and the concrete canyons ominously empty.

Outside it's business as usual, with an uncharacteristic bonhomie thrown in for good measure. Bones asks two strangers for directions and they're more than happy to help. (Is this the *new* New York? I was quite looking forward to the customary rudeness!) We look for our usual old-style deli, only to find that it's now a self-serve joint with paper plates, Styrofoam cups and plastic cutlery, operated by a young Korean guy who looks like he could use some sleep. In desperation I call a friendly local, a publicist who tells me that she's just written a bio for a band named Marah. ('Are they a religious group?' I ask. 'No,' she replies, without missing a beat, 'they're from Philadelphia.') She advises that the Comfort Diner on East 45th Street is the closest example of the real thing, with booths and Laminex tables, and where the first word uttered after 'How many?' is 'Kawfee?'

Otherwise, the pretzels, fruit stands, books and dodgy watches are all back on the streets, and as cheap as chips. I buy two watches in a wooden box with 'Manhattan' written on it, for the exorbitant sum of ten dollars US, just to see if either would keep going. (They do!) I also pick up a white t-shirt with a photo of Osama bin Laden's face, with 'Wanted: Dead or Alive' written underneath, then, as an apparent afterthought, the word 'Dead' plastered over his face, and 'Terrorism Sucks' thrown in for good measure down the side.

Avoiding the dreaded 49th Street musical-instrument stores, I stride instead through Central Park, past Roxy Paine's brilliant stainless-steel tree sculpture and over to the Boathouse, where I spot many fine examples of NYC's most endangered species – children. Yes, kids of all sizes, shapes and colours, running, falling over, crying and being helped up by their nannies. Every kind of mobile youngster is on display, from rollerblading rug rats to high-tech stroller–ing infants adopted from China, now happily resident in multi-million-dollar Upper West Side apartments, and sporting brand-new names like Lark-Song Schwarz and Li Lin Weintraub.

Somehow I end up outside the Hayden Planetarium at the Natural History Museum on Central Park West, where I decide to abandon myself for a while in the esoteric world of quasars, black holes, supernovas, spiral galaxies, redshift and the intriguingly named 'virgo super clusters' (not a cosmic convention of pedants as I imagine). The tour begins with a spiral walk, from the Big Bang – 13 billion years ago, give or take a day – to the present, every step representing 45 million years. (I can relate to this after the Milwaukee show.) You can touch a meteorite that weighs over four tonnes, a hellish lump of space rock that must have really given the Native Americans something to think about when it fell out of the sky.

The highlight, though, is the Space Show, where you're 'shot' into the heavens by an invisible rocket-powered slingshot, out of our solar system, and into a vacuum where even the deputy commissioner of Taxation won't find you. You then return to Mother Earth via a black hole, an unpleasant journey that brings to mind a camera fast retreating from a colonoscopy. None other than Tom Hanks narrates the whole celestial journey, sticking tightly to the script, and not lapsing into Forrest Gump even once.

It's great to be back on the ground in New York City, major music town that it is. New York, New York, where Ella Fitzgerald once sang at the Savoy Ballroom in Harlem, where Billie Holliday performed at the Cafe Society nightclub in Greenwich Village, and where Gene Krupa played with Benny Goodman at Carnegie Hall. Then in the '60s and '70s, the Velvet Underground, the Ramones, the Dictators, the New York Dolls, Television and Patti Smith made NYC the centre of underground rock, paving the way for the mainstream success in the '80s of Talking Heads and Blondie, and the Strokes in the naughties.

Before we get too settled in New York though, there are shows to do in Philadelphia and New Jersey. The latter turns out to be at the alcohol-free Birch Hill Nightclub, in a forest at Old Bridge, where we change clothes in a table-dancing bar and are called 'Assholes!' by one of the staff for failing to keep a door closed (he over-apologises later). We then suffer waves of on-stage nausea from the cooking smells emanating from the kitchen. As Jim says later: 'When you can smell the bain-marie from the stage, you know you're on your way out.'

During the show, I let my mind drift back to 1993, when, in a momentary loss of clarity, we made it known before the Philly gig that we'd individually autograph our single at the time, 'Outbreak of Love', if it was brought along after the concert. Well ... 340 people and seventy minutes later, we emerged stonkered from the signing session, only to scrawl our names on a similar number of copies the following night in *Joisey*. And so on, every night, for the following six weeks.

We've recently revived these post-gig signing sessions, an idea that has since taken off here like an unmanned Predator spy-plane, so that they're now 'expected' at many radio-sponsored concerts (apparently). The process involves installing oneself at a long table, armed with a sharpie (a felt-tip pen, not a manchild with a mullet) and preferably with a beer, while members of the audience file past with their single, album, ticket, poster and/or t-shirt. All this takes place under the stern gaze of a phalanx of security men and women, whose love for turning chaos into order is demonstrably greater than for life itself. None of us is spared this nightly ritual, but each of us handles it in our own fashion, Bones telling jokes behind his cool, blue sunglasses, 'Gentleman' Jim greeting everyone with warmth and sincerity.

As for the fans, Americans are generally very adept at striking up conversations with strangers, so these 'grip 'n' grins' usually proceed fairly smoothly. Some of the most devout fans arrive clutching arcane memorabilia from the Triassic period of Oz rock. A guy in Minneapolis produces a large black and white photo of the band, taken by Bob King in 1977 at

Parramatta's War and Peace in western Sydney, featuring our little blue lightbox set-up behind us.

Other folk hand over their own CDs, which come with bios making extraordinary claims, such as a recent one from the band members of Atlantis: 'We are crusaders of rock, missionaries, if you like, that support all life on Planet Earth and Mother Nature as a whole.' (Whoa! Something tells me that Atlantis may remain submerged for a little longer.) Then there are the sullen teenagers, who just spin their ticket down in front of you to sign, with hardly a grunt, displaying a distinct lack of 'people skills', as politicians like to say.

And let's not forget the stoner dudes who 'just want to shake your hand, man', and 'share the good vibes' (man); or the biker couples who want your moniker on their matching Harley bandanas. And the open-pored, clear-eyed greenies wearing smokeable hemp hats who discuss the Arctic wilderness between bouts of vigorous flossing; the powdered white American Gothic girls wearing all black, fastidiously avoiding direct sunlight; and the hand-trembling obsessives, with their compulsive, manic intensity. And even the occasional brazen hussies, demanding that their suntanned breasts be signed. We oblige, naturally, pressing lightly so as not to puncture anything pneumatic. (Hey, it's a living ...)

The Australians in the line are always easy to pick, their flat accents with final rising inflexion cutting through the smooth American drawl like a hot knife through Vegemite. Curiously, most of the Aussies I meet seem to come from Adelaide. I now know where South Australia's young population has gone: to the USA, married to men called Travis or Jared, or engaged to women named Kelly or Bri. One of the most common subjects is the time and place of our first encounter.

'I first saw youse at the Thebbo, and then at the Ark,' one bloke tells me. 'Youse was great! And I'm not just pissin' in yer pocket!'

'I appreciate that. Where did you say you saw us?'

'You know, at the Thebarton Theatre and the Arkaba. Just down from that place that used to have the mud-wrestlin' chicks.'

The most troublesome punters are the drunks, who can turn these close-up and personals into a bacterial jungle. One unhygienic bozo manages to gob in Martin's eye and mouth while slobbering out his greeting, while in Kansas City a *Noo Yawker*, with one too many libations under his ample belt, grabs me by both shoulders.

'Don ever shtop doin wha yer doin, Rarb – Promish me! I'm jusht a builder from Long Island but you guysh ar *the greatesht band ever*!!'

'Thanks, mate. You've got a lovely way about you,' I reply, before attempting to escape, but his nail-gun grip holds me even tighter.

'And Rarb!' he blusters. 'I love the Ghoshtwriters album, the one with that sarng ... you know ... the really *dark* one!'

THE ONLY LIVING BOY IN NEW YORK

Who can stop the hail
When human senses fail
There was never any warning
No escape
from 'My Country'

New York City is a tough town, make no mistake. They've got steel-tipped sidewalks and gingko trees, which have survived on Earth for at least 200 million years. There's a Hellgate Railway Bridge, a Fresh Kills Landfill, a Dante's Inferno Horror Ride at Coney Island, and a ferocious, Styrofoam-munching garbage truck called a Dumpasaurus. There are expressway signs that read 'Time is Money is an Insult to Time', and an investment bank with 'We helped Einstein make his money. What makes you think you can do it alone?' strung up in the lobby. And when they recently sprayed the city for West Nile virus, the Long Island lobsters marched on City Hall demanding more. Well, almost.

Mayor Giuliani was right when, after the September 11 attacks, he said that 'The people of New York ... are stronger than these barbarians.' This is a town where even the

accountants sound like wise guys. When we first met Bert
Padell (of Padell, Nadell, Fine and Weinberger), he bran-
dished our deal, joking: 'Take a look at this contract! You
guys fuck up and *I* go to jail!'

Born in the Bronx and a former bat boy for the New
York Yankees, Bert has been '*the* accountant to the stars'
for the last few decades, as well as a business manager to
people such as Madonna, Alicia Keys, Robert De Niro and
Faye Dunaway. He's a keen collector of show-biz and sporting
memorabilia, and ... a poet. As Talking Heads' David Byrne
wrote in *Thoughts ... The Poetry of Bert Padell:* 'When I
was younger, the concept of an accountant did not enter my
mind, and an accountant who wrote poetry was not within
the realm of possibilities. WELL NOT ANY MORE.'

Bert pens casual observations on a vast array of topics, as
well as dedications to John Lennon, James Dean and Judy
Garland. The huge collection of memorabilia in 'Bert's Place',
at his West 56th Street goon-guarded office, includes
Madonna's pointy bra with the tassles, on a headless glass
bust, Rolling Stones tour posters and Beatles signatures, gold
records (including one for Pink Floyd's *Dark Side of the
Moon*), Babe Ruth's original uniform (signed), Joe
DiMaggio's 1950 World Series baseball bat, Yankees caps and
gloves, and one of the twelve turnstyles from the old Ebbets
Field ballpark. I seem to remember that Bert also once pos-
sessed the Japanese WWII surrender documents signed on the
USS *Missouri,* but perhaps I dreamt it. He *does* have the didjeridu we gave him in the '80s. Next door, Bert's associate
Jake Fine has a 'Stick the IRS' board game, with Cuban tax
havens included.

New York is full of such forthright characters. Like the
pair of profoundly deaf 'grumpy old men' from Brooklyn I
encounter having a cross-restaurant yelling match over breakfast, rendering futile everyone else's quiet chatter.

'A lotta people like hardwood floors. I don't,' stated one man, leaving zero room for disagreement.

'I love boats as much as you love the law,' replied his non-sequential friend.

'I was livin' like that fourteen hundred a week was never gonna stop.'

'You were just runnin' around chasin' women, throwin' it away.'

'Where I grew up there was just a dirt road. We had a cow, a pig, a peach tree. We *had* no money.'

'Things have changed ... Look at you now – you're walkin' like you're ninety years old.'

'Why don't you just crawl away and die!' (Ad infinitum.)

One of the city's colourful musical identities comes to our show, the multi-talented Steve Van Zandt, or 'Little Steven', who was responsible for 1985's *Sun City* album by the Artists United Against Apartheid (which included a line sung by Pete). Steve also has five albums under his own name, and plays guitar in the E Street Band with Bruce Springsteen. He recently created a new nationally syndicated radio program, *Little Steven's Underground Garage*, where you can hear everyone from the Dictators to Dylan to the Dave Clark Five, and has landed an acting role as the Pacino-quoting mobster Silvio Dante on HBO's *The Sopranos*.

On Halloween the band is invited to the Australian Embassy in Manhattan, to fill out absentee ballot forms for the (ill-fated) Federal election at home. The ambassador, an old school buddy of Pete's, kindly throws a drinks party for us, so we wander around the conference room meeting friendly merchant bankers and company suits. Others in attendance include an ex-pat artiste, an Australian wine export representative, and many bright young things attached to the embassy. Meanwhile, the VB and Rosemount flow, Midnight Oil music pumps away in the background, and business cards are handed out like chook-raffle numbers in a pub. We even remember to vote, kissing our postal votes farewell and wishing them godspeed on their return to Australia, convinced that commonsense and compassion would once again reign o'er the lucky country.

Just as we're reaching a networking climax, the grog's abruptly cut off. In true Aussie tradition, we bail out, with 'Forgotten Years' still playing – for the third time on high rotation – as the elevator doors close behind us. Down on the streets of New York everyone looks even crazier than usual ('No beer, and now this!' groans Craig), perhaps a result of the full moon rising up through the skyscrapers, or because they're fancy-dressed for Alice Cooper's Halloween concert. As Jim and I make our way up to Smith and Wollensky's for a steak and a Sam Adams ('brewer-patriot'), a man is selling t-shirts with the slogan 'These Colours Don't Run', written over a US map painted in red, white and blue stripes, 'They Just Bleed a Lot These Days.'

In the morning we join the curious, the respectful, the voyeuristic and the shell-shocked at the World Trade Center site. To avoid the road blocks, we take a cab down FDR Drive, skirting the edge of Alphabet City, where Jim, Martin and I once made $22.50 busking during the 'Bedlam Bridge' film clip. We race past rat-infested U Thant Island (where Pete filmed the 'Bedlam' chopper shots) and walk the rest of the way from the junction of the Brooklyn Bridge and the East River.

Ground Zero is surrounded by barricades covered in flowers, flags and tributes. There are cops in cars and on horseback, firemen walking to and from their shifts, and, in the centre, a tortured sculpture of twisted steel and crumbling concrete. Nearby buildings are covered in what appears to be red hessian, as if Christo has already wrapped up the 'holy place', to borrow Barbara Walters's description. Heavy machinery is grinding away, and smoke is still rising into an atmosphere pungent with fumes and fine white dust. The scale of the destruction is immense – much larger than the TV cameras suggest – like an entire neighbourhood has been clear-felled by giants with tungsten chainsaws, then set alight.

The stunned onlookers are mostly hushed into silence. One woman hands me some Christian literature, which contains stories from the relatives of the victims. Another slips a pamphlet by 'St Michael's World Apostolate' into my hand, which is full of dire prophecies from the Virgin Mary, 'transmitted through this seer named by Heaven, Veronica of the Cross'. A party of Japanese tourists arrive in face masks, which makes the rest of us feel irresponsible for not wearing one. One guy with a guitar feels the need to add his own charitable contribution, and begins moaning a 'We're all doomed' diatribe right next to the viewing spot – the kind of apocalyptic nonsense that New Yorkers are really receptive to at present. Actually, people are responding to the spectre of Mr Armageddon in a variety of ways, from tolerance and pity to annoyance or open hostility.

I follow the other Oils in a circuitous route away from the scene, still totally unable to grasp the enormity of the disaster at the southern tip of Manhattan Island. As Rhonda, a New Yorker friend, puts it: 'It's like punching your mother – you just don't do it.' One shoe salesman has already created a 'museum' from his premises, refusing to remove the 9/11 dust from a neat row of leather shoes lined up inside his window. I sincerely hope that he isn't selling them to souvenir hunters as *objets de terror*, to put on someone's mantelpiece next to pieces of the Berlin Wall.

I grab a *New York Times* and take the yellow subway up to Midtown. According to the paper, an unlikely alliance (including Woody Allen, Henry Kissinger and Barbara Walters) is busy making NYC tourist promotion advertisements, to encourage people back to the recovering city. Later that day, tempers rise between the firefighters and the cops, and punches are thrown between the two rescue teams. It seems that the firies want to maintain their numbers at the site, so that they can continue searching for the remains of their fallen brothers, against local government attempts to scale down the effort. A compromise is reached, with the firefighters giving the cops a standing ovation at City Hall, but chanting 'Rudi [Giuliani] must go' at the soon-to-retire New York City mayor.

New York's incoming mayor, Michael Bloomberg, admits that the city still has a long way to go before its emergency response is up to scratch. As it stands, the present alert level is Code Orange, one step down from the highest, Code Red. A symbolic moment passes later, on 30 May 2002, when the World Trade Center site clean-up is completed (by an Australian company, incidentally) at a cost of 750 million dollars, well below expectations and ahead of schedule. For now, everything's being transferred by barge to the grimly named Fresh Kills Landfill on Staten Island. All that remains upright is a homemade cross fashioned from rusty girders, standing defiantly where 3 billion tonnes of steel, glass and concrete recently made up a cluster of New York's greatest towers.

I walk up Second Avenue past the www.imnoslob dry cleaners, and cut across to Times Square, where children's letters are taped onto the NY Police Department's booth. 'Dear rescue dogs,' writes Amanda Neumann, 'I think you were really brave for saveing [sic] the people the [sic] were alive and sniffing the people out.' A handwritten sign on Prospect Park station echoes the pride which New Yorkers have in their own: 'Be Brave, Helpful, Kind, Compassionate. "Be" New York.'

We don't get a soundcheck at the gig in Times Square, inside the World Wrestling Federation Headquarters no less. And all because of Britney bloody Spears, whose dancers are still rehearsing their foxy moves for the nineteen-year-old star's upcoming Las Vegas extravaganza. (Vegas was once where you ended your career, not began it.) I must confess to not being a huge Britney Spears fan, and I'm certainly not over her oeuvre, preferring the work of the late, great Stewie Speer, colossal drummer with Max Merritt and the Meteors. *Whatever,* I'm sure the sweet Southern ingenue has no interest whatsoever in the extra work that our road crew, the indefatigable Baz Woods and the boys, have to put in to get our seminal East Coast gig up and running, dodging the wrath of the toughest of unions, and finishing the line check, PA and monitor EQ only moments before we're due on stage.

As a result, Tim Millican, well accustomed by now to sonic doctoring of dysfunctional house PAs, has to grapple with front-of-house gremlins from the beginning of the show to the end. During the gig Pete, in between finetuning the venue's air-conditioning levels, invites audience members up on stage during 'King of the Mountain', where they dance wildly on Ms Spears's phallic catwalk. 'If Britney can have dancers, so can we,' reasons Pete, pushing one muscle-bound maniac back into the audience, as the ego-ramp begins to palpitate provocatively under fifteen hot shakin' butts.

We leave New York City at 10 am sharp the following morning, with a five-hour bus ride to Boston up ahead. As it turns out, the Boston hotel is right downtown, and a ritzy joint at that, with lots of darkened bars and self-important

Bostonians in penguin suits. The only problem is, I can't get in. Loaded down with suitcase, guitar and shoulder bag I get stuck in the revolving door, unable to move backwards or forwards. I reason that the management must have installed a kind of venus fly trap for guests who haven't paid their extras, releasing them only on the production of a MasterCard. Eventually extricated by a chuckling concierge, I salvage what's left of my pride and stride purposefully into the lift.

It's soundcheck time as soon as we check in, so there's no chance for a walk around the Boston Common, Beacon Hill, Back Bay, Quincy Market or the Freedom Trail, or to even throw down some Legal Sea Food's clam chowder. In any case, the hotel is now cordoned off by Boston Park Rangers, sitting tall on immaculate horses, plus a lone Irish piper. Assuming that one of the remaining Kennedys is about to arrive for a drinkathon, we run the gauntlet to our bus, which has been circling the block since we left. One woman approaches Slim, the driver, peers inside the cabin at the four leather-jacketed hombres, and asks, 'Is this the airport shuttle?'

'This is a half-million-dollar motorhome, dumb ass,' Slim replies, always in character.

Tonight's gig is the Avalon Ballroom, in the shadow of the famous Fenway Park, home since 1912 to Willie's own baseball team, the Boston Red Sox. On the way back to the hotel from the soundcheck there's a snake man on the bus, an old friend of Willie's, who tells us that he raises 'corn snakes' and 'king snakes' for sale as pets (no doubt useful for when the Jehovah's Witnesses call around). He treats the snakes to rodent suppers and a chilled 'artificial winter' environment, so that they hibernate and breed, and is on his way to New Jersey to release a particularly aggressive snake in the woods. I suggest somewhere close to our recent Jersey gig with the fascist doorman, the Birch Hill Nightclub.

This time I've no trouble getting inside the hotel – I just can't find my room. If you leave your key in a hotel room in America right now, or forget your room number (I do both), the people at reception go into terrorist-suspect alert mode. This involves the pressing of a buzzer discreetly placed under the desk, which automatically summons a security monster. He then escorts you to your door like a Turkish jailer with his hash-smuggling prisoner. Next, you have to play a little guessing game, called What's in your Room?

'What will I see when I enter your room, sir?' demands the brick with eyes.

I'm so tired that I want to say 'My new best friend Cindy', but decide against it when I catch his expression. 'Black guitar on the bed, green bag in the corner, clothes thrown all over the room.'

'Okay, let's go in and see,' says the man from *Midnight Express,* sounding unconvinced. I follow him in, backing along the wall, hoping like hell that my guitar hasn't changed colour.

'You have a nice day,' he commands, as he spins around and locks me securely in my cell, leaving me with a severe case of deja vu. There I am, back in 1981, sitting alone in the Diplomat Motor Inn in Acland Street, St Kilda, Melbourne; I'm going crazy in a room stinking of Winfields and Pine-o-Clean, with Chinese-restaurant wallpaper all around and the remains of a fettucine alfredo on the floor, scrawling the words for 'Only the Strong'.

Songwriting isn't always inspired by frustration and solitude – although all songwriters endure bucketloads of both. On the contrary, writing songs is usually the most satisfying part of the whole trip, something Jim and I started when we were still at school, with early versions of 'Surfing with a Spoon', 'Powderworks', 'Used and Abused' and our first nano-hit, 'Run By Night'.

For me, the band's strongest songs have been the result of the two of us joining forces, bringing together words and music that are written alone but find a common thread. We then map out the basic song, adding Martin's guitar parts, arrangement suggestions and 'quality-control', Bones's (and previously Giffo's) grooves and golden-tonsil harmonies and, sometimes, Pete's vocal 'punctuation marks' or additional verse lyrics. Songs like 'No Time For Games' ('Some Kids'), 'Read About It', 'The Power and the Passion', 'Short Memory', 'When the Generals Talk', 'Kosciuszko', 'The Best of Both Worlds', 'Beds Are Burning', 'The Dead Heart', 'Forgotten Years', 'King of the Mountain', 'Truganini' and many others were written in this way.

It can be a convoluted process. One of guiding the words and melodies, verses and choruses, chords, riffs and rhythms through different arrangements, feels, keys, tempos and instrumentation. The whole process then continues through to the final recording, editing, mixing and mastering. Sometimes it comes in a 'heated rush', to quote Springsteen; other times it's as if you need to be a small child again, picking tiny jewels from a beach of broken shells. However the songs evolve, it's Jim and Martin's inestimable musical talent, coupled with a rare humility and patience, that guides them to full realisation – and which has always been Midnight Oil's most potent secret weapon.

The Boston show is one of the tour's best, with people travelling from New York and Connecticut to see us, and driving all the way home after the show. Americans are very mobile in this way. Almost everyone you meet was born in one city, went to college in another, and got a job somewhere else again, so the idea of crossing a few states to catch a band is not a huge deal. Presents arrive in the form of a didjeridu painted in Midnight Oil artwork – one for the archives – eco-theme t-shirts, and a few pages of 'musician jokes' to keep us amused on the bus. Naturally, the drummer jokes are the best (there's a lot to work with), and include one I haven't heard before:

What do you say to a drummer in a three-piece suit?
'Will the defendant please rise.'

DAMN YANKEES

Oh, the power and the passion
Oh, the temper of the times
Oh, the power and the passion
Sometimes you've got to take the hardest line
from 'The Power and the Passion'

A new fever has got America in its sway, and it's got nothing to do with the near pathological urge to destroy bin Laden and al-Qaeda, or the anthrax virus. It is fundamentalist, but doesn't involve religious extremists. It's obsessive, visceral, atavistic. It takes priority over any foreign skirmish or nation-wide terrorist man-hunt. It is, of course, the Ball Game, and it's succeeded, temporarily at least, in wiping the Taliban and all their works clean off the front pages of *USA Today*.

This is clearly a country that's got its priorities right: base-ball before guns before butter. Tonight's game is the seventh and final of the World Series, with the New York Yankees playing the Arizona Diamondbacks in Phoenix. The Yankees had to beat the Oakland As then the Seattle Mariners to get into the final play-off. Both teams are steeling themselves to play all night if necessary to decide a winner.

Fortunately we have the ever-helpful US sports-meister Willie MacInnes on the bus to explain the finer points of the game to the baseball *ignorames* from Australia, a country burdened by the twin misfortunes of first being colonised by the Poms (La Perouse, where were you?), then being foisted with one ... long ... cricket match every summer – arriving at the same time as bushfires, mosquitos and the noisy koel outside my window.

Evidently, baseball has been doing it tough recently. Falling attendances, wealth imbalances between teams (particularly vis-a-vis the cashed-up Yankees), mistrust between the players and the owners, looming battles with the unions, and a potential steroids scandal all plague the game at present.

Nor is baseball the all-American game it used to be back in the glory days of Babe Ruth and Joe DiMaggio. Willie points out that nowadays many young players are fostered in Venezuela, Mexico and the Caribbean (particularly in the Dominican Republic, Puerto Rico and Cuba) where they're put on a survival wage until a major US team decides to sign them up. At which time they presumably paddle furiously to Florida on rafts made from lashed-together baseball bats.

Detroit Tigers hitter Randall Simon is a good example of a poor boy made good, growing up in the Dutch Antilles, swinging at bottle tops with a broomstick when a bat and ball couldn't be found. Simon was eventually signed to the Atlanta Braves a decade ago, reaching the majors in 1997. Not bad for a young bloke in a new country, as my father would say.

Unlike Australia, where talented, enterprising people arriving from poor countries by sea can currently look forward to a barbed-wire-on-the-beach kind of reception, these newcomers to North America are warmly welcomed. Some day they could be making up to 13 million US per annum, like Yankee pitcher Roger 'Rocket' Clemens, or his Arizona counterpart, Curt Schilling. By the time our bus has circumnavigated greater New York City on our Boston-to-Washington day trip, Clemens and Schilling have mowed down a succession of hitters with balls travelling at over 155 kilometres an hour. During the previous night, the Diamondbacks' Randy Johnson had been firing them down at an unbelievable 163 km/h. And both these men are perilously close to forty years young ...

The reception on our satellite TV comes and goes, as do the first five innings, and still there's no score. Arizona have their hometown advantage and finally use it in the sixth, when Danny Bautista scrapes home. When the Yankees score in the seventh innings, 'St Rudi' Giuliani springs to his feet in the stand and cheers wildly. More than anyone, Giuliani knows that a Yankees win is just the shot in the arm that his beleaguered city needs right now.

After the seventh-innings stretch, New York brings in Mendoza to pitch; then, in the eighth, Soriano hits a home run, making it NY 2, Arizona 1. The excitement level on the bus, plus the constant interrogation, is too much for Willie. He retreats to his bunk, only to be driven back later by loud yahooing in the final amazing minutes.

Pitcher Schilling, a perfectionist who claims he plays better with a ballpark's roof closed, is next to retire, after a ball clips his finger – the TV close-up revealing a man in a world of pain. He's replaced by the formidable left-hander Randy Johnson, star power-arm for the desert state, who winds up like the Bugs Bunny coyote, then uses his 208-centimetre height to fire a succession of volleys down at the Yankee hitters. By the ninth and last innings, the Diamondbacks have first and second base; Womack evens the score, leaving Luis Gonzalez to win the World Series for Arizona, for the first time ever.

The Phoenicians go mad. George W. Bush (or 'Shrub' as Australian writer Phillip Adams has taken to calling him) gets on the phone to congratulate the team, and America's sixth-largest city has a collective hangover for days, with 300 000 people lining the streets of Phoenix to cheer the local heroes. The Yankees' only consolation prize is the prestigious Cy Young award, later presented to Roger Clemens for his pitching (his sixth such award).

Personally, I'm beside myself during the game, pacing anxiously around the bus then sitting back down on the edge of the front lounge seats. I haven't seen a crowd go so ballistic over a sporting event since the hot-blooded 1994 World Cup final, fought to the bitter end by Italy and Brazil. At the time, we were in Saratoga Springs on the WOMAD USA Don't Blink Or You'll Miss It tour, featuring Peter Gabriel, Lucky Dube, Live, and Arrested Development. That night, most of the entourage squeezed around a backstage TV as the match went into overtime, and the penalty shoot-out began. While the goals and misses followed one after another, someone noticed that a woman was performing oral sex on her blissful boyfriend in the woods behind the venue. In groups of twos and threes, people in the touring party became transfixed by the simultaneously climaxing distractions, spinning their heads from the screen to the woods, until in an audible explosion of euphoria, gratitude, relief and dismay, Italy's Roberto Baggio booted his ultimate shot away from the goal posts at exactly the same moment that our unwitting porn stars reached their own denouement, collapsing exhausted into the undergrowth.

On this occasion, though, the mood in the Midnight Oil camp is subdued. A sleepless night in Boston's Park Plaza Hotel, where a bar fight progressed into a drunken street brawl right outside our windows, made for an underwhelming start to the day. Since then, horrendous traffic on the Interstate around New York City, and the Yankees' loss have conspired to create some restlessness in the ranks. The thought of spending any time at all at the epicentre of the other target of the terrorist attacks, Washington DC, has left the band lost in thought, even after we finally dock in the illuminated sleeping capital around midnight.

Later we find out that our concerns are shared by the power brokers at 1600 Pennsylvania Avenue, who've allegedly established a 'shadow administration' in subterranean bunkers distant from the White House. That way, America can continue to operate even if the king pins are hit.

***

The next morning is cool and clear. Martin, Jim, Bones and I battle a cold wind across the Mall near the Reflecting Pool. We stop to admire the scale and portence of a site so identifiable with forty years of people power – from the civil-rights marches, antiwar demonstrations, equal-opportunity and pro-choice rallies, to anti-firearm protests, veterans awards marches, Black Pride processions and International Aids Day. Our own invaluable contribution is to take pictures of the Washington Monument, lining it up so that it looks like it's growing out of our heads.

We then wander around America's favourite space junkyard, the National Air and Space Museum, which is chock-full of missiles, rockets, shuttles and space stations. Our fellow visitors are mainly men in uniform: polo-shirted dads in bone-coloured Chinos and boat shoes, and kids in sloppy t-shirts, baseball caps, baggy jeans and Wal*Mart sneakers.

We retreat to the Henry Moore exhibition at the nearby National Art Gallery, only to find that Henry's solid nudes are also a big favourite with European art documentarians, who've laid siege to some of the English sculptor's best-loved works. We head for another wing of the massive gallery, one filled with gilt-edged, keenly guarded masterworks of the great American classicists – Whistler, Sargent and Homer (Winslow, not Simpson). I find myself wondering about the figures in the portraits, whether these privileged folk were ever troubled by the nineteenth-century equivalent of sound-checks, interviews and dirty laundry.

As it turns out, Pete has come up with an innovative solution to the laundry problem, combining it with an invitation to a Melbourne Cup Day lunch from the people at the Australian Embassy in DC. While the rest of us catch up on lost sleep, sending our apologies, Pete arrives at the embassy carrying a large bag of dirty clothes, hopeful for some Omo action.

We run our own Melbourne Cup sweep on arrival at the gig, the famous 9:30 Club at number 999 9th Street. We're in the Shaw neighbourhood of north-west Washington, once home to Duke Ellington, and still feeling the effects of the 1968 riots (the staff advise us, 'Only go outside the building if it's on fire'). We explain to the Americans, including the Will Hoge band, that on Cup Day – the first Tuesday of every November – the whole country stops what they're doing, if anything, and tunes in to a horserace that will almost certainly make them poorer in just over three minutes.

The winner of the sweep is Marshall, our American truck driver and advance co-ordinator, who walks around beaming until he's told that there's been a mistake. Afterwards he's seen muttering about 'the gross inequities of Arzzie horse-flesh'. Bones is the new winner with Ethereal, and celebrates enthusiastically with the blonde and friendly embassy staff who, bearing gifts of Victoria Bitter and Vegemite, have escaped the Cup Day drinking marathon and made it down to the show. (Perhaps they finished Pete's laundry.)

The concert is imbued with the sweet smell of dope, and propelled by a roof-raisin' audience, who sing 'Shor-or-ort

Memoree' with such gusto that we can no longer hear ourselves play (the Afghanistan reference elicits a few 'woops!' and 'yeahs!' from the crowd). In fact, many of the song lyrics seem to have a new context, particularly 'When the Generals Talk', 'Forgotten Years', 'Armistice Day' and 'Hercules'. 'One Country', with its military snare-drum rolls and march time beat, now sounds to me like a last-ditch plea for peace, a foreboding soundtrack to a menacing war.

Otherwise, the band locks into gig mode. Martin travels freely around stage right, while Jim constantly swaps electric guitars for the acoustic, the Dobro, the piano, the organ, the synth or the sequencer – or plays a combination of several of them at the same time – in between singing harmony vocals in 'Capricornia', 'Too Much Sunshine' and 'Been Away Too Long'. Bones skips over to banter with Ben at the monitor desk, and jumps up behind me to play the tympani at the end of 'The Dead Heart'. At one point, Pete has a few private words with some of the gridiron players near the front, who are unwittingly throwing around their cubic metres and making life a misery for the people around them.

At the after show grip 'n' grimace; I overhear some of the expats talking about the merits of the new songs in the live set, including 'Too Much Sunshine': 'Typical bloody Midnight Oil, they must have run out of things to complain about,' says one bloke. 'It's always too much this, too much that, and now it's too much bloody *sunshine*!'

We do a quick pack at the hotel and drive out of town towards Atlanta, Georgia past the Pentagon, with its huge gaping hole, floodlights and heavy machinery – the so-called Phoenix Project. On the bus we watch a mini-movie called *American Dummy,* about a ventriloquist on the skids who happens upon a foul-mouthed dummy who saves his act, and then proceeds to destroy everyone around him. So whatever did happen to Ronald Reagan and Rush Limbaugh?

THE NIGHT THEY DROVE OLD DIXIE DOWN

Older than Kosciuszko
Darwin down to Alice Springs
Dealers in the clearinghouse the
settlements explode
High up in the homelands
Miners drive across the land
Encounter no resistance when the people
block the road
from 'Kosciuszko'

Atlanta, home of Coca-Cola, Delta Airlines, Turner Broadcasting System and the giant fossil-fuel-burning power utility Southern Company, is warm and clear, unusual for a city second only to Los Angeles for air pollution.

Atlanta sprawls like LA too, with distinct and segregated neighbourhoods, including Sweet Auburn, where Martin Luther King Jr grew up, and Midtown, home to *Gone With the Wind's* Margaret Mitchell from 1925. Another area is Downtown, where in the underground you can see some of the only dwellings left standing by General William T. Sherman after his infamous building-burnin', property-lootin'

March to the Sea in the final months of 'the War of Northern Aggression'. All of these sites are open to the public, as is the golf range at the nearby granite monolith known as Stone Mountain. On a previous tour, it was here we crumpled under the vastly superior stroke play of our companions in Hunters and Collectors.

I walk down Peachtree Street to Mick's Diner, a former apothecary with a high pressed-metal ceiling, and order the most exotic-looking breakfast on the menu – a fried-green-tomato sandwich. Jim, Pete, Deborah and I then decide to take a look at Martin Luther King Jr's birthplace, which turns out to be a well-preserved, double-storey, Queen Anne–style timber home, with chocolate-coloured trim, opposite a neat line of shotgun-row houses. Young ML, as he was known, lived here until he was twelve, later becoming co-pastor with his father for eight years at the Ebenezer Baptist Church on the corner. On the day we arrive the church is being renovated and is thus off limits to visitors, even incomprehensible ones from strange lands across the seven seas. I buy an MLK badge from the elderly black lady who's pottering around inside, then drift over the road to the historical site dedicated to the progress of the civil-rights movement. The site honours all the milestones, from the bus boycott in Montgomery, Alabama, through the Freedom Rides, desegregation, Vietnam protests, the riots in Watts and Detroit, to King's assassination on 4 April 1968 in the Lorraine Hotel in Memphis.

Dr King's grave lies next to the Freedom Walkway, adjacent to a series of shallow memorial pools. When you reach the top you can see items of his clothing and travel accessories, along with representations of his mentor Mahatma Gandhi, whose independence struggle in British India became a model for King's own non-violent actions. Also featured is Rosa Parks, who triggered the Montgomery Bus Boycott in 1955 by refusing to give up her seat to a white man on an

Alabama bus. As I walk around the exhibits, the racism and brutality of those years come sharply into focus. I remember my parents' dismay as first John Kennedy then Martin Luther King Jr were assassinated, as US cities burned, as the old order was savagely, justly, up-ended in the name of 'a dream'.

We walk back to the Georgian Terrace Hotel, rest for a while, then jump into a minibus bound for our evening show at Earthlink Live. Our driver introduces himself as 'the Cowboy, man', and seems even more excited about the night's prospects than we are.

'Wow! Earthlink, eh? A lot of out-of-town honeys will be there. Lotsa pussy, pink and furry ... Man, they could suck the chrome off a –'

'Thanks, Cowboy,' interrupts Pete, as we pull into the gig.

The concert is in a small, wrap-around theatre. On stage we experience the odd sensation of having half the audience breathing down the sides of our necks, while the show feels more like an audition than a real gig – though a crowded one at least. Afterwards we meet up with a few friends, including drummer Michael Cartellone, whom I met in Sydney after he played a mind-blowing set with John Fogerty a few years back. Michael's now playing with one of the South's best-loved bands, Lynyrd Skynyrd.

Back at the hotel I catch a news grab about 'the Freedom Riders of '61', who are gathering this very weekend in Jackson, Mississippi, for their first reunion. 'Many have paid a high price for their convictions, alienated from their families, hampered by prison records,' the reporter informs me. I summon up a few vague memories of Australia's own freedom ride, in 1965, when a group of Sydney University students, including Charles Perkins, drove around New South

Wales to expose discrimination in country towns. For their trouble, the thirty-strong group were driven off the road in Walgett, and assaulted in Moree, after Charlie led some of the local Koori kids to the segregated swimming pool.

Two years later, Australia's Commonwealth Referendum for Indigenous Citizenship was passed, recognising Aboriginal people for the first time as part of the official Australian population and including Aborigines in the census. The referendum was passed by a 90-per-cent 'Yes' vote, a great victory for Faith Bandler, Nugget Coombs and all those who'd fought to have the original Australians enfranchised and counted. I recall the then leader of the opposition, Gough Whitlam, predicting a referendum victory, saying that there could no longer be any excuse for the terrible conditions suffered by Aborigines. ('Which one the Whitlam man?' ask Aborigines from the remote Top End communities even today, before they cast their vote.)

At the start of the new millennium, though, and after the heady promises of Native Title, Mabo, Wik and the symbolic 'Sorry' Day marches for the stolen generation and the 'Sea of Hands' for reconciliation, the problem is far from over. The 'nation within another' still finds 14 per cent of its number in prison, a jobless rate three times the national average, a life expectancy twenty years less than that for white Australians, and an ongoing health and violence crisis in its communities. The Federal Government's response? 'A sense of fatalistic helplessness,' according to Reconciliation Australia co-chair Fred Chaney.

On the invitation of Northern Territory outback teacher Wes Whitmore, in the winter of 2000 Martin and I threw a couple of guitars and a bagful of percussion into a Toyota Troopie bound for Utopia. The remote settlement is home to celebrated desert artists Gloria and Kathleen Petyarre (as it was to the late Emily Kngwarreye) and situated half a day's drive north-east of Alice Springs.

The idea was to play a handful of music workshops in the satellite schools around the former cattle station, so we barrelled down red dirt roads flanked by paddy melons and surrounded by abundant bush tucker, scaring finches and galahs into the mallee. On the way, we gathered up children from settlements such as Mulga Bore and Soapy Bore, and drove them to the schoolhouse at Aniltji, as they sang along to their favourite tape, Linda Ronstadt's *Greatest Hits*.

At the school, everyone was given a pair of drumsticks, a tambourine, a cowbell or some clapsticks, and were soon belting away so enthusiastically that Martin and I, the bush buskers up the front, wondered whether the din would break the school's newly acquired windows (glass ones, not the PC software). So vigorous was the musical contribution, in fact, that some of the instruments were shredded and later abandoned, bound to join an old upright piano lying on its side behind the hall, its ivories looking like the broken bones of a buffalo carcass bleaching in the sun.

A few months later the whole band returned to the Western Desert, camping out under the magnificent Macdonnell Ranges near the township of Papunya, which we'd visited with the Warumpi Band and (didjeridu-meister) Charlie McMahon fourteen years earlier. Warumpi's guitarist Sammy Butcher was now council president of the community, and as such had organised a complete set of musical instruments for the local bands, one of whom, a desert reggae outfit, showed great promise.

We played a concert with these groups, outside in the school courtyard at night, with scabby township dogs wandering freely around the amps and drums, and the younger kids rushing up to the makeshift stage and dancing wildly

– until the music stopped and the great quiet resumed, at which moment they'd dive headlong back into the safety of darkness. The only other dancers were a clandestine mob of bush zombies, young petrol sniffers frying their brains on cans of gasoline, perhaps tragically destined to inhabit their own nightmarish never-never. The fast-moving members of Midnight Oil were kicking up the dust too, trying our best to work off the huge quantities of beef, buffalo, emu and kangaroo that Gary Morris had purchased from Woolworths at Alice Springs.

On 10 December 1977, in the dressing room of Sydney's legendary Bondi Lifesaver Club, we decided not to accept the recording deal being waved at us by one of the 'Big Six' A&R guys outside. Instead, in the independent spirit of the times, we created our own label within a division of 7 Records, called it Powderworks after the first song on our debut album, and hit the road.

Four years ago, on our twentieth birthday, the band found itself in Disney World, Orlando, Florida, standing on an outdoor stage in light, warm rain in front of a few hundred hard-core fans, halfway through a pre-recorded live radio broadcast across America. Asking ourselves, in the words of Talking Heads, 'How did we get here?'

I recall surveying the dismal scene from behind the drum kit. Huge families four axe-handles across were clasping pink candy and barging like D9 Dozers through our audience, who were resolutely standing their ground against the march of the primates. Actually, some of these truculent interlopers did fit the description of the Japanese macaque monkeys I'd just seen at the Milwaukee Zoo: 'Adults have red faces and rumps that deepen in colour during fall breeding season.'

Meanwhile, up on stage, Pete was barely spitting out the words, so *pissed off* was he that we'd ended up in 'Wally world' on our twentieth birthday. For the band, the gig was rapidly disintegrating into one of the least memorable moments since we'd played *that* Christian festival in the British Midlands, arriving on stage after Samantha Fox and a U2 covers band. As for me, I was already a basket case, being in the early stages of pneumonia from repeated nights of passive chainsmoking at the Mercury Lounge in New York City.

Earlier that day I'd been visited by the Disney World doctor and his girlfriend. ('It's okay,' he'd said, 'she's also a doctor.') They'd inspected me for a full thirty seconds, ordered me back on solids, then charged me 150 dollars cash, plus another 200 bucks for strong antibiotics, asthma drugs and a course of steroids – the latter causing my balls to ache, my jaw and frontal lobes to protrude, and reducing my vocal abilities to short, simian shrieks. 'This is serious,' said the doctor, with as much gravitas as one can muster in a Mickey Mouse tie.

The 2001 show in Orlando is a far more enjoyable affair, at the House of Blues. Everyone is in good spirits on this warm Florida evening. Bones meanders off around the front of the PA during 'The Dead Heart', bantering with the front row of the audience and the security guy, before darting back just in time for the final 'doo doo doo doo doo doo-doo's. ('When the band goes "doo doo", make it *red*,' manager Gary once famously told lighting man Nick Elvin.) Bones then throws his bass guitar to Pete, who plays the Big Rock Ending while spinning on the spot. After the gig a thoughtful bloke gives us some rare 7"-vinyl Midnight Oil singles – to keep for the archives, rather than just to sign, return and then come across the next day for sale on the Net.

The next morning we're all jolted awake, as the hotel's fire alarms are tested room by room. I give up trying to sleep, throw open the heavy curtains, and notice that the first Christmas decorations are up, in the shape of sparkling red, white and blue Confederate Santas strung around the mall. They're truly a welcome sight, beacons of innocence among the daily barrage of post-9/11 gloom and fear. But there's no other evidence of fun outside, just more carparks, shops, freeways and a Kipling-esque swamp – a 'great grey-green greasy Limpopo River, all set about with fever trees' – steaming listlessly in the sun.

Jim and I decide to visit Celebration, a model town conceived and constructed by the Walt Disney Company, with the aim of 'creating a better place and, ultimately, a better way to live'. The guiding principles, a worthy manifesto known as 'the Celebration Cornerstones', are clearly outlined in the brochure: 'Community, Place, Education, Health and Technology.'

A large black limo arrives at the Radisson Inn to take us to Celebration, which makes us a little uneasy, coming from a country where the only people swanning around in limousines are usually total wankers. More unnerving, it's driven by a man who's either had a laryngectomy, or whose sandpaper voice, filing-cabinet frame, tight dark suit and black Italian sunglasses would get him lots of work as a gangland thug in mob movies. When we arrive at the town centre he croaks something unintelligible, the kind of sound an alien might make as it disembarks from a spaceship. Assuming that he means that he'll wait for us, we set off to see what a real-life *Truman Show* has to offer.

Our first stop is the clean, cheerful shopping village, painted the colour of ripe persimmons. Here, contented-looking people of various colours, shapes and sizes are grazing at upmarket restaurants around an artificial lake. A walk around the residential streets confirms the impression, where rows of similar-style homes with neat clipped gardens, white picket fences and American flags are dotted with 'Armed Response' warning signs.

I get the real estate rag and discover that 'from the mid $100 000s' you can buy a terrace; while an 'estate home', some of which look like Southern plantation mansions, will set you back up to 700 000 big ones (price excludes fields, crops, tools and slaves). Once you're settled in, you can keep an eye on your neighbours via a private cable TV channel, which schedules community events and 'live broadcasts of town meetings'. (My local council in Sydney should do the same. The level of abuse at the regular Monday-night meetings would make great reality TV.) I must admit, the longer we're here, the more seductive the whole package becomes. The Disney town planners have thought of everything: schools, healthcare facilities, parks, a golf course, a Presbyterian church, a university and a 'children's learning center'. What more could you want?

Except to jump back into the limo and leave, immediately – before they wind up the drawbridge. A disturbing thought takes hold of me, that just behind this shiny veneer there's a gulag waiting for residents who permit their poodles to foul the perfect lawns, with death by fire-ants for repeat offenders. Actually, in the case of Celebration, situated as it is in the *deepest* South, this probably isn't so far from the truth. Florida is currently the third-highest state – after Texas and Virginia – to make use of the death penalty. And since George W. Bush's brother Jeb took over as governor, the chance of 'ridin' the lightnin'' (execution by electric chair) is greater than ever.

Tonight's gig, an outdoor show at St Petersburg's Jannus Landing, is a *real* celebration. It makes up for everything else – the switchblade in the lower spine, the whitewater-rafting in the ears, the hungry, horny heart. It 'almost makes up for the strip search', as Woody Allen said at the Oscars. The punters are in great spirits on the warm Florida evening, and the sound from our amps and drums is thick and gritty as it tussles with the humidity.

Actually, the atmosphere reminds me a little of the toad-racin' sensibilities at our old regular gig on Australia's Gold Coast, the Playroom. In between our sets there, sun-blasted surfers sucking Bundy and Coke ('Queensland fighting foam', as Nick Elvin calls it) would yell out scores at the Best Butt competition babes, while 'What I Like About You' and 'Start Me Up' were cranked through the massive house PA at hair-parting volume.

At the end of a great show you can feel on top of the world. Literally. On our first and only tour of South Africa, which began at Ellis Park footy field in Johannesburg (1753 metres above sea level), we felt a collective sense of euphoria – the kind that keeps you hooked on live performance forever. The concert that evening, which included South African stars Brenda Fassi, Lucky Dube and Johnny Clegg, as well as a flu-ridden Sting, was one of the first big, multi-race outdoor music festivals since the end of Apartheid, with black folk from Soweto bussed to and from the stadium. I stood by the side of the stage all afternoon, watching a succession of amazing drummers, percussionists and bass players, and, in the case of Clegg, brilliant dancers. It dawned on me that bringing my drums to Africa was as illogical as someone shipping didjeridus to Australia.

A monumental roar went up as we descended the long set of stairs to the stage, where Bones and I began a rambling introduction to 'The Dead Heart'. After two songs Pete and I were gasping for oxygen, but the thrill of playing in the heart-land of Nelson Mandela's newly liberated South Africa more than countered the effects of altitude. Didj player Charlie McMahon set off one of his homemade Roman candles, a gun-powdered 'shooter' that ricocheted off Martin and landed in the crowd, causing the gun-shy South African secur-ity guards to reach for their revolvers. 'That's the last time I use the mongrel,' said Charlie afterwards.

'Beds Are Burning', always the best-known song, had the audience singing along in rich Highveld harmonies, which left our own slight, white efforts somewhere in the shade, and we finished the long day of great music amid a tangible spirit of optimism and brotherhood. On a mile-high kind of high.

RAMPART STREET BLUES

The drums are playing louder up
on Military Road
The Bakerman is laughing as he's rolling
in the gold
from 'Bakerman' (demo version)

Recording is an entirely different beast from touring. For one thing, it can be over before you know it, exploding like a mind bomb, leaving casualties sprawled over the mixing desk, bleeding on the control-room floor, screaming, 'Did anyone get the number of that track?' Our first, eponymous record, aka 'the Blue Meanie', was made in a five-night blitz between pub gigs. Some say that it sounds like it. A few years passed and the process became somewhat different. After the third month of recording *Red Sails in the Sunset* in Tokyo we began to crawl up the rice-paper walls, to gaze forlornly over the Buddhist cemetery on the overpass behind the studio, to fantasise about escaping from a hotel room so small that if something went wrong with the shower, they'd replace the entire bathroom. We threw so many sounds in the pot – a Sumo wrestler's soup of samples, cheesy keyboards, gongs and a saki-soaked orchestra – that producer Nick Launay, struggling to lock-up two 24-track tape machines, took five full days to perfect the mix of songs like 'Kosciuszko', before abandoning it and completing the album in London. Eventually the friendly studio engineers, Shigeo and Yoshi, succeeded in *scaring* us out, concocting stories about an *obake*, a ghost, which they claimed was maliciously erasing the tapes.

Actually, the time we spent in Japan was priceless, unforgettable – and often incredibly funny. The trip would have been worth it alone to see the look of astonishment on the face of Victor JVC studio boss Isamu Hachiguchi – dubbed 'Ice-creamu san' from his generous daily gifts of frozen desserts – when he found me playing the drum kit in the third-floor restroom, which we'd discovered had a cacophonous drum sound. 'Too roud!' he exclaimed in the English I'd been helping him with, although unfortunately I couldn't stop drumming right there and then, being halfway through the definitive take of 'The Best of Both Worlds'. I apologised later, however, when I discovered that the drums had been leaking into the downstairs studio, where a pristine recording of shamisen and koto was being performed by a living national treasure and his wife.

Tokyo in the '80s was like a set from *Happy Days*, a yen-driven explosion of pop culture, cars, clothes and baseball, with the added attraction of pachinko parlours, beer-vending machines and computer games, where hair-perfect Japanese Fonzarellis mimed to Carl Perkins and met their girlfriends for thirty-minute trysts in 'love hotels'. We learned enough Japanese to record the album, to order in cafes specialising in *ebi, unagi* and *tonkatsu*, and later to stay in *minshukus* in southern Honshu, Shikoku and Kyushu. My wife Lesley and I travelled to Kobe on the Shinkansen, followed by a spectacular overnight voyage on the Inland Sea, dotted with the lights of hundreds of fishing boats. Most people we met were helpful, kind and polite, including everyone in the record company, who stood up on cue and applauded us enthusiastically, for a solid minute, when we visited their open-plan office, after which we were treated to a traditional twelve-course dinner in a garden restaurant illuminated by fireflies.

Of course, there were the less romantic aspects, the kind of stuff that sometimes left us gob-smacked in disbelief: the sado-sexual comics, the 'cruelty TV', the *karoshi* – death from overwork – of the *sarary*-men, the scale of teenage prostitution, the barbaric exploits of the *yakuza*, the epidemic of student suicides, the subjugation of women, the whitewashing of history and the slavish devotion to everything American. I remember laughing out loud, though, when the collision of Japanese and English – 'Janglish' – resulted in such sights as a safety-pin pierced punk snarling through the crowded Shinjuku lunch-hour, with 'I FUK LIKE A BEEST' hand-painted on the back of his studded leather jacket.

By comparison, the few weeks we spent on *Breathe* in June 1996 should've been a walk in the swampy woods. Part of the album was recorded in New Orleans at the now-defunct Kingsway Studio, an atmospheric old mansion converted to a live-in recording studio by songwriter/performer/producer Daniel Lanois.

But 'Nawlins' has its own hungry ghosts, potent enough to frighten their Japanese counterparts back into the underworld. We became convinced that the grand old two-storey house was seriously haunted, beholden to murderous secrets and malevolent spells, home to seditious spirits and hellhound horrors, all ensnared within the perimeter walls as if incarcerated in a cajun *cauchemar*. It was decorated to match, with pantheistic imagery and voodoo iconography in every room, and lit dimly, so that we ate, drank, worked and relaxed in a perpetual twilight zone.

Since our arrival, Bones had been winding up Grant Pudig, our then stage manager, with lurid tales he'd heard about glowing apparitions standing at the ends of beds and bursting through doors. So on the first night at Kingsway I scared Grant half to death when, disoriented in the black of night, I mistakenly forced open his connecting bedroom door instead of my bathroom door, and stood there momentarily, a naked shadowy spectre, at which moment he let out a blood-curdling scream which echoed down the ancient corridors and woke up the entire household. Grant hardly slept at all from that moment on.

We set up our instruments around the house, with the drums in the dining room, amps in the lounge and study, the mixing desk and tape machines in the lobby. The rooms themselves weren't huge, but had lofty ceilings, and were arranged around a dark polished timber stairwell which led upstairs to a rabbit warren of bedrooms. Soon, in an attempt to use the coolest part of the day, and fuelled by garlic pizza, melatonin and wheat beer, we began recording later and later into the night, producer Malcolm Burn wearing his 'Robert Crumb' hat, telling stories and playing a range of instruments. Including your *own*, if you left the studio for anything longer than a quick piss.

The weeks in Kingsway became a blur of debilitating daytime heat and cooler darkened rooms, and in truth, this was not the happiest time of my musical life. Perhaps the studio's foulest ghosts had permeated my soul, so that what I needed, as my friend Rick Grossman might say, was 'a spiritual enema'. I spent most of the time at Kingsway like sad bastard Eeyore in his gloomy place, unsure of who was the more decaying and distressed, the house or its miserable occupant.

You can still see the heel marks where they had to drag me to the drum kit. Soon I was experiencing similar anxiety attacks to those which had plagued me in 1981, during the recording of '10 to 1', when dizziness, heart palpitations and sweaty palms made London even less appealing than usual.

Perhaps to relieve the claustrophobia, Malcolm Burn, Canadian born but living in New Orleans, suggested an excursion to a southern gospel church in the suburbs. Initially we lost our way, finding ourselves caught up in a local protest march, only to be rescued by some helpful church ladies dressed in their best Sunday dresses and hats, who guided us in their car through the burnt-out 'hood to the chapel's front door. As the only whites at the service, and strangers at that, we were formally welcomed to the congregation and encouraged to join in the singing and praying as the preacher paced the aisles in his splend'rous robes, saving souls and forgiving sins, howlin' and hollerin' and praisin' the All-marty, while the two organists blew the roof off the old church, battling with each other for greater power and volume, as if to demonstrate the struggle of the Lawd 'gainst the peril of perdition.

Afterwards we sat in the gutter outside and feasted on a real gospel brunch – fried chicken, coleslaw and root beer – then drove back to the Quarter in an ancient yank tank, squeezed up in the front seat with Lesley, Malcolm and his French girlfriend, cruising past the above sea-level sarcophagi of the St Louis Cemetery, marvelling at the hospitality that we'd encountered throughout the morning, and wondering whether the same spirit of acceptance would have been shown to a group of black folk who turned up unannounced at a white church in the South.

As I make my way through town on the current trip, enjoying the city much more this time in the cool of the November evening, I hear the unmistakable strains of that old traditional 'Rampart Street Blues'. It's a sad and sexy lament I first enjoyed in the darkness of the original Basement in Sydney, at age sixteen, while my girlfriend and I drank Vermouth rosso and rested our hands in each other's thighs. ('Haven't you two got a home?' asked the manager.)

The song was soon expropriated by the Stanley Street Jazz Band, a high school group I joined, formed by ambitious trombonist (another oxymoron) Michael Stenning. The young band actually got a lot of gigs, playing harbour cruises, school assemblies, jazz clubs, a shopping-mall opening – even a function I hardly dare mention in the grounds of the nuclear facility at Lucas Heights ('Don't play in the dirt,' warned my father). Our set list was trad jazz and ragtime in the style of the Original Dixieland Jazz Band, and included 'Tiger Rag', which featured the inevitable drum solo. It must've sounded more like a drum kit being thrown down a stairwell but still, the stunned crowd would usually applaud vigorously – a motor reflex triggered by traumatic shock – which was all the encouragement I needed to increase the solo's length and volume on the following weekend. Suffice to say, though, that New Orleans's own Baby Dodds, and master skins-man Chick Webb, never had *anything* to fear.

Tonight's version of 'Rampart Street Blues' is coming from a hole-in-the-wall jazz dive, and sounds just like the recording made in 1923 by the Georgia Peach herself, Lucille Hegamin, and the spectacularly entitled Blue Flame Syncopaters. (I suppose you had to make your own entertainment in those days.)

Way down on Rampart Street in New Orleans,
Somebody's callin' me,
and I can hear that gang of jelly beans,

Are singing harmony!
I get lonesome by my ownsome,
Here in this one-horse town!
My heart beats
For Rampart Street,
And for my teasin' brown!

I'm still not certain what was meant by 'my teasin' brown', but I'm pretty sure I never want to wake up next to one. Whatever it is, there's obviously plenty of 'it' still going around, because as every Saturday night gets older and dirtier the scene around Bourbon Street turns ugly, with marauding tribes of horny young men wearing 'I'm here about the blowjob' t-shirts stumbling past the tap dancers and palm readers, spilling beer from plastic cups, and bellowing 'show uz yer tits!' to the females partying on the balconies above. (The response to this cute mating ritual appears to be in direct proportion to the quantity of absinthe or rum 'hurricanes' imbibed.)

New Orleans's French Quarter is a curious melange of history and fakery, authenticity and opportunism, hex and hoax. It's the remains of a navy brothel and smugglers' port built on a swamp, with Bourbon Street – a kind of drunken, dodgy Disneyland for grown-ups – seething like a chilli-dog in its gut. Early maps of 'Storeyville' show saloons, honky tonks, prisons and pawn shops standing side by side with hospitals, churches and cemeteries, an intoxicating gumbo of saints and sinners that continues today. These few square kilometres also form the epicentre of American blues roots and traditions, with their rich folklore, unique provenance and boundless influence on almost all forms of modern music, including our own. The locals, who cherish the Quarter and treasure their heritage homes, either tolerate the tourists, stay clear of Bourbon Street, or leave town altogether during the peak periods and the stifling summer months.

You can still hear real 'jass' and blues in the tradition of Louis Armstrong, Kid Ory, Ma Rainey and Bessie Smith anytime at Preservation Hall, and at the annual Jazz and Heritage Festival in late April or May. If you're lucky, you might also stumble across zydeco and cajun music on a street corner, along with the kind of rough and ready delta blues that I've recently been joyfully playing with the Backsliders in Australia.

Bourbon Street aside, a walk around the French Quarter can be a delight to the senses. The antique shops, second-hand books and clothes stores, art galleries and well-preserved French and Spanish colonial architecture are often shaded by spreading magnolias and decorated by flower-box petunias tumbling over the iron-lace railings. Add to this the intoxicating smells of cajun cooking that seep out of hidden court-yards. One waiter tells us that 'You jus' keep on addin' sparces [spices] til ya valves slam shurt', which sounded quite promising after five weeks of bland road food. We make the most of it, feasting on ribs with Jack Daniel's BBQ sauce, voo-doo shrimp in Dixie beer reduction, and 'Loosiana' crawfish, po'boys and beans, all the while swilling the local ales, spirits, and lots and lots of tap water, which was surprisingly clean and clear.

As we sit outside in the warm breeze, I try to imagine what it might have been like here 150 years ago, sipping mint juleps on the porch of an antebellum-plantation mansion, gazing out over fields whistling with sugar cane and indigo. 'Fore they 'drove ol' Dixie down'. Perhaps the drums of the coming war against the abolitionist Yankees would have been as deafening back then as they seem today against the terrorists, whose whereabouts are once again dominating the international news – even in this far Southern, yet strategically important, river port. George 'John Wayne' Bush recently delivered a tough-guy screen performance worthy of the Duke:

'Osama bin Laden, he may be alive. If he is, we'll get 'im. If he's not alive, we got 'im.'

Eventually we have to go to work, so on day three of con-spicuous consumption we drag ourselves to the intimate House of Blues on Decatur Street. As this is the last night on this tour with Will Hoge as the support group, the crew de-cide to ensure that the Southern gentlemen's tour memories with Midnight Oil will be happy ones.

In the middle of Will Hoge's show, lighting tech Nick Elvin, dressed only in tiny satin shorts and carrying a towel, ap-pears on stage next to Kirk, where he proceeds to 'talk' the drummer through the next song like a boxer's corner-man. When Will breaks a string on his Rickenbacker he finds that his spare, a Telecaster, has been securely gaffer-taped into the guitar rack. Then I crawl inside the water tank (as one does), initiating a metallurgical 'drum battle' with Kirk.

During our encore, both bands combine for a version of Neil Young's 'Rockin' in the Free World' – loud and rough in the manner of Crazy Horse – with Pete and Will sharing lead vocals, and Bones cruising around the stage in the latest foot-wear, rolled cigarette behind the ear, shooting film. By the end of the show, New Orleans already rates as one of our finest evenings of shared music and practical jokes since 1990, when our smoke machine became mysteriously jammed in the 'max' position during a Hunters and Collectors set, with the result that the Hunners disappeared under a thick blanket of San Francisco–style fog.

After the show we meet 'the Hogies' at the Irish Bar on Toulouse Street, for a long night of Guinness, pool and, eventually, arm wrestling (Craig 'Crocodile Dundee' Allen is the man to beat). Mr Fahy, the publican, is clearly delighted to have a pub full of happy, slurring customers – 'Very well-behaved crowd,' he tells a friend of ours the following day. It's sad to see Will and co. drive away in their van, but a record deal with a major label is in the offing, so I'm quietly glad that Kirk will soon be able to afford a pair of shoes, and no longer have to play the drums in his socks.

The next morning there's just enough time before our flight (we abandoned the tour bus in Florida) to walk along the riverfront, where the paddle-steamer *Natchez* is rollin' on the river. I make my way through the French Market, with its trestle-tables groaning under African masks, Mardi Gras beads, tie-dyed t-shirts and craftworks, the latter including some little wire dream-catchers, being made on the spot by 'Lalo' from Guadalajara. I buy four, one for myself and three as presents, as well as some five-cent beads – about the same amount that Jefferson paid Napoleon in 1803 for each acre of the land we're standing on. The so-called Louisiana Purchase, or more correctly the Louisiana Horse-Theft of the Century, doubled in one quill-stroke the size of the land then known as America. (The French emperor must have been in a particularly good mood that day. Perhaps his legendary haemorrhoids had stopped giving him hell.)

A few hours later we're climbing over the mighty, muddy Mississippi River bound for Seattle, Washington, flying over angular atolls dissected by rivers and lakes that look from above like Chinese dragons and basking geckoes. I spot two speeding air-boats, and imagine a mobster from a James Lee Burke thriller being pursued by detective Dave Robicheaux through an alligator-infested mudflat. And with that thought I fall asleep, bayou country dreaming.

ONLY HAPPY WHEN IT RAINS

Under the waterline
No place to retire
To another time
The eyes of the world still turn
from 'Put Down That Weapon'

The first thing I see when I awake is the close-up of flight attendant Val, her tiny plastic face suffocating underneath a parachute of Phyllis Diller hair. Then I realise that Val's lips, though stapled into a slick commercial smile, are also moving in time with some vaguely familiar language, a language which, at that groggy moment, I find entirely indecipherable.

Fortunately, the kind woman sitting on my left helps me with the translation, which turns out to be a simple request for a drink order. With bladder health in mind, I croak, 'Cranberry juice, please,' then start chatting with Donna, my translator, a vital grandmother who flies every Tuesday and Wednesday to different states to encourage her company's employees to eat well and stay fit. She resumed her schedule on the first flight out after 9/11, when the pilot thanked the few nervous passengers for their loyalty and trust, then suggested that anyone lunging at the cockpit should be met with a feather-storm of 'the additional pillows provided'.

We get talking about the whys and wherefores of arming airline pilots, a proposal which is to be debated in Washington over the next few months. Donna believes that a pilot could easily be overpowered, and his weapon taken and used against airline staff and passengers, or to critically damage the plane. She's convinced that a combination of increased security, passenger 'profiling', reinforced cockpits and air-marshalls is the way to go. I tell her that, as a last resort, pilots should be able to defend the cockpit, and that in these days of terror, providing them with guns, for use only on the aircraft, is an acceptable risk. We both agree that any of the above would be considerably more effective than a midair pillow fight.

As a nutritionist, Donna admits that she's fighting a losing battle. With a clinically depressed nation literally crawling over itself to reach the comfort-food cupboard, more of her charges are developing heart disease, diabetes and obesity than ever. At the same time, binge drinking is getting out of control. She sighs: '9/11 has made things even worse.' Even the US military has a high proportion of personnel classified as 'too fat to fight'.

Production and stage manager Barry Woods, who boards the Seattle flight only to find that his seat has disappeared beneath the gelatinous girth of another passenger, would doubtless have sympathised with Donna. When Barry complains that his full-fare place has ceased to exist, the highly drilled diplomatic corps at Delta go into fleshy-cabin-crisis mode, knowing that their already shaky airline's very survival depends on avoiding a fattist cause celebre at any cost. They take 'Mr Woods' discreetly aside, and offer him a US$361 travel voucher to be used at any time in the next twelve months, anywhere within the United States, if he just 'leaves quietly and catches the very next flight'. Baz, not one to miss an opportunity and in no particular rush, accepts the bribe and de-planes.

This is not an isolated case. Only days ago, Craig found himself behind an unfortunate lass trapped by her size in a Disney World turnstyle. By the time our accountant arrived, the poor woman had stopped attempting to move forwards or backwards, and was resigned to the idea of being surgically removed by one of Mickey's front-end loaders. It sounded like a most regrettable incident – one of the least-appealing carnal episodes I've heard of since Iggy Jones and Joylene Hairmouth's 'Night of the Raw Meat' at Sydney's Balmain Town Hall.

Responding to the curse of the West, the World Health Organisation is suggesting that eating greens in restaurants become the law, following successful campaigns in Finland and the Netherlands, while McDonald's has recently resolved to use a less cardiac-arresting oil for its fries. Americans, however, have a long history in resisting any move aimed at regulating the freedom of the individual, whether that be the constitutional right to bear arms or the non-wearing of a car seat belt or motorbike crash helmet, so it's a safe bet that any dietary harassment from the bully pulpit will come to an equally miserable end. Anyway, who could blame young Ky or Kylene for being keen on the canteen, when so many schools have deals with the big soft-drink companies to stock their sugary syrups exclusively? And if diets, drugs and treadmills ultimately fail, revenge can be sweet, through America's best-loved get-rich-quick scheme: litigation, an option being pursued by the gormless git who's suing several fast-food chains for not disclosing how unhealthy their food is. Durrr!

We arrive in Seattle to cold, constant rain. The last time we collectively witnessed such an unceasing deluge was during the prophetic Breaking of the Dry tour in Australia with Crowded House and Hunters and Collectors, in the early 1990s, when, no doubt angered by the presumptuous tour title, the heavens opened and the drought became a flood, then a vast inland sea, within a matter of days.

Before we can discuss the weather, though, we have to bundle our gear into radio station KMTT 'the Mountain', for a live-to-air show and interview. We play an ironic, acoustic version of 'Too Much Sunshine' for the first time, then stand around while the callers' questions come through. One woman isn't sure who we are – 'So just what kind of lubricant is Midnight Oil?' she asks boldly. Further questions are just as stimulating, so we pack away the gear and get the hell out. 'I'm not sure these radio shows do us much good,' says Martin, on the way back to the hotel.

Certainly, the busking nature of many of these thrown-together radio spots are worlds apart from the extensive preparation we did for the MTV Unplugged we recorded in New York City in 1993. That show was our first big-time opportunity to present the songs in a less-frantic, stripped-back form, so we rehearsed countless times in hotel rooms, sound stages and in the MTV studio itself. Joining us was our regular guest pianist/organist Chris Abrahams, along with percussionist Bashiri Johnson (on loan from the Whitney Houston band) and Aussie didjeridu player Adam Plack, who we bumped into on the streets of Manhattan.

As it turned out, the audience was really supportive, making that 'whoo-whoo-whoo-whoo' sound and open clenched-fist thing that only New Yorkers ever used to do, so the recording was fun, and came alive with later mixes by Nick Launay in London's Townhouse Studio. (My favourite part is Chris's 'typist-on-speed' piano hammering in the middle of

'Short Memory' in the lead-up to the final choruses, and Pete's stirring ad-libs over the top.)

I walk down to Seattle's Pike Place Market looking for a decent feed. (All those good-eating lessons from Donna, and they gave us nothing on the three-hour flight except a lousy packet of pretzels; then they tried to charge us five dollars for a headset. Things must be crook in the airline racket!) Down on the waterfront I find a place that sells some of the city's legendary coffee, order a spa pool–sized mug of the stuff plus soup and olive bread, and seat myself at a formica table by the window. As I wait, I gaze absently out over the harbour, hoping that the weather will break long enough to catch the outline of the Olympic Mountains or the aptly named Mount Rainier. It doesn't.

The local newspaper is full of war talk. A Pentagon agency is evidently exploring the various methods that could be employed to destroy underground bunkers of biological weapons, without simply blowing them to pieces and risking the contamination of nearby civilians and soldiers. Suggestions include a warhead which would surround the weapons with a sticky foam, or incinerate them. Another option is the painful-sounding 'Robust Nuclear Earth Penetrator', which could burrow mole-like into the ground, explode, and emit a violent shockwave that could burst open the target (and presumably empty its chemical contents into the local aquifer used for drinking water ...).

After lunch I drift around the market, a labyrinth of quirky shops selling clothes, CDs, curios, fresh fruit and seafood. I stop in amazement next to perfect slabs of glistening salmon lying on an icy mattress.

'We can box one up and send it to Heathrow for you,' says the cheerful fishmonger, mistaking my accent.

'That's fine,' I reply, 'but wouldn't it be faster to send it directly to Sydney?'

'We can do that too,' he laughs. 'It'll be there about seven tomorrow morning!' Except that he doesn't say 'about', he says 'a boat', in that delightful nor-western brogue which becomes even stronger by the time you reach central Canada.

'A boat'll never make it,' I observe, walking away, leaving us both in a state of contented confusion.

I soon come across another salmon, a ceramic one for hanging on a sportsman's trophy wall, but I baulk once again, suspecting that the blokes at the airport would almost certainly reduce it to roe. Instead I buy a checked flannelette shirt, in honour of all those local bands that borrowed John Fogerty's uniform and made it a symbol of grungy *attitood*. As I leave the market, dodging heavy showers, it dawns on me why the musicians from Washington state, from Hendrix to Nirvana, Pearl Jam and beyond, have often been so musically accomplished: every time they feel like giving their instruments a rest and going outside for a smoke, they're driven back inside for more rehearsal by blinding rain.

The stores on the way back to the hotel are typically empty – bin Laden has sure knocked the hell out of retail. As we noticed the last time here, there's always a lot of homeless people in the market area asking for change ('Large bills accepted as well,' says one guy). This must be one of the worst places in America to be ceiling-challenged with all this inclement weather. Other than that, Seattle reminds me a little of Sydney, with its hills, harbour and separation of port and city by the Alaskan Way, not unlike our own ageing Cahill Expressway. Set our cities free, I say! Get rid of these eyesores! Both are ugly, noisy stinkways strung like dental braces across the crooked teeth of the otherwise attractive cities. (Have the solution on my desk, first thing Monday morning.)

Actually, Seattle should be a modern, well-planned metropolis since they had two goes at getting it right. The great fire of 1889 destroyed the old town but gave the city fathers a golden opportunity to solve a pressing problem: shit. Built from the dawn of western settlement on low-lying mudflats and marshes, malaria and other nasties plagued the port for decades, so with the ashes of old Seattle still warm, the builders started work on the previous first floor, thereby elevating the new city above the sickly swamp. A new public water supply was built underneath the pavement, while townsfolk could now install 'Thomas Crapper's patent Waterfall No. 1' – a modern flushing toilet – connected to the sanitation system. Chief Seattle himself couldn't have been prouder.

Just what the esteemed chief would have made of Seattle's latest addition to the skyline, the Experience Music Project, is anyone's guess. Microsoft *billionerd* Paul Allen's fixation with Jimi Hendrix has seen him fork out 240 million dollars US (beware of geeks bearing gifts!) for the EMP, a Frank Gehry–designed paean to American pop culture that stands right under the city's unique Space Needle. (Well, it used to be unique; now even Auckland's got one.)

Like much of Gehry's work, the EMP is a visually arresting structure. From the outside, it's 'a pile of guitar-shop trash' with an undulating roof made from laser-cut metal shingles in silver gold, red, duck-egg blue and translucent 'purple haze'; its disjointed interior is rumoured to be inspired by shards of Hendrix's smashed guitars. The current 'Un-common Objects' exhibition features the Beatles' 1967 Granny Smith Apple, plus sartorial *objets*, from Patti Smith's priceless ripped t-shirt at one end of the scale, to Liberace's Louis XIV gold jacket at the other.

Along with Cleveland's Rock and Roll Hall of Fame, Nashville's Country Music Hall of Fame and the new Stax Museum of American Soul Music in Memphis, Seattle's EMP is a grand gesture in the great American tradition, clearly conceived by a man who'd swap his grey mouse for a sunburst Strat any day of the week. Of course, Seattle's grunge-capital credentials will now forever distinguish the city as an oracle of originality, but as rock stars become the new royalty, as legends are lionised and dopes are deified and myths crystallise into 'history', you get the feeling that soon there won't be a city left standing across the USA without its own musical Big Banana.

Have you heard the one about the Aussie who walks into a bar and gets dragged into a long, drunken rave with another Aussie and a Kiwi, both professional rugby players? Well, it happens to me on the evening after our two-show stand at the Commodore Ballroom in downtown Vancouver, gigs captured by a ten-camera film shoot, but which nonetheless never manage to eclipse the Capitol Theatre concerts (fearlessly documented by David Bradbury) in Sydney in 1981.

The bloke from 'In Zid' turns out to be a multi-talent. Though sporting a broken finger, he plays some nimble piano, and evidently is also skilled at hauling king crabs into fishing boats from the freezing coastal waters off Alaska, making 'big money' for his trouble. He tells me that the crew has to work non-stop without sleep when the bell sounds – i.e. when the crabs are 'on' – in all kinds of unspeakable weather, including mountainous swells of liquid ice.

Kiwis are a resilient lot, especially those from the frozen tundra of the lower South Island. After recording *Head Injuries* in 1979, Midnight Oil was booked for a five-week tour of New Zealand, even though then, as now, five weeks of viable gigs within the entire length of both main islands simply do not exist! Our crewmen back then, Colin Lee

Hong and Glenn 'Pig' Lloyd, had to construct stages in the corners of pubs, explain the concept of three-phase power to the publicans, as well as fend off threats from the Mongrel Mob gang and other rev-head sociopaths. One night after a show at the Hillcrest Tavern in Hamilton, they accidently backed the truck into one of the giant entrance way rocks of the Stonehenge Motel. It toppled over with an earth-splitting thud, creating tiny ripples on the surface of the oh-so-inviting 'tepid pool' several blocks away, and causing a permanent seismic shift in the geomorphology of the Hamilton basin.

By week four we were so bored with the tour that we took to stoning sheep from the minibus. Even the Wizard of Christchurch, the city's self-appointed brains-trust, non-citizen and soapbox soothsayer, seemed interesting. Then a rumour went around that our manager had resigned, denounced rock 'n' roll as the devil's music and become a born-again Christian. At this point I knew that our band would survive, no matter what.

Eventually we reached the Scottish colonial outpost of Dunedin, our third last show, arriving at about 1.30 am – three hours after the Kiwi TV's goodnight theme (the first melody Bones ever learned to play on the guitar) – and promptly ran out of gas on Mount Cargill, which overlooks the city. So we just coasted the bus down through the bends in the direction of the lights until we came to a halt, then called the manager of the Shoreline Hotel and asked him to pick us up.

Normally this kind of middle-of-the-night phonecall would have resulted in a feisty torrent of vowel-flattened abuse (*yer precks!*); however, the band had gained a reputation as 'Aussie punks' after an incident at Auckland's Gluepot, where out of frustration I'd smashed a hole in the low ceiling above the drum riser and Pete, for his own reasons, had taken the stage apart with his microphone stand. The happy result was that the friendly folks from the pub were there within minutes, fixing us a hot meal, and continually approaching 'Mr Garrett', asking him if everything was all right. 'No worries, mate,' said Pete, throwing down another Lemon and Paeroa.

Back at the Vancouver bar, I'm jolted back into the present by our new opening act, a solo performer known as Bleu, who's explaining some of the more esoteric aspects of America's new political order. 'Bush is a moron!' he exclaims, with terrifying clarity. Bleu's tour manager then arrives with two girls, one of whom bears a remarkable similarity to Renée Zellweger in the film adaptation of *Bridget Jones's Diary*. She informs me that she's a 'part-time masseuse', and to illustrate the fact digs her fingers so deeply into the knotty crevices of my back that it feels like she's applied the World Championship Wrestling sleeper-hold. To distract Renée, I tell her I'm halfway through my first book.

'So what's it gonna be called, honey, *Behind the Skins*?' she asks coquettishly.

'No,' I reply, slightly peeved, 'I mean I'm halfway through *reading* my first book.'

In any case, the combined effect of fatigue, hunger, beer and Renée's fingers have rendered me legless. As soon as I can release myself from her professional grip I slink away like an amoeba, enter my room by osmosis, and fall into a twelve-hour coma. The last words I hear are the rugby guys reminding me that I've left half of my beer unskulled – 'Are youse a real Aussie or *what*?'

The next day the weather is fine so I walk down to meet our long-time producer Warne Livesey at Bryan Adams's Warehouse Studio in Gastown, skirting the crack neighbourhood 'just over there'. (That's the interesting thing about the city maps handed out willy-nilly by hotel concierges in North America: they never draw a big red line around unsafe areas to help you avoid becoming the hapless victim of a major felony just by making one wrong turn.) Once safely inside the studio, I notice that Bryan has collected some of the best old microphones that you'll ever see in one place, all neatly arranged in glass cases (with no hammer provided in case of emergency). One of the Neve mixing consoles used by Sir George Martin is also here, rescued from the cyclonic perils of Montserrat. And there's an assortment of rooms in which to capture *the* perfect snare-drum sound.

I come away hoping that we might record here one day, particularly since the unfortunate demolition of Sydney's famous Festival Studios – where we recorded *Capricornia* – is going ahead as planned. Festival, a veritable rock and pop shrine in a decaying warehouse next to the fishmarkets at Pyrmont, was a recording home to everyone from Johnny O'Keefe to silverchair, and boasted the deadly combination of a great live room, good mics, Neve desk, Studer recorders, Pro-Tools and a nearby cafe selling hand-trembling coffee. Like many irreplaceable inner city music and art studios whose returns are modest, it's on the blocks, up for redevelopment by a posse of progressives and profit junkies.

The *Capricornia* recording sessions were a joy, partly due to the ease of pulling a good sound, and partly because the songs were well rehearsed and, in some cases, already ensconced in the live set. The only interruptions were for album cover conversations, mug-shot photos for a painting by eX de Medici for the National Portrait Gallery, and a mid-song call on my mobile phone, which I'd mistakenly left on in the studio. It was one of the farm forestry blokes in south-east Queensland, where I'm growing a small patch of eucalypts. 'Ah gidday there, Bobby,' said a gnarled Aussie voice. 'We've got a bit of a burn-off goin' on up here today, mate, just in case someone complains about the bloody smoke. Anyway, it's all under control, just thought you'd like to know.' (Click).

The twelve songs (one, 'Your Light', didn't make it through to the final selection) were recorded by Warne with all of us playing together in the one big room – now *there's* a novel concept! – with Pete singing a guide vocal to help with the arrangements. A couple of them, 'Mosquito March' and 'Under the Overpass', even went down in the first take. The lead vocals were added later, along with harmonies by Bones, Jim and myself; as were Martin and Jim's additional guitars, Jim's keyboards and my percussion.

Bones filmed grabs of the different set-ups – the first time we've ever made a visual record of the album process – while Jim brought in a photo of a feisty herd of cows as a suggestion for the album cover. Thus began a protracted discussion, a convoluted bovine polemic, a tangential, existential, multi-national, Socratic debate about the front cover which involved, at different times, the band, the management, the record company, the producer, the engineer, the publicist, the tea-lady, the guy who moves the parking-bay cars ... even the layout and design artists themselves.

In the end, a single calf was separated from the herd, because it was 'cute', 'focused' or would 'look good on a t-shirt'. (Actually, by now she'd be looking good on someone's plate.) Mason was the hardest to convince. The softly spoken gent from Liquid 8 Records in the USA visited us in Sydney to say hello, hear how the songs were going, *prioritise* any hit singles, and to check on the album-cover artwork.

'I gotta tell ya, Rarb,' he confided earnestly, 'I'm having trouble with the cow.'

LIVING ON A PRAYER

The rich get richer
The poor get the picture
The bombs never hit you when you're
down so low
from 'Read About It'

I'm sitting having breakfast in a Vancouver cafe, skimming yesterday's tabloids, when I'm struck by an extraordinary story from New York City. Apparently, the latest target of bio-terrorism is none other than Santa! It seems that the growing threat of the anthrax virus has prompted New York postal authorities to irradiate all letters to Santa this Christmas. It's hard to imagine, really. Someone so sick that they'd actually have a go at everyone's Nordic favourite, Mr Fat 'n' Jolly himself.

Folks sure are mighty jumpy here right now, so anything remotely suspicious or irregular is greeted with an avalanche of overreaction. Just the other day they shut down Atlanta Airport, the biggest in the country, after someone ran backwards up an escalator allegedly 'to retrieve a camera'. The suspect managed to slip away into the crowd, but was later arrested and paraded before an angry lynch mob of humour-less passengers. He was then whisked away by airport security to the relative safety of the local lock-up.

Then a Florida student was suspended from school and charged with a second-degree felony after he sprinkled white powder on a teacher's desk, evidently in the (successful) hope that a bio-terrorism scare would result in cancelled classes. Next, a doughnut store in Toronto was evacuated when a cus-tomer discovered a 'pipe bomb' in the men's washroom. The 'bomb' was later correctly identified as a dildo.

Against such a backdrop of panic and paranoia we expect greater security at airports and other high-risk areas, but nothing prepared us for the thorough bag and body search that we have to endure before our flight back into the United States from Canada (Vancouver to Portland, Oregon). We're red-flagged. We're hand-wanded. We're frisked and prodded and zapped. We remove our shoes, twice. We dismantle our cameras. We're approached by a heavily armed man wearing rubber gloves ... who proceeds only to empty our carry-on luggage piece by piece.

Airport security in America is tough right now, and has become even tougher since Washington grabbed the reins in reaction to revelations that some of the private security officers had criminal records. If our own experience is anything to go by, Australians must be on the Dangerous Aliens list, as we're repeatedly singled out for 'secondary screening' – regardless of our tough-as-tungsten prime minister's assurance (to a half-full US Congress) that 'America has no better friend, anywhere in the world, than Australia'. A friend that, not for the first time, was one of the first of America's allies to raise a hand to help ol' Uncle Sam in his darkest hour since Pearl Harbor.

Of course, it's not just harmless Aussies that set off airport alarms; elderly folk clutching American passports are spared no indignity. (The sight of a frail nonagenarian being held up by security and being wanded and shoe-fondled is enough to make you FURIOUS!) At least prohibited carry-on items are now clearly specified. In Denver's new brushed-steel and marble, tornado-proof airport, these items include: 'box-cutters, ice-picks, corkscrews, baseball bats and pool cues'. Similarly, those objects 'allowed after inspection' have been identified: 'syringes (with proof of medical need), nail clippers, walking canes, tweezers and eyelash curlers'. (Now that's a headline you'd never expect to see: 'Boeing Down in Eyelash-Curler Attack'!)

Australians should also be aware that boomerangs are also banned, ever since a professional boomerang thrower was arrested when she insisted on bringing her 'weapon' onto a flight. Even make-up kits can take on a sinister aura (eyelash curlers aside). On a later tour we noticed that one had been revolving on a baggage carousel at Salt Lake City's airport, and had consequently been cordoned off with police tape. A mountainous cop arrived, leading an alsatian, which sniffed the suspicious item and recoiled, evidently preferring another range of flavoured lip-gloss. 'I don't know who looks scarier,' said guitar tech Dave Mayer, 'the dog or the cop.'

Back to Vancouver Airport in 2001, and we finally make it to the gate.

'Wassa name of your group?' enquires the ticket zappatista.

'Midnight Oil,' I reply, totally over the constant interrogation.

'How long have you been playing in da group?' he persists.

'All my life,' I sigh.

'Get a lotta groupies?' he asks eagerly.

'Hundreds,' I lie, as he hands me back my passport.

Eventually allowed to board, and gratefully unviolated, we make a run for the plane, which happens to be a tiny Fokker twin-prop. With a strong headwind, we soar upwards – 'like a fart in a bath', as an Aussie pilot recently described it to me, in terms he must have felt I'd understand. Soon we level off, and fly at such low altitude that Pete and I and twenty other largely nonchalant passengers get fantastic views of the snowy remains of Mount St Helens, which blew its top off in a major tantrum in May 1980. (Australians become very excited when we see real mountains, having only a few pimply ones ourselves.)

The bloke in the seat next to me utters not a word for the entire flight, in stark contrast to my chatty travelling companions on every other recent flight to and from and within North America. On the trip over, for example, I sat next to a Singalese woman now living in Nelson, New Zealand, who, with her doctor husband, had built the first Buddhist temple in the city. Sova (I believe that was her name) described the five rules of her religion: 'No killing, no stealing, no lying, no adultery, and as for getting pissed, that's *right* out.' Competing with the jet roar, she stressed that: 'The breath is the life constant', and that meditation 'can be achieved by simply focusing on breathing in and out'. I told her that I was certain to get the hang of it, since, having suffered from mild asthma since early childhood, I'd been concentrating on breathing in and out for as long as I could remember.

Other interesting itinerants were to follow. I found myself sitting (facing *backwards*!) opposite a Mexican–American floor-coverings salesman with an infectious laugh, whose father bred cockfighting hens, and who fancied himself as a 'lady'th man'. Then there was a Nepalese economics professor who compared and contrasted the fiscal implications on his country's GDP of the quarrelsome Maoist guerrillas and the freak assassination of most of Nepal's royal family. Next came a director of physics at the Northern Illinois Center for Accelerator and Detector Development, who explained the impact of protons and anti-protons colliding in a four-mile underground 'racetrack' at nearly the speed of light. There was also a young female army recruit making her uncertain way to a two-year training course at Fort Wainwright in Fairbanks, Alaska. Then, on the trip home to Australia, two young guys from Wisconsin are travelling to an international herpes conference in Cairns (or so they *said*).

Not every flight is as stimulating or comfortable as these. One South West shuttle was so cramped that the co-pilot had to make a joke out of it. 'This is a no-whining, no-complaining, zero-leg-room service to Nawlins,' he said over the intercom. 'No smoking in the toilets, and remember, damage to the smoke detector will incur a 2000-dollar fine. And we know that if you had 2000 dollars you'd be flying with Delta. And for those of you travelling today with children … we're sorry!'

I spent the rest of that miserable flight squashed like a bug against the window of the third-last seat. Pete seemed particularly surprised by the conditions down at the back. 'These planes are really long,' he remarked. To make matters worse, sitting next to me (and *on* me) was a colossus of a man who fell asleep immediately, and in doing so became even wider as his ample body relaxed. At one point I thought that he'd expired altogether, like the Indian woman who, on an earlier tour, wheezed her final breath next to our former guitar tech Spanky, at the beginning of a Vancouver-to-London flight. (Much to Spanky's horror she was left there for over an hour, covered head to toe by an airline blanket.)

I yearned shamelessly for the one and only time I was upgraded to first class (computer error?) on a trans-Atlantic flight, joining the sombre, hyphenated gentlefolk with expensive suits and complex tax arrangements in the cone of silence up the front. The seats were enormous, real Jason Recliner rockers, and flattened out like dentist's chairs but without the drill. We were offered the *suggestion du jour*, a still-screaming Maine lobster a la thermidor, washed from between our perfect rows of teeth by a naughty Chateaux Pricure-Lichine '86. We were so close to the pilots that we could have reached over their shoulders and plotted our own way home to our country estates. The only other passenger who looked like a fraud in this old-money milieu was none other than English actor Bob Hoskins, seated in front of me in a tight-fitting tan leather jacket: "'Ere,' he said as we held up the other passengers whilst leisurely disembarking, 'you weren't supposed to be up 'ere either, were you?'

Today's short hop, by comparison, is comfortable and scenic, even if my fellow passenger is as dull as a coach-class lunch. I keep an eye out for Mount Hood, which overlooks Portland and can actually be seen from the city on the odd clear day. Hood is another peak not to be trifled with, claiming the lives of three climbers the following summer, a helicopter crashing in the rescue attempt. This spectacular country is where the famous Oregon Trail ended and the new world's promised land was supposed to begin. At least that's what thousands of westward-headed folks were led to believe before they set out on their buffalo-dodging, Indian-fighting trek across the Great Plains.

I imagine that I see the descendants of these nineteenth-century hopefuls, adventurers, trappers and fur traders as I wander around the town. What I do see are a couple of Deadheads from the nearby town of Eugene tucking into a vegetarian meal at the Greek restaurant near our hotel; and a pick-up truck bursting with rednecks doing burn-outs on the road next to the Willamette River. There are also a number of cold and hungry-looking backpackers hanging out down near the Saturday Market.

The stall vendors appear to be universally frozen, yet resolute and ever optimistic. There's a table covered with badges, brooches and stickers. 'I love my country,' one claims. 'It's the government I'm afraid of.' One man is dressed up as a huge dalmatian, selling 'reversible dog scarves'. I decide that the market for these must be extremely limited – after all, how many reversible dogs are there? (Boom boom.)

On the return trip through the city I come across several shops in the Skidmore/Old Town districts specialising in obscure vinyl and other arcane band memorabilia. I enter one of them on the slim chance that I'll be insulted by the Jack Black character from *High Fidelity*. No such luck. The number of guitar and drum stores is a promising sign, though, particularly for the Australians playing in town tonight at the Roseland Theater. This is clearly a place where the guitar band still lives, perhaps even prospers, evidenced by Portland's own Everclear, Elliott Smith and the Dandy Warhols (whose drummer/vocalist Brent DeBoer sits next to me on the following day's flight to LA). 'I don't like the idea of bands travelling on the same plane,' says the Dandys songwriter/vocalist Courtney Taylor-Taylor, referring to the crash that killed Buddy Holly, Ritchie Valens and the Big Bopper on 3 February 1959 – 'the day the music died', as Don McLean famously sang.

I decide that Portland is a very liveable medium-size town, with its exquisite Japanese Garden, boutique breweries – and no sales tax. What's more, the folk we meet are generous and friendly, with design artist Gary Houston giving all of us copies of the excellent dot-painting posters he'd made for our concert. Heart-warming also is the sight of the newly erected Christmas tree in Pioneer Courthouse Square, although its arrival marks the beginning of the best and the worst of the Visa season.

In America, hardly has Grandpa woken from his Thanksgiving afternoon nap than the Christmas juggernaut gets going and proceeds undiminished for a full month. That is, as long as no shopping-mall Santas are struck down by some Machiavellian Dr Strangelove's chemistry set. (As it transpires later, this wasn't such a crazy notion. In October 2002, in what he described as 'a defining day in the War Against Terror', US Attorney-General John Ashcroft claimed that 'a potential terrorist cell within our borders' had been 'neutralised'. Where? None other than Portland, Oregon.)

As this is the last show of the tour, I say my advance good-byes to Willie and Deborah before we head off in different directions in the morning. In a moment of weakness, I allow opening act Bleu to talk me into joining him on stage for his nightly piss-take of Bon Jovi's excruciating 'Living on a Prayer'. There's a signature drum fill before *every* chorus that *everyone* knows that I manage to get wrong *every* time. It's a train wreck.

Later, however, I feel curiously satisfied. I so obviously didn't know the song, and this must surely count in my favour. Nonetheless, I'm convinced that our most hard-core fans, the self-anointed Powderworkers, will condemn me on their website for this reckless, capricious gesture. A judas. A pariah. A desperate drumming doppleganger sentenced to tour the USA forever in a Bon Jovi covers band.

AND THE BAND PLAYED WALTZING MATILDA

The real world is not as calm as it appears to
be from here
The small world is not as strong and the
testing ground is near
The Old World is not as safe as the one we
could have seen
The Great South Land can be as great as the one
it could have been
from 'The Best of Both Worlds'

We're heading home for the summer. Home to the smooth-barked apple gums, the Norfolk Island pines, the Moreton Bay figs, the flannel flowers, the banksias, the bottlebrush, the Sydney sandstone, the southerly busters, the nor-easters, the sulphur-crested cockatoos, the kookaburras, the pelicans, the white-faced herons, the cormorants, the rainbow lorikeets, the fruit bats, the cicadas, the Christmas beetles, the funnel-web spiders, the water dragons, the bandicoots, the possums, the geckoes, the fairy penguins, the bull sharks, the blue swimmers, the bluebottles, the blackfish and the bream.

We'll soon be back in town. Back to the quarter-acre block, the brick veneer, the double garage, the 'deck', the perg'la, the fibro shack, the four-be-two, the paling fence, the backyard barbie, the footy, the Test, the Coopers ale, the Hills Hoist, the piss-warm pool, the Mr Whippy van, the Sunday roast, the Vegemite toast, the Billy tea, the Humble Pies, the flies, the mozzies, tomatoes with taste and sane-cow beef (plus Don's blue heeler, Sonia's rooster and Nelson, our terrorist terrier).

We're touching down in Australia. The land of the Diggers, the mateship, the yarn, the fair-go, the 'ave-a-go!, the 'round or two for a pound or two', the 'she'll be right', the 'no worries mate', the tyranny of distance, the hard yakka, the n.i.m.b.y., Tim Winton, David Williamson, Michael Leunig, Cathy 'cos I'm free' Freeman, Pat Rafter, the John Butler Trio, the Blundstone boot, the Chesty Bond, the Billabong boardy, the 'Pacific Solution', the Republic!, the Australian crawl, the sandcastle, the sunburnt back, the surfboat wedgie, the skinny-dip, the summer sex, the bushfire sunset, the Southern Cross, the ... the ... SERENITY!

It's great to sail through the 'Australian Passports Only' side of customs, with other smug Aussies, while the behemoth in the Stars-and-Stripes bandana who sat behind me on the plane, whose uber-gut prevented me from moving my seat back beyond the vertical, and who farted belligerently and wheezed malod'rous breath down my neck for the past thirteen hours, is now languishing at the back of a queue snaking past Sans Souci (French for 'no worries'). Oh *yes*! Wonderful to escape a flying cylinder full of desperate, dehydrated people whose idea of an anti-thrombotic exercise was to lower their bottom jaw for another feed. Yes indeed! Marvellous to leave behind an overbooked, overdue, overtired planeload of peripatetic passengers, haggard hosties, lethal lunches and an ever-rotating film about sharks tearing apart dead and dying killer whales. Ah, the romance of travel ...

Holy moly, it's terrific to be home! For the last hour of the trip, I watched the rainbow arc of dawn increase in intensity outside my window, until it broke into a celestial gallop over the sandstone shoreline, chasing the Jumbo into still, sleeping Sydney town, then ceding to a brilliant sunrise as we touched down just after the 6 am curfew. I feel a huge sense of relief, although I know from previous homecomings not to expect everything to be perfect, or you just set yourself up for a big slump. This adopted country of ours is a mere work-in-progress, a tortuous, stumbling and often painful on-going journey. A dystopia with a fairer future just beyond the horizon. A long-orphaned child of an ever-scornful parent, whose flag we still fly obsequiously in the top left-hand corner of our own. A promising student in need of wise counsel, currently plagued by a cynically orchestrated, paralysing inertia. Australia is like a never-ending series of *Neighbours* – you can stay away for years, come back, and pick up the plot immediately.

Bidding the boys farewell, I drive through the city and the Harbour Tunnel, following a suspicious-looking Charger XL in camouflage paint and a 'Baby in Boot' warning sign on the rear window. Mmm … (Snap out of it. You're *home*!)

Motoring past Balgowlah's suburban shopping strip, with its numerous restaurants and neglected banks and a real estate agent named Yorick, I arrive home to real tea, Vegemite toast, a hot bath and much-anticipated, grateful sex (not with a real estate agent named Yorick). I unpack my bag and stow it in the attic, thereby mentally eradicating the tour and all its works. Then, having been starved of the mundane things in life for the best part of two months, I dig out my boom-box radio, relocate my pruning shears, and throw myself straight into some savage gardening.

Ever supportive of new Australian talent, Triple J is blasting out a fresh bunch of songs by young local bands (and the occasional older act still deemed cool enough to play), including great newies by Grinspoon, Regurgitator, Screamfeeder and Eskimo Joe. The blunt Aussie accents on the call-back line fill me with the inestimable 'joy of belonging'. One blokey caller is already tanked to the eyeballs when they put him on air: 'Mate, I'm as full as Shirvos's lycra,' he gurgles.

I'm outside the house up a ladder, chopping away happily at the hedge, when a neighbour pulls up.

'Been to Canada have you great place Vancouver great place,' he says, without drawing breath. 'We were staying near Stanley Park and saw the skunks you know what you've got to do if you get sprayed by a skunk jump in a bath of tomato juice that's the only way of getting rid of the stink.'

I thank him for the advice and head inside to write it down. A short while later I re-emerge to wash the car. I've just got a healthy lather up when I hear a voice behind me.

'Tony and Joy just copped a $1500 fine for doing that.' Alarmed, I turn to face my accuser, one of the colourful local identities.

'Doing what?' I ask.

'You're not allowed to wash your car on the street, you've got to wash it on the grass,' he explains.

'But there's hardly any grass!' I protest.

'Don't worry,' he reassures me, 'I'm not going to dob you in.'

Fearing a turtle-wax citation, I hot-foot it from the crime scene. I speed around the foreshore bushland to the lookout at Dobroyd Head, racing up the dirt track through wind-stunted casuarinas and banksias, chasing water dragons and scattering the welcome swallows and noisy mynahs back into the scrub as I pass. Steaming in through the Heads is a blue and white floating tool-box, a rectangular-sided container ship with 'NHK line' written immodestly on the hull. I regard the featureless tub for a few minutes, thinking how much more rewarding boat-spotting must have been during the great age of sail. Back then, clippers with brains, brawn and beauty would have made majestic entrances into Port Jackson, and graceful timber schooners and cutters, ketches and yawls, barques and barquentines would have billowed like square-rigged cumulus clouds down to the docks of Circular Quay.

A few months later I'm rewarded with a magnificent sight, as the Chilean four-masted white training ship *Esmeralda* slips quietly into port, curiously unhindered by protests about its role as one of Pinochet's prisons and torture chambers in the 1970s. My sixteen-year-old daughter Alex even goes on board later that evening, invited by the commanding officer to a reception at Woolloomooloo Bay. All the while, I maintain a good watch from the wharf, checking for any sign of rum, sodomy or the lash. And making damn sure that 'Enrique' keeps his salty, suntanned, homesick hands to himself.

On the way back from my run I stop to admire a solid-timber fishing boat on the slipway, and ask one of the marina skippers if the owner is working on the vessel.

'You can't put one foot onto the slips now,' he says grimly, 'because of the public liability insurance. They can't afford to cover you if you have an accident. It's all happened in the last few months.'

'Well, what about over at the other boatshed?' I ask, pointing to the empty cradles on the opposite side of the bay, where I used to scrub down my own fishing boat.

'He's gone,' he replies, and walks off to start the tender launch.

As soon as I get home I collapse into the couch, eager to catch up on some local news. There's a disturbing article in the paper concerning Australian writer and ABC broadcaster

Phillip Adams. Incredibly, Adams has been the subject of a complaint by a card-carrying member of the American *antagonistas*, who wants to have him investigated, for 'racial vilification', by the Human Rights and Equal Opportunity Commission. Apparently 'the Man in Black', in his column in the *Weekend Australian*, dared to suggest that US foreign policy in countries such as Cambodia, Chile and Iraq had been flawed. Similarly, author and self-described 'gnarled hippie' Richard Neville has been lambasted at home and abroad following an earlier piece on 'the dark side of Uncle Sam', entitled 'American Psycho'.

Hopefully, freedom of speech will triumph before either writer becomes the subject of a latter-day Dreyfus Affair. Adams is suitably uncowered by the incident, writing six months later that 'What happened in Chile reminds us that the US has a long record of sponsoring terrorism on an awesome scale'. But it seems extraordinary that the near-total America-wide media blackout on anything other than the Washington party line is seeking also to gag us at home in Australia.

Of course, attitudes have always been noticeably different on either side of the Pacific. The text message left on my mobile phone from one of my erudite companions in the Ghostwriters is not atypical: 'hope your kicken sepo butt!! cya [sic].' A friend currently living in New Zealand has sent me a redrawn global map, entitled 'the World According to the USA'. On this map, Britain is a 'new best friend', as is Pakistan, Uzbekistan and Turkey. China and Cuba remain 'evil communists', while over the entire Middle East – with the exception of Israel – is the word 'baddies'. 'Kangaroos' is the only Australian label, with an arrow pointing to the Gold Coast. 'Movie studio', it says.

Our shows in Australia the following year often begin with 'US Forces', prefaced by a few well-received words from

Pete, part caution, part fact, part wishful thinking: 'I'll say it again – Australia is *not* a suburb of the USA!' The posters plastered over the outside walls of our Melbourne gig, at the Forum Theatre, remind me of the glorious blunt-speak of my university days: 'American imperialism is an obese villainy thriving on war,' they read. 'It is a confederacy of hate dictated by selfish oligarchs contemptuous of the world, its culture and its environment.'

New York Times writer Paul Krugman highlights this chasm of perspective by quoting a Pew survey of 'opinion leaders', which found that 52 per cent of Americans think that their country is liked because it 'does a lot of good', while only 21 per cent of foreigners agreed. Many Americans are genuinely baffled by their poor international reputation, which may have prompted CNN to pose the open question, 'Can America's image in the Muslim world be improved?' ('Not as long as its foreign policy is directed at supporting Israel' was one reply.)

Perhaps this confirms just how little many Americans know about the outside world, a world nonetheless strongly affected by its actions. Barbara Walters, anchor for the *20/20* program on (American) ABC, admitted that prior to the Incident her ratings-driven weekly slot concentrated on 'film stars in trouble'–type stories – because no-one was interested in Russia's President Putin, or knew the name of the leader of Pakistan. Including Bush the Younger himself.

There's not much interest in Australia, either, something for which we can perhaps be thankful. With the exception of a story about a shark-feeding frenzy on the Gold Coast, a three-second grab of our gloating prime minister and his lick-spittles after their election 'victory', and a music rag snippet that Kiwi band Shihad have changed their name to something that sounds less like *jihad* (Pacifier, actually), there was zip on any US network or newspaper about Down Under for our entire seven-week tour. The only antipodean news I saw was an article in the *Wall Street Journal* about the explosion of fake didjeridus being sold in America, and a *USA Today* piece throwing light on the 'tidal wave' of cheap Aussie wines now breaking over America. Subsequent tours were much the same – at least until the terrorist bombings in Bali the following October, which received huge international attention.

Neither did I hear a whole lot of Australian music on the US airwaves, apart from dance-floor pop by the all-conquering Kylie ('Just like a real woman, only smaller', as Bones once observed), whose spin-doctored formula (class + arse = brass) seems to have struck butt-shakin' gold. The only other songs I heard were Crowded House's timeless 'Don't Dream it's Over', in a shop at Salt Lake City Airport, and INXS's 'New Sensation', on high rotation as a McDonald's ad.

It's not as if the Aussies and Kiwis aren't out and about, playing, promoting and, in the case of the Wiggles, taking the free world's short people by strategy. During the tour we met up with Neil Finn and his wife Sharon in LA, as well as David Bridie and his band, while Nikka Costa had just toured through some of the same venues. We didn't cross paths with crocodile-botherer Steve Irwin, however, who's single-handedly (ir)responsible for introducing 'Crikey!' and 'She's a bewdy!' into the American vernacular.

Before the October–November 2001 tour becomes another distant, garbled memory, I decide to scribble down a mnemonic, a pseudo-inventory of cautionary tales for would-be travellers to the USA:

a Never eat airline breakfast sausages.

b Never open the plastic orange-juice containers towards you.

c Never send back a cattle-class dinner – the replacement will almost certainly be just as bad, if not worse.

d Never attempt to bust through airport security.

e Never play frisbee with a sniffer dog.

f Never tick the box on the Visa Waiver form that asks if you've 'ever been involved in terrorist activities, or genocide, or between 1933 and 1945 were involved, in any way, in persecutions associated with Nazi Germany or its allies' (even if you have been).

g Never attempt humour with a fully armed National Guardsman.

h Never poke fun at a Republican president.

i Never count out restaurant tips in one-cent pieces.

j Never make international calls direct from a hotel phone.

k Never disbelieve the weather channel – it's more reliable than the sky, the birds or that ache in your elbow.

l Never order the cocktail known locally as a Cock-Sucking Cowboy anywhere in Texas.

m Did I mention the sausages?

APPENDIX A: MISCELLANEOUS OBSERVATIONS

1 American men are no more capable than Australian men of transferring the contents of their bladders to a urinal, without spilling at least half over the surrounding floor. (One late-for-a-meeting guy attempted and failed the notoriously difficult 'walk-up wee', and was already in mid-micturation as he approached the bowl at the ambitious stretch of one metre.)

2 People shout things to each other from cars that they'd never say face to face in the street.

3 There are three things which must *never* come back: headbands, gongs and playing slide guitar with a beer bottle.

4 Drummers are capable of wearing gloves, or going without a shirt, but never at the same time.

5 Never believe a promoter who tells you, when ticket sales are down, 'Don't worry. It's a walk-up town,' or trust anyone in the music biz who says, 'Trust me.'

6 It's better to play complaint rock than compliant rock. Fortunately, I'm thrown into a clutch of end-of-year school and family engagements which, for the first time in months, take my mind off the terrorists, the media, the USA and the band. It's terrific to be doing 'normal' things again, meeting people with different lives who don't care about American chart positions or the number of bums on seats. There's a 'School Spectacular' at the Entertainment Centre that features an earnest young tenor destined for the cruiseship circuit, and dancers from country New South Wales aping gangstas from LA. And at a school prize-giving night at Sydney Town Hall, the guest of honour from HMAS Penguin enthrals the soundly sleeping audience with a history of the naval base, including such riveting, classified information as the fact that the swimming pool was once the sewage works. And there's my daughter's water-polo team barbecue, where I discover at considerable length from one of the other dads that he's organised venture capital for a company that has invented a warning device indicating when industrial ball bearings are about to wear out.

Predictably, the family's Christmas eat-and-booze-a-thon starts well enough, with peace and goodwill to all mankind, then quickly descends into a trifle-stained, bacchanalian brawl. I take bets with my brother-in-law, to determine whether it'll be the adults' political jousting or the children's green cordial-fuelled aggression that will be the first to end in tears. Uncle Joe reminds me of a quote by American spokesman William Allen White: 'Politics is, after all, a minor branch of harlotry.' Uncle Ronnie, another disillusioned 'true believer', alludes to the tragic loss of strong Federal Labor Party leadership in Australia – the barely flickering light on the hill – addressing anyone in earshot: 'All I can say is, comrades, that whirring sound you can hear as you pass through Bathurst is Joseph Benedict Chifley turning in his grave.'

Of course, it's the simple pleasures of life that make all the difference. It's thrilling to see the progress my teenage daughters have made, in just two months, on the piano and guitar – although in the case of Alex, the advent of boys, booze and the Big Day Out fills me with a profound and visceral fear. It's marvellous to stride through the heavy-oak foyer of the cathedral in which my daughters' end-of-year carol service is being held (rather than skulking up to the stage door via a squalid back lane reeking of garbage, through a kitchen slippery with grease and fat and piled high with boxes of plastic cups and straws, to change clothes in a staff toilet between the urinals and the Evening Magic condom machine). And even oddly comforting that our own 'Brolgas-are-dancing' Aussie Christmas carols are overlooked once again in favour of the execrable 'In the Bleak Midwinter'.

Later the same evening, there's a rare moment of epiphany as the organist pulls out all the stops in the final verse of 'The First Noel'. The earth trembles with the bass pedals, the walls resonate with the pulsating pipes as mortar dust cascades like angelic dandruff on the congregation. The choir's descant soars like celestial seraphim and mine eyes fill like waterfalls with wonder, as goodness triumphs over evil once more – and all is well with the world.

Here endeth the first lesson.

ENCORE: ONCE IN A LIFETIME

By the time you make up your mind
If ever you do
I hear the drums of heaven too
from 'The Drums of Heaven'

The tulips are up in Chicago, their density, vigour and depth of colour a good indication that since the last time we were in town, in October 2001, the ground temperature must have fallen below freezing point, and hovered there for at least a few days. In fact, the winter here has been comparatively mild, with only one heavy snowfall. The city itself appears to be virtually recession-proof, with springtime skyscrapers popping up almost as fast as the bulbs.

We've just arrived from Boston, where the weather was equally stunning for our Earthfest concert at the Hatch Shell, on the banks of the Charles River. Along with Bonnie Raitt, Lisa Loeb, and Garbage, we played to a large, blissed-out crowd in blazing sunshine. As if the earth had decided that, for one day at least, she bore us no grudge.

So here we are again, back in North America for another five-week, high-mileage road trip, which began, inexplicably, in Bangor, Maine, on the far north-east coast, and will span the continent to Vancouver in the far north-west, returning to New York City via the Canadian Rockies and prairies. With us is our regular crew – bribed, bullied or blackbirded onto the bus – although one of our previous bus drivers, the sweet-natured Dominic, has replaced Slim at the big wheel, while his son Dominic Jr is driving the crew. Truck driver Marshall (or 'Hattie Jacques', as Bones has been calling him) has been gratefully promoted to US production manager, making way for a new truck driver, the affable Gronk, to steer the giant rig.

The band has a new stage set made by the Flying Goolie folks at Byron Bay, New South Wales. There are corrugated-iron panels featuring a windmill and a lizard, scrap-metal parrots that hover like pterodactyls above the band, and an impressive, tongue-lolling cow named Michael, in honour of our former long-serving stage and production manager, Michael Lippold. It's the best looking set we've carried for quite some time; far preferable to the Spinal Tap–esque Easter Island Statues that we had made for the *Earth and Sun and Moon* tour in 1994. Gross polystyrene carvings they were, strangely resembling the band members, and standing tall and dead-pan at the rear of the stage while we ran around in front, paying them frantic homage. (The statues were soon defaced by graffiti, then unceremoniously dumped in an LA warehouse, where they doubtless ended their short lives as surfboards and beanbags.)

The intro tape has also been changed. 'The Demolition of Dresden' has been mothballed and replaced by the sound of a herd of panicky cows being loaded onto trucks (or onto stage), compiled by audio-meister Tim Millican (from 'the original cow concept' by Jim). It must be the Year of the Cow. Even one of the latest mobile phones comes with a cow ringing tone.

The leit-motiv for our return is to play the key cities again, plus a list of places we somehow managed to miss last time we were through. In North America, it's not that the population centres are so vast, it's just that there's so darn many of them, and you have to play in *everyone's* backyard unless you're happy to be ignored. After all, there's always another band who *will* show up if you don't. This country is the natural home of the quid pro quo – no quo, no quid. If you're prepared to 'say hello to the folks' at every major radio station and retail outlet, then you never know your luck in a big city.

This is actually our second time in the USA since 'the 9/11 tour', having performed 'Golden Age' on *The Late Show with David Letterman* in late March, an invitation that coincided neatly with a handful of our own shows and radio broadcasts. We've appeared on *Letterman* a few times over the years, once playing a rocking 'Sometimes', on another occasion, a laboured 'Outbreak of Love', and the experience has been remarkably similar in each case. You rehearse and tape the live recording in the New York studios, which are chilled down to near freezing – the guitar picks are printed with '48 degrees' – because 'that's the way Dave likes it' (perhaps it keeps the guests and the audience alert, their arses frozen onto their seats). We're introduced by the host as 'bushmen from Australia', with Letterman holding up the current CD, after which we play a song 'lasting no more than four minutes'. As we finish, the audience applauds on cue, Dave jumps up and shakes our hands, Paul Shaffer counts the studio band into a medley of our greatest hit (i.e. 'Beds'), and the credits roll: 'The LATE SHOW is a production of WORLDWIDE PANTS INCORPORATED'. And th-th-that's all, folks!

Later we played 'Luritja Way' on the LA show that immediately follows Letterman's, *The Late, Late Show with Craig Kilborn* (aka the 'western' *Letterman*), arriving at CBS's

'Television City' under such tough security that we had to produce our passports. I wondered if the studio apparatchiks remembered our appearance on *Thicke of the Night* years ago, when we set fire to the newspaper-covered studio floor during the taping of 'Read About It'. ('We're *really* pissed!' said the floor manager, brandishing a fire extinguisher like a weapon in the Green Room afterwards.) As a result of this little prank, this time I half-expected to find a big sign at the entrance: 'You Are Now Entering Kilbornia, Produce Your Papers And Lose Your Lighters!' As it turned out, there was just a lone guard, who quizzed Willie half-jokingly as the tour manager charged through: 'You haven't got a machine gun in that guitar case, have you?'

LA's mood had brightened significantly, with fresh faces on the billboards and a lot less flag-waving. Financial considerations have rapidly reclaimed their rightful place in the cosmos; near Genghis Cohen's Chinese restaurant on Fairfax a man was holding a placard mysteriously reading 'Anatoly Tenenbaum Owes Me $20 000'.

While in Los Angeles, I accepted an invitation, on behalf of the band, to an 'Aussie Oscars' bash in Beverly Hills, where, for the first time in my life, I didn't find myself on the fuck-off side of the velvet rope. Pleased as punch, I proceeded to wander aimlessly around the sumptuous house and garden like Peter Sellers in *The Party*, approaching strangers with 'Howdy, pardener' and the like. There were plenty of recognisable A- and B-list celebrities (I believe I was the only F-lister) including many tongue-and-groovin' yuppies, well-connected dinkies and sybaritic skinnies, plus a few shiny gawbbs (God, another white bald bloke) and at least one lombard (lots of money but a real dickhead). Eventually I found a clutch of familiar faces, literally stumbling into ex-Noiseworks writer/producer/keyboard player Justin Stanley, singer/actor Kate Ceberano and actor Ben Mendelsohn.

Best Actress nominee Nicole Kidman made a classy entrance, her statuesque figure and alabaster complexion in stark contrast to much of the ruddy, beer-swilling, ex-pat rabble, who 'burned tunnels in the air adoring her from afar', to borrow a line from Clive James (another ex-pat). As soon as Nicole had been duly lionised by the host, and before she was mobbed by a drooling throng of 'cultural attachés' à la Les Patterson, I approached her, drew myself up to my fullest height, and whispered an invitation in her shell-like ear to our concert later that night at the House of Blues. (Which she couldn't attend, of course, her place at the HOB reserved table being taken later by feisty drumming band leader Mick Fleetwood.) I left the party soon afterwards, but it was only in the hotel-bound taxi that I realised that my fly had been undone the entire evening.

On Bones's birthday we catch the ferry to Larkspur Landing on the northern shore of San Francisco Bay. It's a scenic trip, with views of the city, the Golden Gate Bridge, Alcatraz and Angel islands and the forbidding San Quentin State Prison, with its fortress walls, razor wire, floodlights – and most infamous guest, one Charles Manson. When Bones wanders off to 'talk to an Irishman about a bass', I stay on board for the return trip, a surprisingly complicated, quasi-military operation which involves disembarkation, re-embarkation and then re-occupation of the exact same lookout point. I get chatting with the deckhand, Bill Hamilton, a sprightly octogenarian who worked in the local navy shipyard during World War II, before joining the merchant navy.

As it turns out, our paths may have crossed years ago. Bill visited Sydney on several occasions, on the Matson Lines cargo ships named after the Bay Area counties – *Ventura*,

Sierra and *Alameda* – as well as the company's passenger
liners *Monterey* and *Mariposa,* vessels duly logged into my
ships register as I scanned the harbour, when I was a young
boat-mad kid sleeping over at his grandparents' flat.

In 1960 Bill met an Australian girl, who he's certain bore
his child, a daughter he was never permitted to see. 'I probably should have married her, but that's in the past,' he says
wistfully, before battling his way back inside the cabin, out of
the chill wind.

As for me, I stay out in the gale, taking shelter under
the gunwales as we shudder back to port, loving the salt,
the sway, the freedom, the romance. Rewinding images from
twenty-five years of writing, recording and touring with
Midnight Oil. Of *living* Midnight Oil with five other
musicians and their families. Of being part of a cast of
contradictory characters – right-brain and left-brain people,
alpha and omega males, optimists and realists, musicians and
politicians, autodidacts and over-achievers. Of shaping the
band, fighting for it, sweating over it – almost always salva-
ging it, as if it was one of those grand steel ships of a Sydney
Harbour childhood.

LAST DRINKS: POETS AND SLAVES

The Tuckerbox is empty now
The heart of Kelly's Country cleared
The gangers on the southern line
Like the steam trains have disappeared
from 'Mountains of Burma'

Pete leaves the band shortly after the final concert of the Australian *Capricornia* tour. 'They've been belting out their patriotic hits for 25 years and still going strong,' reads the flyer for the last two gigs, at Twin Towns Services Club on the New South Wales–Queensland border. In fact, we're still a few weeks away from our official quarter-century together, and our charismatic lead vocalist and frontman has already told us that he's calling it a day.

'Citizens of the Republic of Australia, we come to play songs which are written in the heart!' declares Pete at the beginning of what proves to be our last show, before letting rip with a paint-stripping blast of blues harp. Jim and Martin are next on stage, perfectly synchronising the opening chords of 'US Forces', followed by Bones and me, pushing each other towards our microphones just in time to join in the 'Sing me songs of no denying' first chorus. The audience is in fine spirits, perhaps sensing that this is a special gig when, near the end, drum tech Clem Ryan is lured out from behind Bones's speakerbox and handed a thank-you present for all the years of hard work ... a drum!

Two days ago we set aside Pete's Y-fronts – which Craig Allen usually picks up off the changing room floor after every show and dutifully drops into the laundry bag with the rest of our sweat-soaked clothes – and asked Johnno the lighting rigger to attach them to a cable and lower them onto the stage during our final song of the tour – as a symbolic Spinal Tap–style gesture. So, as the band charges through the end themes of 'The Power and the Passion', and a big fat moon rises high above the RSL, the aforementioned white underpants descend slowly onto centre-stage, where they hover portentously like a surrender sign, fluttering slightly in the breeze, before dropping to the floor for the ultimate time. As a last hurrah, we link arms on the lip of the stage, wave farewell to the crowd, and collapse heavily into a dressing room covered with signed posters of Gerry and the Pacemakers, the Delltones and Glen Campbell. We then shake hands as gentlemen do.

'Thanks, Pete,' I pant, 'it's been fun.'

'If it wasn't for the enduring power of the music, I wouldn't have made it this far,' he gasps.

By 6.15 the following morning, Pete's gone, jetting to Melbourne for the Australian Conservation Foundation's annual general meeting.

Pete's departure leaves us multi-skilled renaissance men in Midnight Oil to contemplate our own futures – to find a new place in the firmament. Spurious suggestions for a new lead singer bounce off the windows of the Tarago, including everyone from Sister Janet Mead ('The Lord's Prayer'), ex-ABC newsreader Richard Morecroft, the Reverend Tim Costello,

SBS's Mary Kostakidis, Chopper Read and our ANZ banker, Mike Feltscheer. (Later we got an irresistible offer from a 'nude bootscooter' in Wagga, and from my writer friend David Leser.)

'We should get a poet!' cries Jim. 'Les Murray would be great.'

'Or Bob Ellis,' I add. 'Imagine – both of the bastards from the bush!'

A few seconds of silence pass.

'How about a politician?' I suggest. 'Keating, for example. We could be PK's first band since the Ramrods. Then again, as he once asked of Andrew Peacock, does a soufflé rise twice?'

'What about you, Craig?' Bones asks our tour accountant. 'How's your singing coming along? You must know the words by now – you type them out every night. And you could do your own massages ...'

A few chuckles, then silence.

'And the press release?' I persist. 'We should figure out what we're gonna say.'

'We should *all* release statements,' says Martin, 'to throw them off the scent.'

'"Oils Rhythm Section in Sordid Love Tryst",' I venture.

Hoots. Cackles. More silence. Brooding.

'So what's everyone going to do, now that Pete's left?' I ask finally. 'I mean, we can't just hang around lighting farts.'

'I'm gonna shave off my beard and take bids on eBay,' says Jim, 'then get in my Samsonite and bury myself in the yard.'

'I'm off to Byron and going into competition with Giffo. Except I'm gonna make really *big* underwear!' laughs Bones.

'"Urgent Pantaloon Delivery!"' adds Jim.

'We could always hire ourselves out to do soundchecks for other groups,' says Martin.

'Don't wanna do media or wait in the lobby?' Bones chimes in, using his best radio announcer's voice. 'Call Midnight Oil! We'll do it for you!'

Half-hearted laughter, followed by quiet contemplation all around.

'We should all get together and do some playing,' I offer. 'The middle of next year maybe, when Jim's studio's up and running, and, all things being equal, the Backsliders' blues festival gigs are done.'

Positive murmurs.

'If we do a farewell show, what should the last song be?' I ask eventually.

'An instrumental,' says Bones.

www.ingramcontent.com/pod-product-compliance
Lightning Source LLC
Chambersburg PA
CBHW022121080426
42734CB00006B/207